REMEMBERING The KANJI 2

BY THE SAME AUTHOR

Remembering the Kana: A Guide to Reading and Writing the Japanese Syllabaries in 3 Hours Each. Honolulu: University of Hawai'i Press, 2007 (1987)

Remembering the Kanji 1: A Complete Course on How Not to Forget the Meaning and Writing of Japanese Characters. Honolulu: University of Hawai'i Press, 2011 (1977)

Remembering the Kanji 3: Writing and Reading Japanese Characters for Upper-Level Proficiency (with Tanya Sienko). Honolulu: University of Hawai'i Press, 2008 (1994) [third edition in press 2012]

Kanji para recordar I: Curso mnemotécnico para el aprendizaje de la escritura y el significado de los caracteres japoneses (with Marc Bernabé and Verònica Calafell). Barcelona: Herder Editorial, 2005 (2001)

Kanji para recordar II: Guía sistemática para la lectura de los caracteres japoneses (with Marc Bernabé and Verònica Calafell). Barcelona: Herder Editorial, 2004

Kana para recordar: Curso mnemotécnico para el aprendizaje de los silabarios japoneses (with Marc Bernabé and Verònica Calafell). Barcelona: Herder Editorial, 2005 (2003)

Die Kanji lernen und behalten 1. Bedeutung und Schreibweise der japanischen Schriftzeichen (with Robert Rauther). Frankfurt am Main: Vittorio Klostermann Verlag, 2006 (2005)

Die Kanji lernen und behalten 2. Systematische Anleitung zu den Lesungen der japanischen Schriftzeichen (with Robert Rauther). Frankfurt am Main: Vittorio Klostermann Verlag, 2006

Die Kana lernen und behalten. Die japanische Silbenschrift lesen und schreiben in je drei Stunden (with Klaus Gresbrand). Frankfurt am Main: Vittorio Klostermann Verlag, 2006

Kana. Snel Japans leren lezen en schrijven (with Sarah Van Camp). Antwerpen: Garant, 2009

Kanji. Snel Japans leren schrijven en onthouden door de kracht van verbeelding (with Sarah Van Camp). Antwerpen: Garant, 2010

Megjegyezhető kandzsik, Első kötet. A japán írásjegyek jelentése és írásmódja (with Rácz Zoltán). Budapest: Shirokuma, 2011

REMEMBERING THE KANJI

VOL. 2

A Systematic Guide to Reading Japanese Characters

James W. Heisig

FOURTH EDITION

University of Hawai'i Press

HONOLULU

17 16 15 14 13 12   6 5 4 3 2 1

Library of Congress Cataloging-in-Publication Data

Heisig, James W., 1944-
     Remembering the kanji / James W. Heisig.
     p. cm.
     Includes indexes.

     Contents:
     v. 1 A complete course on how not to forget the meaning and writing of
          Japanese characters
     v. 2 A systematic guide to reading the Japanese characters
     v. 3 Writing and reading Japanese characters for upper-level proficiency;
          James W. Heisig and Tanya Sienko

     1. Japanese language—Orthography and spelling. 2. Chinese characters—
Japan. 3. Japanese language—Textbooks for foreign speakers—English. I. Title.
PL547.H4 2012
495.6'82421—dc22

                                                                    2010049981

v. 1 6th edition   ISBN 978-0-8248-3592-7   (pbk. : alk paper)
v. 2 4th edition   ISBN 978-0-8248-3669-6   (pbk. : alk paper)
v. 3 2nd edition   ISBN 978-0-8248-3167-7   (pbk. : alk paper)

The typesetting for this book was done at the Nanzan Institute for Religion and Culture.

Contents

Introduction

As THE TITLE SUGGESTS, the present book has been prepared as a companion volume to *Remembering the Kanji: A Complete Course on How Not to Forget the Meaning and Writing of Japanese Characters.* It presumes that the material covered in the first book has already been mastered and concentrates exclusively on the pronunciation of the Japanese characters. Those who approached the study of the kanji in a different manner may find what is in these pages of some use, but it has not been designed with them in mind.

As I explained in the Introduction to the previous volume, if it is the student's goal to acquire proficiency in using the Japanese writing system, the entire set of "general-use characters" (常用漢字) need to be learned. To insist on studying them in the or+er of importance or frequency generally followed in Japanese schools is pointless if some other order is more effective as a means to that final goal. A moment's reflection on the matter is enough to dispose of the common bias that the methods employed by those who come to Japanese as a foreign language should mirror the methods used by the Japanese themselves to learn how to read and write. Accumulated experience and education—and in most cases an energetic impatience with one's own ignorance—distinguish the older student too radically from Japanese schoolchildren to permit basic study habits to be taken over with only cosmetic changes. A clearer focus on the destination should help the older student chart a course more suited to his or her time, resources, and learning abilities—and not just run harder and faster around the same track.

Perhaps the single greatest obstacle to taking full advantage of one's privileged position as an adult foreigner is a healthy fear of imposing alien systems on Japanese language structures. But to impose a system on ways of learning a language does not necessarily mean to impose a system on the language itself. To miss this distinction is to risk condemning oneself to the worst sorts of inefficiency for the worst sorts of reasons.

Obviously the *simplest* way to learn Japanese is as the Japanese themselves do: by constant repetition, without interference, in a closed cultural environment. Applied to the kanji, this involves drilling and drilling and drilling until the forms and sounds become habitual. The simplest way, alas, is also the most

1

time-consuming and frustrating. By adding a bit of organized complexity to one's study investments, the same level of proficiency can be gained in a fraction of the time. This was demonstrated in the first volume as far as the meaning and writing of the characters are concerned. By isolating these skills and abstracting from any relationship they have to the rest of the language, a firm foundation was laid for the next step, the assignation of sounds or "readings" to the individual characters. That is the subject of this book.

The earlier volume was described as a "complete course"; the present volume is offered as a "guide." The differences between the two books are as important as the similarities. While both books are intended to be self-taught and allow individual readers to progress at their own pace, the former traced out a path step by step, in a clearly defined order. Here, however, the material is presented in such a way that it may be followed frame by frame or may be rearranged freely to suit the particular student's needs. The reason is that the readings of the kanji do not allow for any more than a *discontinuous* systematization: blocks of repeating patterns and clusters of unpatterned material organized under a variety of rubrics. In fact, the only thing ironclad about the method is the assumption that the student already knows what the characters mean and how they are written. Without that knowledge, the systematization becomes all but opaque. In any event, it is important to gain some understanding of how the book as a whole is laid out before deciding how best to make use of it.

The book falls into two parts of wildly disproportionate length. The first ten chapters cover the Chinese or *on* readings (音読み); the last chapter, the Japanese or *kun* readings (訓読み). This should not give the impression that the *on* readings themselves are so much more difficult than the *kun* readings, but only that their systematization requires much more attention. What is more, the method followed in CHAPTER 11 is closer to that followed in volume 1 and can thus be treated in relatively short shrift.

One of the chief reasons for frustration with the Chinese readings is not that there are so many kanji to read, but that there are so few readings to go around, creating a massive confusion of homonyms to the uninitiated. No sooner does one attempt to establish a set of rules to rein in this phenomenon than exceptions begin to nibble away at one's principles like termites until the entire construction begins to look like a colossal waste of effort.

True enough, there are exceptions. A lot of them. But there is also a great deal of consistency which can be sifted out and structured for the learning. The principal aim of the first ten chapters is to isolate these patterns of consistency and use them to the fullest, holding brute memory at bay as long as possible. To this end I have introduced what are called "signal primitives." By this I mean *primitive elements within the written form which signal a particular*

Chinese reading. Since most of these primitive forms were already assigned a meaning in the first book, the strategy should come as a welcome relief and carry you well over one-third of your way through the *on* readings. Whatever readings fall outside the compass of this method are introduced through a variety of devices of uneven difficulty, each assigned its own chapter.

CHAPTER 1 presents 56 kanji which form the parent-kanji for the forms of the *hiragana* and *katakana* syllabaries and whose readings are directly related to the modern *kana* sounds. 49 of them are Chinese readings, 7 are Japanese.

CHAPTER 2 covers a large group of characters belonging to "pure groups" in which the presence of a given signal primitive entails a uniform sound.

CHAPTER 3 presents the small group of kanji whose readings are *not* homonyms and may therefore be learned in conjunction with a particular character. CHAPTER 4, conversely, lists characters with no *on* reading.

CHAPTER 5 returns to the signal primitives, this time gathering together those groups in which a signal primitive entails a uniform sound—but with a single exception to the pattern. These are called "semi-pure" groups.

CHAPTER 6 brings together readings drawn from everyday words, all or nearly all of which should have been learned during the course of a general introduction to Japanese conversation. Allowing for occasional slight shifts of meaning from those assigned the kanji in the first volume, the only work that remains to be done is to see how Japanese puts the pieces together to create new meanings.

CHAPTER 7 returns one final time to the use of signal primitives, picking up what characters can still make use of the device and subdividing them into three classes of "mixed-groups" where a given primitive element can signal two or more different sounds.

CHAPTERS 8 and 9 follow the pattern of CHAPTER 6, except that the compounds will be less familiar and require learning some new vocabulary. The only thing these kanji have in common is that they do *not* belong to any natural phonetic group. The most useful compounds are presented in CHAPTER 8. The generally less useful compounds of CHAPTER 9 are all introduced with explanatory comments.

CHAPTER 10 is a wastepaper basket into which I have thrown the remaining readings: uncommon, rare, or generally restricted to proper names.

All the kanji from CHAPTERS 1 through 10 are arranged in a frame of uniform design (see FIGURE 1 on the following page). Taken together, they cover the entire range of *on* readings established as standard by Japan's Ministry of Education. Five indexes have been added to facilitate reference and review.

INDEX 1 lists all the signal primitives, arranged according to number of strokes, and the frame in which they first appear.

INDEX II presents a listing of all the kanji treated in this and the former volume, arranged according to the number of strokes.

INDEX III lists, in syllabic order, all the *on* readings, their respective kanji, and the number of their respective frames.

INDEX IV lists all the *kun* readings and their respective kanji. Together these two indexes constitute a complete dictionary of readings for the general-use kanji.

INDEX V follows the frame sequence of the first book, giving the *kun* readings and the frame(s) in which the *on* reading is introduced in this book.

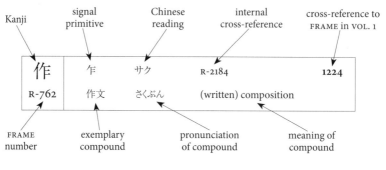

FIGURE 1

The frames have been arranged to facilitate reviewing: if you block out everything to the right of the compound used as an example, you are able to run a simple self-test from time to time. For more thoroughgoing review, the flash cards that were prepared according to the design given in CHAPTER 5 of the first volume can be completed, with the aid of the indexes. A complete explanation is provided in CHAPTER 11.

Although the principles that govern the structure of this book will become clearer as the student grows more familiar with the content, there are a few points that seem worthy of mention at the outset. They represent both the courtesies I paid my own memory in learning to read Japanese and the pitfalls I watched fellow students fall into following other methods. As time goes on, you may or may not choose to follow them, but at least you should know what they are.

First, relating one compound to another by means of similarities of sound is to be avoided at any cost. It merely clutters the mind with useless information. The fact that the two syllables *sensei* can mean teacher (先生) or astrology (占星) or despotism (専制) or oath (宣誓), depending on the kanji assigned to them, may come as such a surprise that you are tempted to make some use of the coincidence. Resist the temptation.

Second, it is best not to try to learn *on* and *kun* readings at the same time for the same character. The idea of "conquering" a character in its entirety will be supported by nearly every textbook on the kanji that you pick up, but is nearly as mistaken as trying to learn to write and read the kanji at the same time. Once you have learned the general-use characters, you will have a much better base from which to learn the meaning, writing, and readings of new characters *en bloc* as you meet them. Until then, cling to the Caesarean principle of "divide and conquer."

Third, with few exceptions, it seems preferable to learn the several possible Chinese readings of a given character as they come up, in isolation from one another. When second or third readings appear, reference to earlier frames will inform you of the fact. You will no doubt notice that the quickest way to complete the information on your flash cards is to rush to INDEX V and start filling them in. If you do, you might end up with a tidy set of cards that are no longer of any use for review, or else find yourself reviewing what you haven't yet studied. In either case, you would be sidestepping the entire method on which this book is based. Be sure to read the instructions on pages 297–99 before doing anything with your cards.

Fourth, certain Japanese sounds undergo phonetic alterations when set alongside other sounds. For example, 一本, 二本, 三本 are read *ippon, nihon, sambon,* the syllable *hon* being like a chameleon that changes to suit its environment. Some of these alterations are regional, some standard. In any case, they are best learned by trial-and-error rather than by a set of rules that are more complex than they are worth.

Fifth, a word about Chinese compounds (熟語, じゅくご). With a grain of salt, one might compare the blend of Japanese (*kun*) and Chinese (*on*) words to the blend of Anglo-Saxon and Latin-Greek words in English. Generally, our words of Anglo-Saxon root are richer in meaning, vaguer, and more evocative than those of Latin-Greek root, which tend to precision and clarity. For instance, the word "glass" can suggest a whole range of possible images and meanings, but as soon as we substitute its Latin equivalent, "vitrine," we have narrowed it down to a more concrete meaning. The presence of Chinese words (generally a compound of two or more *on* readings) in Japanese performs a similar narrowing, specifying function, while the native Japanese words reverberate wider and deeper meanings.

In much the same way that we combine Anglo-Saxon words with Latin and Greek words (for example, in the term "fiberglass"), Japanese will occasionally mix *on* and *kun* readings in the same compound. As a rule, I have avoided these in the exemplary compounds. The order of preference in choosing examples was roughly as follows:

1. a compound that includes a reading appearing in a previous frame;
2. a compound in ordinary use;
3. a compound that uses a reading to appear soon after the frame in question;
4. the most common or instructive compound;
5. a name of a person or place;
6. rare or archaic compounds.

The student is encouraged to substitute familiar compounds at any time for the examples I have chosen.

Sixth, the use of signal primitives demands the same rigor applied to primitive elements in volume 1. Where a single jot or tittle of difference is present, the element is excluded. Additional attention will have to be paid to the *position* of the primitive, which was not important in the earlier book.

Seventh, I would register a plea against trying to begin with the two volumes of *Remembering the Kanji* at the same time. I wash my hands (or as Japanese would have it, my feet) of all responsibility for the results. That having been said, there is no reason that these pages cannot be used in conjunction with a set of graded readers. I would only advise that you begin this *after* having worked your way through CHAPTERS 2 and 5. The benefit of such an approach is that it enables you to take full advantage of the grammatical and vocabulary drills that such readers provide.

At the same time, the commonly heard advice about learning characters "in context" is one that is not as sensible as it sounds. Even if I learn the English word "troglodytic" in sentences such as "I can trace my ancestors back to the troglodytic age" or "There's a family of troglodytes in my tool shed," the word still needs to be learned in the first place. New Japanese vocabulary falls on the foreign ear with much the same impact—totally unrelated to anything we already know. The benefit of a context is that it enables one to drill a number of words and assimilate something of how they relate to one another grammatically and connotatively. Context defines the finer nuances that usage and tradition have affixed to the kanji, but the compounds themselves still need to be learned. For this reason, students who wish systematically to make their way through this book frame by frame need not trouble themselves over the absence of context provided they do not abandon all reading practice in the process.

Eighth and finally, a vigorous warning against the use of *rōmaji* in learning to read Japanese kanji. Get the idea out of your mind that the Roman alphabet is a "crutch" to help you hobble along until you master the *hiragana* and *kata-*

kana syllabaries. It is nothing of the kind. It is rather a slow and self-inflicted amputation that will leave you crippled for the rest of your Japanese-reading years. Not only does the Roman alphabet inflict quirks on your pronunciation, it cultivates a systematic bias against the *kana* that gets harder and harder to uproot. Be patient with the *kana,* and never write Roman letters beneath them. The stricter you are in expelling all *rōmaji* from your study of Japanese words, the quicker you will find that Roman letters become an obstacle to reading and writing, which they are for the Japanese and should be for anyone learning the language.

In the fall of 2010, the Japanese Ministry of Education, Sports, Science, and Technology approved the addition of 196 new kanji to the official list of 1,945 established in 1981. These changes were reflected in the sixth edition of volume 1 of *Remembering the Kanji,* which now comprises 2,200 characters. The readings for all these kanji are covered in this fourth edition of volume 2.

Nagoya, Japan
1 August 2011

PART ONE

Chinese Readings

CHAPTER 1

The Kana and Their Kanji

THE TWO JAPANESE syllabaries known as the *hiragana* and the *katakana* (or collectively, the *kana*) originated as stylized versions of Chinese characters used to represent the sounds of Japanese without any reference to the original meaning of those characters. In modern Japanese not all of the *kana* retain the sound of their parent-kanji, but there are a number that do, whether as *kun-yomi* or *on-yomi*. This means that if you can recognize these kanji, learning at least one of their readings is almost automatic.

Many of the calligraphic transformations will be immediately apparent; others require some knowledge of calligraphy. In these cases, a calligraphic drawing has been included for the sake of completeness.[1] The letters H and K, set off in parentheses and inserted in the location of the internal cross-reference numbers, indicate whether the kanji in the frame is parent to *hiragana* or *katakana* or both. *On-yomi* in this chapter are given in parentheses where necessary to distinguish them from the kana based on the frame's kanji.

To make a representative listing, it has been necessary to include a number of rare exemplary compounds and compounds that mix *on* and *kun* readings. These deviations have been indicated in each case. Despite these difficulties, the frames presented in this brief initial chapter are worth studying carefully before moving on to the simpler material in the next chapter.

As stated in the introduction, *on-yomi* are listed in *katakana* and *kun-yomi* in *hiragana,* a common convention in Japanese dictionaries. The readings of example compounds are uniformly given in *hiragana.*

一		二	(K) R-247	**2**
R-1	二世	にせい	second-generation	

---

1. For a clearer idea of the connection between the *kana* and the kanji, see my *Remembering the Kana* (Honolulu: University of Hawai'i Press, 2006), where the original forms of both the *hiragana* and the *katakana* are included.

三 R-2		ミ (サン)	(κ) R-1184	3
	三つ子	みつご	three-year-old child; triplets	
女 R-3	め	め・メ (ジョ)	(H/K) R-1044, 2179, 2315	102
	女神	めがみ	goddess	
千 R-4		チ (セン)	(κ) R-1067	40
	千島	ちしま	Kuril Islands, north of Japan	
左 R-5	さ	さ (サ)	(H) R-997	81
	左右	さゆう	right and left; on both sides	
不 R-6	ふ、	ふ・フ	(H/K) R-2182	1302
	不安	ふあん	uneasiness	
	The *katakana* form comes from the first 2 strokes only.			
世 R-7	せ	セ	(H/K) R-1713	28
	世界	せかい	world	
多 R-8		タ	(κ)	113
	多少	たしょう	more or less	
知 R-9	ち	ち (チ)	(H) R-208	1308
	知人	ちじん	an acquaintance	
利 R-10		リ	(H/K) R-387	972
	利用	りよう	use	
	The *kana* forms come from the right side of the kanji.			

以 R-11	いろ 以上	い (イ) いじょう	(H) above; more than	1105
和 R-12	和 平和	わ・ワ へいわ	(H/K) R-2402 peace	963
部 R-13	へ 部屋	へ へや	(H/K) R-1178 a room	1988

The *kana* forms come from the right side of the kanji.

由 R-14	ゆ 由来	ゆ・ユ ゆらい	(H/K) R-1103, 1460, 2316 reason; origin	1186
流 R-15	流転	ル るてん	(K) R-521 metempsychosis	826

The *katakana* form comes from the last two strokes of the kanji only.

保 R-16	ほ 保安	ほ・ホ ほあん	(H/K) security; keeping the peace	1072

The *hiragana* form is based on the entire kanji; the *katakana* comes only from the last 4 strokes.

留 R-17	る 留守	る (ル) るす	(H) R-1822 absence (from home or work)	1527
波 R-18	は 電波	は (ハ) でんぱ	(H) R-1545 radio waves; electric waves	866

太	た	た (タ)	(H) R-1246	126
R-19		丸太 まるた	log	
	The example combines *on* and *kun* readings.			

止	と	と (シ)	(H/K) R-1683	396
R-20		止まる とまる	to stop; halt	
	The *katakana* comes from the first 2 strokes.			

比	ひ	ひ・ヒ	(H/K) R-381	482
R-21		比較 ひかく	comparison	

武	む	む (ム)	(H) R-1240	403
R-22		武者 むしゃ	warrior	

衣	え	え (エ)	(H) R-1695	423
R-23		白衣 びゃくえ	white robe	

己		コ	(H/K) R-1323	564
R-24		自己 じこ	oneself; the self	
	The *kana* forms come from the first 2 strokes of the parent-kanji.			

加	りつ	か・カ	(H/K) R-891	932
R-25		加入 かにゅう	admission (as to a group)	
	The *katakana* is based on the left side of the kanji only.			

為	ゐ	ゐ (イ)	(H)	2067
R-26		行為 こうい	conduct; actions; deeds	

与 R-27	ら	よ (ヨ)	(H/K)	1335
	与党	よとう	ruling political party	

The *katakana* comes from the bottom half of the kanji.

江 R-28		え (コウ)	(K) R-118	148
	江戸	えど	Edo (old name for Tokyo)	

Only the right half of the kanji is used for the *kana*.

幾 R-29	省	き・キ	(H/K) R-334	1481
	幾何学	きかがく	geometry	

宇 R-30	ᄀ	う・ウ	(H/K)	1785
	宇宙	うちゅう	cosmos; universe	

The *katakana* comes from the first 3 strokes of the kanji.

恵 R-31	恵	ゑ・エ	(H) R-1688	659
	知恵	ちえ	wisdom	

The *hiragana* in question is, of course, the old form.

仁 R-32		に・ニ	(H) R-249, 2210	1063
	仁王門	におうもん	Buddhist temple gate with fierce Deva Kings	

伊 R-33		イ	(K)	1245
	伊太利	いたり	Italy	

Only the left side of the kanji is used to form the *katakana*. The example compound is older usage. Modern Japanese prefers to use *katakana* for the names of Western countries.

之	乀	シ	(H/K)	1299
R-34		之字形	しじけい	zigzag (like the kanji 之)

須	ス		(K)	1854
R-35	急須	きゅうす	Japanese teapot	
	The *katakana* comes from the stylization of the right side.			

乃	ノ	の (ナイ)	(H/K) (R-2372)	741
R-36	乃木坂	のぎざか	Nogizaka (place-name)	
	The *katakana* comes from the first stroke of the kanji.			

奈	な	な・ナ	(H/K)	1175
R-37	奈良	なら	Nara (place-name)	
	The *katakana* is based on the first 2 strokes only.			

也		ヤ	(H/K) R-1398	2236
R-38	也寸志	やすし	Yasushi (man's personal name)	
	This kanji only appeared in VOL. 1 as a primitive (page 181).			

呂	ろ	ロ	(H/K)	24
R-39	風呂	ふろ	Japanese bath	
	The *katakana* uses only the first 3 strokes of the kanji.			

於	お	お	(H/K)	2909
R-40	於ける	おける	in; at	
	The *katakana* form is based on the left side of the kanji only. The character featured here did not appear in VOL. 1, but its primitive elements should be easy to recognize.			

牟 R-41	ム	(K)	2965
	牟田　むた	Muta (surname)	

The *katakana* form is based on the first 2 strokes of the kanji. This character, rare in modern Japanese except for names, was not introduced in VOL. 1.

祢 R-42	ね・ネ	(H/K)	2647
	祢宜　ねぎ	low-ranking Shinto priest	

The *katakana* form is based on the left side of the kanji only. It is rare and did not appear in VOL. 1.

久 R-43	ク	(H/K) R-1768, 2310	1092
	久遠　くおん	eternity	

井 R-44	ヰ (ショウ)	(K) R-1838, 2091	1946
	井戸　いど	a well	

The *katakana* based on this character has become obsolete.

美 R-45	み (ミ)	(H) R-1207, 1578	587
	新美　にいみ	Niimi (surname)	

The *hiragana* form is based on the final 3 strokes of the kanji. The readings of both characters in the exemplary compound are rare, except for names.

良 R-46	ら・ラ	(H/K) R-993	1578
	奈良　なら	Nara (place-name)	

奴 R-47	ぬ (ド)	(H/K) R-211	758
	奴田　ぬだ	Nuda (surname)	

The *katakana* form is clearly drawn from the right side of

			the kanji only. The reading of the parent-kanji is rare, except in proper names.	

曽 R-48	旹	そ・ソ	(H/K) R-594, 1289	540
	中曽根	なかそね	Nakasone (surname)	
	The reading shown here is used only in names. Note that the reading combines *kun* and *on* readings.			

Of the 48 kanji given above, a number were indicated as having rare readings or readings chiefly used in proper names. Those that happen to be general-use kanji will be assigned more common readings in later chapters, as you will notice from the inclusion of an internal cross-reference number.

We now turn to kanji whose readings differ from the pronunciation of the *kana* which they serve as parent-kanji by virtue of an extra syllable which is present in the kanji but not in the *kana* that comes from it. We begin with 3 characters whose readings lengthen the vowel of the *kana* syllable, making it a diphthong.

計 R-49	け	け (ケイ)	(H)	359
	計画	けいかく	scheme; plan	
毛 R-50		も (モウ)	(H/K) R-903	2062
	毛布	もうふ	blanket	
礼 R-51	礻	れ (レイ)	(H/K) R-2265	1168
	失礼	しつれい	discourtesy; impoliteness	
	The *hiragana* form is based on the whole kanji, the *katakana* on the right side only.			

As in the last 3 frames, the readings of the kanji in the following 5 frames add a final syllable ん, which is absent in their *kana* pronunciation.

安 R-52	あ 安心	あ (アン) あんしん	(H/K) R-351 peace of mind	202
寸 R-53	寸 寸法	す (スン) すんぽう	(H) measurement	45
天 R-54	乞 天国	テン てんごく	(H/K) heaven; paradise	457
散 R-55	散歩	サン さんぽ	(K) a walk; stroll	1273

The *katakana* comes from the first 3 strokes of the kanji.

遠 R-56	を 久遠	を (オン) くおん	(H) R-295 eternity	429

This reading is rare, even in place-names.

The list of characters treated above does not cover all the *kana*, nor does it begin to include all the possible alternative kanji that have served the function now restricted to the *kana*. Unless you plan to start penning *waka* and haiku poems in the classical style, the 56 characters of this chapter should more than suffice as a background to the relationship between the kanji and the *kana*.

CHAPTER 2

Pure Groups

THE EASIEST groups of character-readings to learn are those that share common *on* readings by virtue of the presence of a common primitive element, called here a signal primitive because it "signals" a particular sound for each character in which it appears. Let us begin with a concrete example.

中		チュウ	R-1113	39
R-57	中国	ちゅうごく	China	

As you learned in VOL. 1, the character in the above frame serves as a primitive element in a number of other characters with the *meaning* of "in."

Conveniently, the character itself also provides those characters with a common *on-yomi,* namely チュウ. In other words, each time you see this primitive element, you can be sure what the Chinese reading will be. Among all the kanji treated in VOL. 1, there are three characters that fit this pattern. All you need do to learn their Chinese reading is to recognize them as possessing the signal primitive.

If all the primitive elements served as signal primitives, things would be easier. It might even make sense to study the reading and writing of the kanji together. Alas, this is not the case, so it is best to forget about primitive elements throughout this book.

忠		チュウ		648
R-58	忠告	ちゅうこく	admonition; warning	

沖		チュウ			**146**
R-59	沖天	ちゅうてん	ascendancy; rising to the sky		

仲		チュウ			**1029**
R-60	仲介	ちゅうかい	agency; mediation		

There are other "pure groups"—and these are clearly the majority—in which the signal primitive is not itself a kanji, or at least not one included in the list of those we studied. In these cases, the signal primitive is set off immediately to the right of the kanji treated in the frame. An example follows immediately.

Unless some other explanation is given, the use of proper names for exemplary compounds is meant to indicate that this reading is used exclusively or chiefly for names in modern Japanese.

舗	甫	ホ	R-1011	**1982**
R-61	店舗	てんぽ	a shop; store	

補		ホ		**1983**
R-62	補助金	ほじょきん	financial subsidy	

捕		ホ		**1978**
R-63	逮捕	たいほ	arrest; capture	

哺		ホ		**1979**
R-64	哺乳動物	ほにゅうどうぶつ	mammal	

The size of particular "pure groups" varies. Some are as large as 8, others as small as 2. Since the larger groups are, obviously, easier to learn, we begin with those containing 4 or more kanji. Be careful to note the special conditions that occasionally accompany the signal primitives.

長 R-65		チョウ		2070
	社長	しゃちょう	company president	

張 R-66		チョウ		2071
	主張	しゅちょう	emphasis; insistence	

帳 R-67		チョウ		2072
	通帳	つうちょう	bankbook; passbook	

脹 R-68		チョウ		2073
	膨脹	ぼうちょう	swelling; inflation	

付 R-69		フ		1075
	付与	ふよ	an allowance; grant	

府 R-70		フ		1077
	政府	せいふ	government	

符 R-71		フ		1076
	符号	ふごう	cipher; mark; symbol	

附 R-72		フ		1400
	附近	ふきん	vicinity	
	This character is still used today as an alternative to that in FRAME 70, as the example illustrates.			

腐 R-73		フ		1099
	豆腐	とうふ	bean curd; tofu	

義 R-74		ギ		**691**
	義理	ぎり	social duty; obligation	
議 R-75		ギ		**692**
	会議	かいぎ	meeting; conference	
儀 R-76		ギ		**1059**
	礼儀	れいぎ	etiquette; courtesy	
犠 R-77		ギ		**693**
	犠牲	ぎせい	sacrifice	

青 R-78		セイ	R-1645	**1654**
	青年	せいねん	young man; youth	
精 R-79		セイ	R-1646	**1655**
	精神	せいしん	mind; psyche	
清 R-80		セイ	R-1647	**1659**
	清潔	せいけつ	clean; cleanliness	
晴 R-81		セイ	R-1649	**1658**
	晴天	せいてん	clear skies	
静 R-82		セイ	R-943, 1650	**1660**
	静止	せいし	a standstill	

請 R-83	申請	セイ しんせい	R-1648 application; petition	1656
情 R-84	風情	セイ ふぜい	R-1651 air; appearance	1657

五 R-85	五人	ゴ ごにん	5 people	5
吾 R-86	吾人	ゴ ごじん	we [rare]	17
悟 R-87	覚悟	ゴ かくご	resolve; preparedness	669
語 R-88	日本語	ゴ にほんご	Japanese language	371

白 R-89	白人	ハク はくじん	R-610 white people; Caucasians	37
泊 R-90	一泊	ハク いっぱく	a night's stay	158
迫 R-91	切迫	ハク せっぱく	to be tense; be imminent	300
拍 R-92	拍手	ハク はくしゅ	R-2190 applause	704

舶 R-93		ハク		2013
	舶来品	はくらいひん	imported goods	

伯 R-94		ハク		1041
	伯仲	はくちゅう	to be equal to; be a match for	

包 R-95		ホウ		569
	包丁	ほうちょう	kitchen knife; cleaver	

砲 R-96		ホウ		571
	鉄砲	てっぽう	cannon	

泡 R-97		ホウ		572
	水泡	すいほう	bubbles; foam	

抱 R-98		ホウ		697
	介抱	かいほう	nursing; care	

胞 R-99		ホウ		570
	同胞	どうほう	compatriots; countrymen	

飽 R-100		ホウ		1592
	飽食	ほうしょく	saturation; gluttony	

嬢 R-101	襄	ジョウ		1650
	嬢	じょう	daughter; girl	

譲 R-102	譲歩	ジョウ じょうほ	concession; compromise	1648
壌 R-103	土壌	ジョウ どじょう	the soil	1649
醸 R-104	醸造	ジョウ じょうぞう	brewing; distillation	1647
可 R-105	可能	カ かのう	possibility	97
何 R-106	幾何学	カ きかがく	geometry	1087
苛 R-107	苛酷	カ かこく	rigor; severity	240
荷 R-108	出荷	カ しゅっか	shipping; consignment	1088
歌 R-109	校歌	カ こうか	school song	510
河 R-110	河川	カ かせん	rivers; rivers and streams	157

化		カ	R-1692	1083
R-111	化学	かがく	chemistry	
	The signal primitive must stand alone, with nothing to its right, in order to carry the sound.			

花		カ		1084
R-112	花壇	かだん	flower bed; flower garden	

貨		カ		1085
R-113	貨物	かもつ	freight	

靴		カ		2042
R-114	製靴	せいか	shoemaking	

工		コウ	R-1673	80
R-115	人工	じんこう	man-made	
	The signal primitive in this group must assume a "prominent position" in the character in order to carry the sound with it. When it is tucked away in a corner of the character as a minor element, as in the kanji 築, it loses that function.			

功		コウ	R-2348	927
R-116	成功	せいこう	success	

攻		コウ		352
R-117	専攻	せんこう	field of specialization	

江		コウ	R-28	148
R-118	長江	ちょうこう	long river	

紅 R-119	紅茶	コウ こうちゃ	R-2356 (black) tea	1455
項 R-120	項目	コウ こうもく	item; clause	86
貢 R-121	貢献	コウ こうけん	R-2245 service; contribution	85
巧 R-122	技巧	コウ ぎこう	technique; skill	1329

司 R-123	司会者	シ しかいしゃ	chairperson; emcee	2007
詞 R-124	歌詞	シ かし	song lyrics	2009
飼 R-125	飼育	シ しいく	breeding (of livestock)	2010
伺 R-126	伺候	シ しこう	attendance; waiting upon	2008
嗣 R-127	嗣子	シ しし	heir; successor	2011

官 R-128	教官	カン きょうかん	teacher; professor	1363

管 R-129	管理	カン かんり	administration; management	1365

棺 R-130	棺車	カン かんしゃ	hearse	1364

館 R-131	館長	カン かんちょう	superintendent of a building	1589

倹 R-132	僉 倹約	ケン けんやく	economizing	1804

験 R-133	試験	ケン しけん	R-2308 test; examination	2134

険 R-134	冒険	ケン ぼうけん	adventure	1802

検 R-135	検査	ケン けんさ	inspection	1803

剣 R-136	剣道	ケン けんどう	Japanese "way of the sword"	1801

麻 R-137	麻薬	マ まやく	narcotics	637

摩 R-138	摩天楼	マ まてんろう	skyscraper	689

磨	マ		638
R-139	研磨 けんま	grinding; polishing	

魔	マ		2178
R-140	魔女 まじょ	witch	

士	シ		341
R-141	士官 しかん	commissioned officer	

仕	シ	R-2358	1033
R-142	出仕 しゅっし	attendance (at work)	

志	シ		645
R-143	寸志 すんし	small token (of gratitude)	

誌	シ		646
R-144	雑誌 ざっし	magazine	

申	シン		1198
R-145	申請 しんせい	application; petition	

神	シン	R-1206	1200
R-146	精神 せいしん	mind; psyche	

伸	シン		1199
R-147	伸張 しんちょう	elongation; extension	

| 紳 R-148 | 紳士 しんし | シン | gentleman | 1461 |

| 組 R-149 | 且 組織 そしき The signal primitive must appear on the right, alone. | ソ | organization | 1914 |

| 祖 R-150 | 祖先 そせん | ソ | ancestors | 1918 |

| 租 R-151 | 租税 そぜい | ソ | taxation | 1916 |

| 粗 R-152 | 粗末 そまつ | ソ | crude; shabby | 1915 |

| 狙 R-153 | 狙撃 そげき | ソ | sniping; sharpshooting | 1917 |

| 阻 R-154 | 阻止 そし | ソ | obstruction; hindrance | 1919 |

| 低 R-155 | 氏 低級 ていきゅう | テイ | low-class | 1973 |

| 抵 R-156 | 大抵 たいてい | テイ | by and large; for the most part | 1974 |

底		テイ	**1975**
R-157	海底	かいてい	bottom of the sea
邸		テイ	**1984**
R-158	私邸	してい	private residence

適	商	テキ	**473**
R-159	適切	てきせつ	apt; fitting
敵		テキ	**475**
R-160	敵地	てきち	enemy territory
摘		テキ	**709**
R-161	指摘	してき	pointing out; indication
滴		テキ	**474**
R-162	一滴	いってき	one drop

倍	音	バイ	**1067**
R-163	三倍	さんばい	triple; three times
	The signal primitive must stand to the right, alone.		
培		バイ	**518**
R-164	培養	ばいよう	nurture; cultivate
陪		バイ	**1396**
R-165	陪食	ばいしょく	dining with a superior

賠 R-166		バイ		517
	賠償	ばいしょう	compensation; indemnity	

半 R-167		ハン	R-1276	1285
	半分	はんぶん	half	
	The signal primitive must stand clearly on its own.			

判 R-168		ハン	R-1274	1289
	判定	はんてい	judgment	

畔 R-169		ハン	R-1277	1288
	湖畔	こはん	lakeside; along a lake	

伴 R-170		ハン	R-1275	1287
	同伴	どうはん	company; companion	

講 R-171	冓	コウ		1957
	講義	こうぎ	lecture	

構 R-172		コウ		1959
	機構	きこう	organization; structure	

購 R-173		コウ		1958
	購入	こうにゅう	purchase; buying	

溝 R-174		コウ		1960
	排水溝	はいすいこう	waterway; drainage ditch	

曹		ソウ	**1257**
R-175	法曹界	ほうそうかい	legal circles; judicial world
槽		ソウ	**1260**
R-176	水槽	すいそう	water tank
遭		ソウ	**1258**
R-177	遭遇	そうぐう	encounter
漕		ソウ	**1259**
R-178	回漕	かいそう	sea carriage; marine transport

皆		カイ	**484**
R-179	皆無	かいむ	nothing at all
階		カイ	**1406**
R-180	階級	かいきゅう	social class
楷		カイ	**485**
R-181	楷書	かいしょ	block (square-style) letters
諧		カイ	**486**
R-182	諧調	かいちょう	melody; concord

僚	寮	リョウ	**1842**
R-183	官僚	かんりょう	bureaucracy

寮 R-184		リョウ		1844
	寮長	りょうちょう	dormitory superintendent	
瞭 R-185		リョウ		1843
	明瞭	めいりょう	clear; apparent	
療 R-186		リョウ		1845
	療養	りょうよう	medical care; recuperation	

采 R-187		サイ		791
	采地	さいち	fief; domain	
採 R-188		サイ		792
	採点	さいてん	grading exams	
菜 R-189		サイ		793
	野菜	やさい	vegetables	
彩 R-190		サイ		1850
	彩色	さいしき	coloring	

喩 R-191	俞	ユ		308
	比喩	ひゆ	metaphor	
輸 R-192		ユ		307
	輸出	ゆしゅつ	exports	
愉 R-193		ユ		675
	愉楽	ゆらく	pleasure; joy	

諭		ユ		376
R-194	教諭	きょうゆ	instructor	

癒		ユ		2193
R-195	癒着	ゆちゃく	conglutination; healing up	

The above group of kanji with their *on* readings represents by far the easiest treated in this book. Still, it is important to master them well before moving on, if for no other reason than to make sure you have understood what signal primitives are and how they work.

When you are reviewing (see INTRODUCTION, p. 4), do so only from the compound (not the character) to the reading and meaning—not the reverse. And remember not to clog your memory with useless information (for example, which signal primitives share the same pronunciation). Once you are confident of your progress so far, you can go on to the next group of 114 kanji. They are also of the "pure" type, but number only 3 to a group.

朱		シュ		235
R-196	朱筆	しゅひつ	red (vermilion) brush	

殊		シュ		873
R-197	特殊	とくしゅ	special; particular	

珠		シュ		274
R-198	真珠	しんじゅ	pearl	

路		ロ		1376
R-199	道路	どうろ	road	

賂		ロ		313
R-200	賄賂	わいろ	bribe	

露		ロ	R-2231	1377
R-201	露骨	ろこつ	frank; plain	

幣	敝	ヘイ		1118
R-202	紙幣	しへい	paper money	

蔽		ヘイ		1120
R-203	隠蔽	いんぺい	cover-up	

弊		ヘイ		1119
R-204	弊害	へいがい	evil; abuse	

及		キュウ		743
R-205	普及	ふきゅう	dissemination	

吸		キュウ		744
R-206	吸収	きゅうしゅう	absorption	

級		キュウ		1453
R-207	高級	こうきゅう	top grade; high quality	

知		チ	R-9	1308
R-208	知恵	ちえ	wisdom	

| 痴 | | チ | | 1814 |
| R-209 | 痴漢 | ちかん | molester (of women) | |

| 智 | | チ | | 1309 |
| R-210 | 上智 | じょうち | supreme wisdom | |

| 奴 | | ド | R-47 | 758 |
| R-211 | 奴隷 | どれい | slave | |

| 怒 | | ド | | 759 |
| R-212 | 怒気 | どき | anger; indignation | |

| 努 | | ド | | 929 |
| R-213 | 努力 | どりょく | effort; exertion | |

| 永 | | エイ | | 139 |
| R-214 | 永遠 | えいえん | eternity | |

| 泳 | | エイ | | 144 |
| R-215 | 水泳 | すいえい | swimming | |

| 詠 | | エイ | | 369 |
| R-216 | 詠歌 | えいか | composing a song or poem | |

| 噴 | 賁 | フン | | 1281 |
| R-217 | 噴水 | ふんすい | fountain | |

憤 R-218	義憤	フン ぎふん	1283 righteous indignation
墳 R-219	古墳	フン こふん	1282 tumulus; old burial grounds

呉 R-220	呉服	ゴ ごふく	2046 dry goods; draperies
娯 R-221	娯楽	ゴ ごらく	2047 amusement; entertainment
誤 R-222	誤解	ゴ ごかい	2048 misunderstanding

編 R-223	扁 編集	ヘン へんしゅう	1966 editing
偏 R-224	偏見	ヘン へんけん	1964 bias
遍 R-225	普遍	ヘン ふへん	1965 universal

慈 R-226	茲 慈愛	ジ じあい	1490 kindness and love

磁		ジ		1491
R-227	磁気	じき	magnetism	

滋		ジ		1489
R-228	滋養	じよう	nourishment	

廷		テイ		547
R-229	出廷	しゅってい	appearance in court	

艇		テイ		2021
R-230	艦艇	かんてい	naval vessels; a fleet	

庭		テイ		634
R-231	校庭	こうてい	school grounds; campus	

過	咼	カ		1389
R-232	通過	つうか	transit; passage	

渦		カ		1387
R-233	渦中	かちゅう	in a whirlpool	

禍		カ		1386
R-234	禍福	かふく	fortune and misfortune	

坑	亢	コウ		328
R-235	坑道	こうどう	mine shaft	

航		コウ	2014
R-236	航海	こうかい	sea voyage; crossing the ocean

抗		コウ	700
R-237	抵抗	ていこう	resistance

巨		キョ	920
R-238	巨人	きょじん	a giant

拒		キョ	921
R-239	拒否	きょひ	denial; rejection

距		キョ	1375
R-240	距離	きょり	distance

燥	梟	ソウ	228
R-241	乾燥	かんそう	dryness

操		ソウ	724
R-242	操縦	そうじゅう	piloting; maneuvering

藻		ソウ	2191
R-243	海藻	かいそう	seaweed

求		キュウ	1004
R-244	要求	ようきゅう	demand; request

| 救 R-245 | | キュウ | | 1006 |
| | 救急車 | きゅうきゅうしゃ | ambulance | |

| 球 R-246 | | キュウ | | 1005 |
| | 野球 | やきゅう | baseball | |

| 二 R-247 | | ニ | R-1 | 2 |
| | 十二 | じゅうに | twelve | |

| 弐 R-248 | | ニ | | 379 |
| | 弐万円 | にまんえん | ¥20,000 | |

| 仁 R-249 | | ニ | R-32, 2210 | 1063 |
| | 仁王門 | におうもん | temple gate with Deva Kings | |

| 縫 R-250 | 夆 | ホウ | | 1685 |
| | 縫合 | ほうごう | suture; stitching | |

| 峰 R-251 | | ホウ | | 1683 |
| | 高峰 | こうほう | lofty peak | |

| 蜂 R-252 | | ホウ | | 1684 |
| | 蜂起 | ほうき | insurrection; uprising | |

| 先 R-253 | | セン | | 263 |
| | 先生 | せんせい | teacher | |

洗		セン	264
R-254	洗車	せんしゃ	car wash

銑		セン	289
R-255	銑鉄	せんてつ	pig iron

新	亲	シン	1619
R-256	新聞	しんぶん	newspaper

薪		シン	1620
R-257	薪水	しんすい	fuel and water

親		シン	1621
R-258	親切	しんせつ	kind; thoughtful

侵	㞒	シン	1231
R-259	侵入	しんにゅう	invasion

浸		シン	1232
R-260	浸水	しんすい	flooding

寝		シン	1233
R-261	寝室	しんしつ	bedroom

章		ショウ	464
R-262	文章	ぶんしょう	a sentence (of writing)

彰		ショウ	1851
R-263	表彰	ひょうしょう	commendation

障		ショウ	1393
R-264	障子	しょうじ	Japanese sliding paper windows

朝		チョウ	53
R-265	朝食	ちょうしょく	breakfast

嘲		チョウ	54
R-266	嘲罵	ちょうば	taunt

潮		チョウ	152
R-267	満潮	まんちょう	high tide

州		シュウ	135
R-268	本州	ほんしゅう	(Japan's) main island

洲		シュウ	2386
R-269	六大洲	ろくだいしゅう	the "6" continents

酬		シュウ	1540
R-270	応酬	おうしゅう	retort; repartee

泉		セン	140
R-271	泉水	せんすい	natural spring

腺		セン		141
R-272	汗腺	かんせん	sweat gland	

線		セン		1438
R-273	線路	せんろ	railroad tracks	

壮		ソウ		343
R-274	壮大	そうだい	grandeur; magnificence	

荘		ソウ		344
R-275	別荘	べっそう	resort; villa	

装		ソウ	R-2288	425
R-276	服装	ふくそう	dress; attire	

相		ソウ	R-1694	222
R-277	相談	そうだん	consultation	

想		ソウ	R-2242	656
R-278	思想	しそう	thought; thinking	

霜		ソウ		455
R-279	霜害	そうがい	frost damage	

則		ソク		92
R-280	反則	はんそく	foul; infraction	

測 R-281	測量	ソク そくりょう		160
			surveying; fathoming	
側 R-282	側面	ソク そくめん		1049
			aspect; facet	

代 R-283	交代	タイ こうたい	R-1195	1080
			taking turns; exchange	
貸 R-284	貸与	タイ たいよ		1082
			loan; lending	
袋 R-285	郵袋	タイ ゆうたい		1081
			mail pouch; mailbag	

丙 R-286	甲乙丙	ヘイ こうおつへい		1096
			A, B, C (old enumeration)	
柄 R-287	横柄	ヘイ おうへい		1097
			arrogance	
病 R-288	疾病	ヘイ しっぺい	R-1254	1813
			illness	

玄 R-289	玄関	ゲン げんかん		1484
			front door; main entrance	

弦		ゲン		1487
R-290	正弦	せいげん	sine (of an angle)	
舷		ゲン		2016
R-291	舷窓	げんそう	porthole	

善		ゼン		1112
R-292	慈善	じぜん	benevolence	
膳		ゼン		1113
R-293	お膳	おぜん	table tray; serving of food	
繕		ゼン		1433
R-294	修繕	しゅうぜん	repair; mending	

遠	袁	エン	R-56	429
R-295	永遠	えいえん	eternity	
園		エン		629
R-296	庭園	ていえん	(Japanese) garden	
猿		エン		430
R-297	野猿	やえん	wild monkey	

帝		テイ		466
R-298	帝国	ていこく	empire	

諦		テイ	**467**
R-299	諦観	ていかん	resignation (to)
締		テイ	**1440**
R-300	締結	ていけつ	conclusion (of a treaty, contract)

足		ソク	**1372**
R-301	不足	ふそく	insufficiency
促		ソク	**1373**
R-302	促進	そくしん	promotion; facilitation
捉		ソク	**1374**
R-303	捕捉	ほそく	capture; apprehension

苗		ビョウ	**249**
R-304	種苗	しゅびょう	seeds and seedlings
描		ビョウ	**723**
R-305	点描	てんびょう	a sketch; profile
猫		ビョウ	**259**
R-306	愛猫	あいびょう	pet cat

家		カ	R-1994	**580**
R-307	家庭	かてい		home

嫁 R-308		カ		**581**
	転嫁	てんか	remarrying (archaic)	

稼 R-309		カ		**959**
	稼動	かどう	operation (of a factory); work	

末 R-310		マツ	R-2319	**230**
	粗末	そまつ	plain; coarse	

沫 R-311		マツ		**232**
	泡沫	ほうまつ	bubbles; foam	

抹 R-312		マツ		**694**
	抹殺	まっさつ	obliteration	

峡 R-313	夾	キョウ		**1355**
	海峡	かいきょう	straits; sound; channel	

狭 R-314		キョウ		**1356**
	偏狭	へんきょう	narrow-minded	

挟 R-315		キョウ		**1357**
	挟撃	きょうげき	catch in a crossfire	

橋 R-316	喬	キョウ		**460**
	鉄橋	てっきょう	iron bridge	

矯		キョウ		1306
R-317	矯正	きょうせい	reform; correction	

嬌		キョウ		461
R-318	愛嬌	あいきょう	affable; charming	

侯	矣	コウ		1767
R-319	王侯	おうこう	kings and princes	

喉		コウ		1768
R-320	咽喉	いんこう	throat	

候		コウ		1769
R-321	候補	こうほ	candidacy	

屈		クツ		1140
R-322	退屈	たいくつ	boredom	

掘		クツ		1141
R-323	採掘	さいくつ	working a mine; mining	

窟		クツ		1420
R-324	洞窟	とうくつ	cavern; grotto	

建		ケン	R-2255	417
R-325	建議	けんぎ	submission of a proposal	

鍵		ケン		418
R-326	鍵盤	けんばん	keyboard	

健		ケン		1048
R-327	保健	ほけん	health protection; hygiene	

凡		ハン	R-2104	66
R-328	凡例	はんれい	introductory remarks	

帆		ハン		434
R-329	帆船	はんせん	sailing vessel	

汎		ハン		147
R-330	汎アメリカ	はんアメリカ	pan-American	

勤	菫	キン	R-2392	1700
R-331	出勤	しゅっきん	going to work	

僅		キン		1699
R-332	僅々	きんきん	only; no more than	

謹		キン		1698
R-333	謹呈	きんてい	compliments of the author	

幾		キ	R-29	1481
R-334	幾何学	きかがく	geometry	

畿 R-335	近畿	キ きんき		1483 capital suburbs (around Kyoto)
機 R-336	機会	キ きかい		1482 opportunity

Having completed the larger of the "pure groups," we now come to the more difficult: those with only 2 kanji. Although the groups are small, learning them by means of their signal primitives will come in useful later, once you have left the confines of the general-use kanji. That is to say, many of the signal primitives we are learning here are not restricted to the characters we treat.

録 R-337	录 記録	ロク きろく		1226 record; annals
緑 R-338	緑青	ロク ろくしょう	R-2345	1471 verdigris; green rust

元 R-339	元日	ガン がんじつ	R-1088	63 New Year's Day
頑 R-340	頑固	ガン がんこ		65 stubborn; hardheaded
協 R-341	劦 協力	キョウ きょうりょく		937 cooperation

脅 R-342	脅迫	キョウ きょうはく	blackmail	936

総 R-343	怱 総計	ソウ そうけい	sum total	1466

窓 R-344	同窓	ソウ どうそう	alumni	811

唱 R-345	昌 唱歌	ショウ しょうか	singing	21

晶 R-346	水晶	ショウ すいしょう	crystal	22

忍 R-347	忍者	ニン にんじゃ	a "ninja" spy	642

認 R-348	否認	ニン ひにん	disapproval; denial	643

貞 R-349	貞操	テイ ていそう	chastity	58

偵 R-350	内偵	テイ ないてい	scouting	1056

安 R-351	安心	アン あんしん	R-52 peace of heart	**202**
案 R-352	案内	アン あんない	guiding; information	**227**

伐 R-353	伐採	バツ ばっさい	felling trees; deforestation	**1069**
閥 R-354	派閥	バツ はばつ	clique; faction	**1746**

暴 R-355	暴露	バク ばくろ	R-1144 disclosure; uncovering	**1941**
爆 R-356	爆発	バク ばくはつ	explosion	**1942**

冒 R-357	冒険	ボウ ぼうけん	adventure	**18**
帽 R-358	帽子	ボウ ぼうし	hat; cap	**436**

塑 R-359	朔 塑像	ソ そぞう	doll or statue molded out of clay	**2110**

遡		ソ		2111
R-360	遡及	そきゅう	retroaction	

離	离	リ	R-971	1605
R-361	離陸	りりく	take off (e.g., an airplane)	

璃		リ		1606
R-362	瑠璃	るり	lapis lazuli gem	

僕	美	ボク		1933
R-363	僕	ぼく	I; me	

撲		ボク		1932
R-364	撲殺	ぼくさつ	clubbing to death	

無	無	ブ	R-1219	1913
R-365	無礼	ぶれい	discourtesy	

舞		ブ		1912
R-366	舞台	ぶたい	(theatre) stage	

畜		チク		1485
R-367	家畜	かちく	domestic animals; livestock	

蓄		チク		1486
R-368	蓄電池	ちくでんち	storage battery cell	

面 R-369		メン	2039
	面倒	めんどう	troublesome
麺 R-370		メン	2040
	麺類	めんるい	noodles

徴 R-371		チョウ	952
	象徴	しょうちょう	symbol
懲 R-372		チョウ	953
	懲罰	ちょうばつ	disciplinary action; punishment

動 R-373		ドウ	1806
	自動車	じどうしゃ	automobile
働 R-374		ドウ	1809
	労働	ろうどう	labor

道 R-375		ドウ	R-1868	295
	華道	かどう		the Japanese "way of flowers"
導 R-376		ドウ		296
	指導	しどう		guidance

我 R-377		ガ	690
	自我	じが	ego

餓 R-378	飢餓	ガ きが	starvation; famishing	1586

普 R-379	普及	フ ふきゅう	dissemination	1925

譜 R-380	楽譜	フ がくふ	musical score	1926

比 R-381	比較	ヒ ひかく	R-21 comparison	482

The signal primitive must stand with nothing above or below it.

批 R-382	批判	ヒ ひはん	criticism	701

卑 R-383	卑屈	ヒ ひくつ	sneaky; obsequious	1629

碑 R-384	碑銘	ヒ ひめい	monument inscription; epitaph	1630

名 R-385	有名	メイ ゆうめい	R-2252 famous	117

銘 R-386	碑銘	メイ ひめい	monument inscription; epitaph	293

利 R-387	利用 りよう	リ R-10 use	972
痢 R-388	下痢 げり	リ diarrhea	1821

朋 R-389	朋友 ほうゆう	ホウ friend; companion	19
崩 R-390	崩壊 ほうかい	ホウ collapse	836

表 R-391	表装 ひょうそう	ヒョウ mounting (a picture or hanging)	1666
俵 R-392	土俵 どひょう	ヒョウ sandbags; sumō ring	1667

尉 R-393	尉官 いかん	イ (low-ranking) company officer	1176
慰 R-394	慰安 いあん	イ solace; comfort	1177

乗 R-395	乗車 じょうしゃ	ジョウ riding in a car	1709

剩		ジョウ		1710
R-396	過剰	かじょう	excess	

受		ジュ		794
R-397	受験	じゅけん	sitting for an exam	

授		ジュ		795
R-398	教授	きょうじゅ	professor	

需		ジュ		1249
R-399	需要	じゅよう	demand (opposite of "supply")	

儒		ジュ		1250
R-400	儒学	じゅがく	Confucianism	

従		ジュウ	R-2243, 2363	942
R-401	従事	じゅうじ	engagement; pursuit	

縦		ジュウ		1436
R-402	操縦	そうじゅう	piloting; maneuvering	

塾	孰	ジュク		331
R-403	塾長	じゅくちょう	principal of a private school	

熟		ジュク		332
R-404	成熟	せいじゅく	ripeness; maturity	

旬 R-405	中旬	ジュン ちゅうじゅん	R-2284 middle ten days of the month	71

殉 R-406	殉死	ジュン じゅんし	martyr's death	872

盾 R-407	矛盾	ジュン むじゅん	contradiction	1997

Literally: a lance that nothing can resist and a shield that nothing can penetrate.

循 R-408	循環	ジュン じゅんかん	cycle; rotation	1998

述 R-409	叙述	ホ ジュツ じょじゅつ	description	1643

術 R-410	技術	ジュツ ぎじゅつ	technology	1644

斬 R-411	斬首	ザン ざんしゅ	decapitation	1215

暫 R-412	暫定	ザン ざんてい	provisional; temporary	1216

介 R-413	仲介	カイ ちゅうかい	mediation; intermediation	265

界		カイ		266
R-414	世界	せかい	world	

戒		カイ		730
R-415	戒律	かいりつ	(Buddhist) precepts	

械		カイ		732
R-416	機械	きかい	machine; mechanism	

壊	褱	カイ		427
R-417	崩壊	ほうかい	destruction; collapse	

懐		カイ		891
R-418	述懐	じゅっかい	reminiscences	

貫		カン		106
R-419	貫通	かんつう	piercing; penetration	

慣		カン		674
R-420	習慣	しゅうかん	custom; habit; convention	

換	奐	カン		1122
R-421	交換	こうかん	interchange; exchange	

喚		カン		1121
R-422	召喚	しょうかん	recall; reclamation	

還 R-423	景 還元	カン かんげん	reduction	900
環 R-424	循環	カン じゅんかん	cycle; rotation	899

間 R-425	時間	カン じかん	R-1710 time	1747
簡 R-426	簡単	カン かんたん	simple; uncomplicated	1749

脳 R-427	凶 首脳	ノウ しゅのう	head of state or government	2084
悩 R-428	苦悩	ノウ くのう	suffering; distress	2085

随 R-429	迶 随分	ズイ ずいぶん	fairly; pretty much	1395
髄 R-430	脳髄	ズイ のうずい	the brains	1385

黄 R-431	黄金	オウ おうごん	R-1979 gold	1887

横 R-432	横断	オウ おうだん	crossing; cutting across	1888

渓 R-433	奚 渓谷	ケイ けいこく	dale; valley	903

鶏 R-434	鶏卵	ケイ けいらん	hen eggs	2097

県 R-435	県庁	ケン けんちょう	prefectural office	552

懸 R-436	懸賞	ケン けんしょう	R-2271 reward or prize	1495

気 R-437	气 天気	キ てんき	R-1867 weather	2030

汽 R-438	汽車	キ きしゃ	(steam) locomotive	2031

高 R-439	高校	コウ こうこう	high school	329

稿 R-440	原稿	コウ げんこう	manuscript; original draft	958

勇 R-441		ユウ		1509
	勇気	ゆうき	bravery; "manhood"	

湧 R-442		ユウ		1510
	湧出	ゆうしゅつ	eruption; gushing forth	

荒 R-443		コウ		529
	荒野	こうや	wasteland	

慌 R-444		コウ		671
	恐慌	きょうこう	panic; alarm	

愛 R-445		アイ		796
	可愛い	かわいい	cute	

曖 R-446		アイ		797
	曖昧	あいまい	vague; unclear	

懇 R-447	狠	コン		2123
	懇親会	こんしんかい	social reunion; reception	

墾 R-448		コン		2124
	開墾	かいこん	reopening a wasteland	

骨 R-449		コツ		1383
	骨髄	こつずい	bone marrow	

滑 R-450	滑稽	コツ こっけい	R-1889 laughable; ridiculous	1384

郎 R-451	新郎	ロウ しんろう	bridegroom	1995

廊 R-452	画廊	ロウ がろう	painting gallery	1996

冊 R-453	短冊	サク たんざく	R-1189 slender slips of paper on which poems are written	1967

柵 R-454	鉄柵	サク てっさく	iron railing	1968

勲 R-455	熏 勲功	クン くんこう	distinguished service	1808

薫 R-456	薫風	クン くんぷう	light, balmy breeze; zephyr	1812

却 R-457	返却	キャク へんきゃく	return; reimbursement	1497

脚 R-458	脚本	キャク きゃくほん	R-582 script; screenplay	1498

郷 R-459	故郷	キョウ こきょう	R-2283 one's native place; hometown	1993
響 R-460	影響	キョウ えいきょう	influence	1994
境 R-461	竟 境界	キョウ きょうかい	R-2150 boundary	525
鏡 R-462	鏡台	キョウ きょうだい	mirror-stand; dresser	524
慢 R-463	曼 我慢	マン がまん	patience; tolerance	892
漫 R-464	漫画	マン まんが	comic book; comics	893
明 R-465	説明	メイ せつめい	R-1691 explanation	20
盟 R-466	同盟	メイ どうめい	association; alliance	1558
民 R-467	国民	ミン こくみん	people (of a country)	1976

眠		ミン		1977
R-468	安眠	あんみん	peaceful sleep	

然		ネン	R-1059	256
R-469	天然	てんねん	natural (not artificial)	

燃		ネン		549
R-470	可燃性	かねんせい	combustibility	

暦	麻	レキ		226
R-471	還暦	かんれき	one's 60th birthday	

歴		レキ		402
R-472	歴史	れきし	history	

農		ノウ		2170
R-473	農学校	のうがっこう	agricultural school	

濃		ノウ		2171
R-474	濃厚	のうこう	thickness; density	

禁		キン		1179
R-475	禁止	きんし	prohibition	

襟		キン		1180
R-476	襟度	きんど	magnanimity	

刑 R-477		ケイ		734
	死刑	しけい	death penalty	

型 R-478		ケイ		735
	原型	げんけい	model; prototype	

察 R-479		サツ		1184
	警察	けいさつ	police	

擦 R-480		サツ		1185
	摩擦	まさつ	friction; chafing	

双 R-481		ソウ		753
	双方	そうほう	both sides	

桑 R-482		ソウ		754
	桑園	そうえん	mulberry farm or orchard	

帯 R-483		タイ		444
	地帯	ちたい	(geographical) zone	

滞 R-484		タイ		445
	滞貨	たいか	backlog of freight or goods	

宅 R-485	モ	タク		2065
	自宅	じたく	private residence	

| 託 R-486 | 神託 | タク しんたく | oracle; revelation | 2066 |

| 呈 R-487 | 謹呈 | テイ きんてい | compliments of the author | 280 |

| 程 R-488 | 程度 | テイ ていど | extent; degree | 960 |

| 班 R-489 | 班長 | ハン はんちょう | squad or section leader | 1315 |

| 斑 R-490 | 斑点 | ハン はんてん | specks; dots | 1865 |

| 亭 R-491 | 料亭 | テイ りょうてい | Japanese-style restaurant | 333 |

| 停 R-492 | 停止 | テイ ていし | suspension; ban | 1051 |

| 徹 R-493 | 育 徹底的 | テツ てっていてき | thoroughgoing; radical | 951 |

| 撤 R-494 | 撤回 | テツ てっかい | withdrawal; revocation | 822 |

度 R-495		ト	R-1117, 2262	**1278**
	法度	はっと	ban	
	The readings of both characters belong to the official list, but are not the most common readings. As throughout the book, their other (in this case, more ordinary) readings are cross-referenced.			

渡 R-496		ト		**1279**
	渡航	とこう	a passage; (sailing) voyage	

唐 R-497		トウ		**1241**
	唐突	とうとつ	abrupt; all of a sudden	

糖 R-498		トウ		**1242**
	砂糖	さとう	sugar	

倉 R-499		ソウ		**1758**
	倉庫	そうこ	warehouse	

創 R-500		ソウ		**1759**
	創造	そうぞう	creation	

謡 R-501	䍃	ヨウ		**2119**
	民謡	みんよう	folk song	

揺 R-502		ヨウ		**2118**
	動揺	どうよう	shaking; tremor	

要 R-503	需要	ヨウ じゅよう		demand (opposite of "supply")	1730
腰 R-504	腰部	ヨウ ようぶ		hips; waist area	1731

容 R-505	内容	ヨウ ないよう		contents	853
溶 R-506	溶解	ヨウ ようかい		melting	854

憂 R-507	憂愁	ユウ ゆうしゅう		gloom; melancholy	663
優 R-508	俳優	ユウ はいゆう		actor	1068

秋 R-509	秋季	シュウ しゅうき		autumn season	966
愁 R-510	憂愁	シュウ ゆうしゅう		gloom; melancholy	967

夏 R-511	百 夏期	カ かき	R-2253	summertime	317

寡 R-512	多寡	カ たか		664 amount; quantity

象 R-513	象	ゾウ ぞう	R-1776	2130 elephant

像 R-514	想像	ゾウ そうぞう		2131 imagination; fantasy

蔵 R-515	蔵書	ゾウ ぞうしょ		913 library; collection of books

臓 R-516	心臓	ゾウ しんぞう		914 heart (the organ)

宿 R-517	宿泊	シュク しゅくはく		1070 room and board

縮 R-518	縮小	シュク しゅくしょう		1434 shrinking

量 R-519	測量	リョウ そくりょう		189 surveying; measurement

糧 R-520	糧食	リョウ りょうしょく	R-2256	995 food provisions

流 R-521	充 流動	リュウ りゅうどう	R-15 a flow; flowing	826
硫 R-522	硫安	リュウ りゅうあん	ammonium sulfate	825
参 R-523	参加	サン さんか	participation	1856
惨 R-524	悲惨	サン ひさん	R-2236 distress; wretchedness	1857
制 R-525	制度	セイ せいど	system	447
製 R-526	製靴	セイ せいか	shoemaking	448
切 R-527	親切	セツ しんせつ	R-2247 kind; thoughtful	89
窃 R-528	窃取	セツ せっしゅ	theft	1419
射 R-529	放射	シヤ ほうしゃ	radiation; emission	1338

謝		シャ		1339
R-530	謝礼	しゃれい	honorarium	

放		ホウ		535
R-531	放射	ほうしゃ	radiation; emission	

倣		ホウ		1053
R-532	模倣	もほう	imitation; copying	

升		ショウ		42
R-533	一升	いっしょう	one measure (of saké)	

昇		ショウ		43
R-534	上昇	じょうしょう	rise; ascent	

焦		ショウ		599
R-535	焦燥	しょうそう	fretting; irritability	

礁		ショウ		600
R-536	岩礁	がんしょう	(offshore) reef	

将		ショウ		789
R-537	将軍	しょうぐん	general; shōgun	

奨		ショウ		790
R-538	奨学金	しょうがくきん	scholarship money	

守		シュ	R-1211	**198**
R-539	保守的	ほしゅてき	conservative	
狩		シュ		**258**
R-540	狩猟	しゅりょう	hunting	

感		カン	**662**
R-541	感謝	かんしゃ	thanks; gratitude
憾		カン	**678**
R-542	遺憾	いかん	regrettable

雇		コ	**1164**
R-543	雇用	こよう	employing; employment
顧		コ	**1165**
R-544	顧問	こもん	advisor

紫	此	シ		**1475**
R-545	紫外線	しがいせん	ultraviolet rays	
雌		シ		**605**
R-546	雌雄	しゆう	males and females	

卒	十	ソツ		**1102**
R-547	卒業	そつぎょう	graduation (from school)	

率		ソツ	R-1812	1874
R-548	率先	そっせん	pioneer; forerunner	

到		トウ		817
R-549	到底	とうてい	absolutely; (not) at all	

倒		トウ		1055
R-550	卒倒	そっとう	swoon; fainting fit	

机	几	キ		223
R-551	机上	きじょう	desktop; on a desk	

飢		キ		1585
R-552	飢餓	きが	starvation	

祭		サイ		1183
R-553	司祭	しさい	priest; ritual celebrant	

際		サイ		1392
R-554	国際	こくさい	international	

密	宓	ミツ		837
R-555	秘密	ひみつ	secret	

蜜		ミツ		838
R-556	蜜房	みつぼう	honeycomb	

塔 R-557	苔	トウ	270
	金字塔	きんじとう	pyramid; monumental work
搭 R-558		トウ	698
	搭乗	とうじょう	boarding (a vessel)

座 R-559	坐	ザ	1999
	座席	ざせき	seat
挫 R-560		ザ	1101
	捻挫	ねんざ	sprain

念 R-561		ネン	1715
	記念	きねん	commemoration
捻 R-562		ネン	1716
	捻挫	ねんざ	sprain

疾 R-563		シツ	1820
	疾風迅雷的	しっぷうじんらいてき	lightning fast
嫉 R-564		シツ	1820
	嫉妬	しっと	jealousy

就 R-565		シュウ　　R-2238	2121
	就職	しゅうしょく	taking up a job

蹴 R-566		シュウ		2122
	蹴球	しゅうきゅう	soccer (old term)	

訃 R-567		フ		363
	訃報	ふほう	death notice	

赴 R-568		フ		412
	赴任	ふにん	post; assignment	

捜 R-569	叟	ソウ		1201
	捜索	そうさく	manhunt; search	

痩 R-570		ソウ		1818
	痩身	そうしん	slender body; lean figure	

The kanji featured in the following two frames are unique in that each allows a common second reading. Learn the next four frames as a unit.

会 R-571		カイ	R-573	814
	会計	かいけい	accounts; accountant	

絵 R-572		カイ	R-574	1446
	絵画	かいが	picture; painting	

会 R-573		エ	R-571	814
	会釈	えしゃく	salutations; a bow	

絵		エ	R-572	1446
R-574	絵本	えほん	picture book	

CHAPTER 3

One-Time Chinese Readings

THE CHARACTERS brought together in this chapter should be learned well before passing on to the rest of the book. Knowing them will remove another obstacle from the long road that lies ahead.

This collection of "one-time" readings sifts out all the *on-yomi* (Chinese readings) that are *not* homonyms, at least not in the confines of the standard readings on which this book is based. We have already learned of these readings in CHAPTER 1:

部 = ヘ　祢 = ネ　寸 = スン　奴 = ヌ

This means that the sounds セ, ヘ, ネ, スン, and ヌ will not appear elsewhere in these pages as a reading for any kanji.

The characters these one-time Chinese readings belong to may, of course, take additional readings (see the cross-reference numbers) and phonetic transformations may in fact yield the same sound in certain cases, but the sounds will not be assigned to any other character of those learned in VOL. 1 as a standard reading.

圧		アツ		163
R-575	圧迫	あっぱく	oppression	
域		イキ		380
R-576	境域	きょういき	precincts	
育		イク		821
R-577	教育	きょういく	education	

鬱 R-578	鬱病	ウツ うつびょう		2120 clinical depression
乙 R-579	甲乙丙	オツ こうおつへい		75 A, B, C (a traditional way of enu-merating)
菊 R-580	菊	キク きく		996 chrysanthemum
吉 R-581	吉日	キチ きちじつ	R-979	342 lucky day
脚 R-582	脚立	キャ きゃたつ	R-458	1498 stepladder

Note that this word combines a Chinese and a Japanese reading. We will other examples in FRAME R-1975.

牛 R-583	牛乳	ギュウ ぎゅうにゅう		260 (cow's) milk
玉 R-584	宝玉	ギョク ほうぎょく		272 precious stones; gems
空 R-585	空気	クウ くうき		1414 air; atmosphere
月 R-586	三ヶ月	ゲツ さんかげつ	R-1062	13 3 months

早		サッ	R-1976	26
R-587	早速	さっそく	in a hurry; at once	

雑		ザツ	R-2188	604
R-588	雑誌	ざっし	magazine	

軸		ジク	R-1464	1193
R-589	車軸	しゃじく	axle; wheel	

出		シュツ	R-2185	829
R-590	出勤	しゅっきん	showing up at work	

辱		ジョク	R-811	2165
R-591	屈辱	くつじょく	humiliation; disgrace	

是		ゼ	R-1608	414
R-592	是非	ぜひ	by all means; at any cost	

節		セチ	R-1825	1574
R-593	お節料理	おせちりょうり	New Year's dishes	

曽		ゾ	R-48, 1289	540
R-594	未曽有	みぞう	unprecedented	

存		ゾン	R-1997	739
R-595	保存	ほぞん	preservation; conservation	

達		タツ		591
R-596	達人	たつじん	expert	

茶 R-597	紅茶	チャ こうちゃ	R-1115 (black) tea	267
弟 R-598	弟子	デ でし	R-1538 disciple	1328
泥 R-599	泥酔	デイ でいすい	dead drunk	1135
溺 R-600	溺死	デキ できし	death by drowning	1324

Though the same primitive element appears in both kanji of this compound, it does not serve as a signal primitive.

納 R-601	納豆	ナッ なっとう	R-1742, 2185, 2321, 2323 fermented soybeans	1456
肉 R-602	肉親	ニク にくしん	blood relative	1098
日 R-603	一日	ニチ いちにち	R-1704 one day	12
若 R-604	老若	ニャク ろうにゃく	R-2101 young and old	237
寧 R-605	丁寧	ネイ ていねい	politeness; courtesy; civility	897

熱 R-606		ネツ		1634
	熱帯	ねったい	the tropics	

八 R-607		ハチ		8
	尺八	しゃくはち	*shakuhachi* flute	

罰 R-608		バチ	R-1707	896
	罰当たり	ばちあたり	cursed; damned	
	The second kanji is read with its *kun-yomi*.			

百 R-609		ヒャク		38
	二百	にひゃく	200	

白 R-610		ビャク	R-89	37
	黒白	こくびゃく	black and white; good and bad	

米 R-611		ベイ	R-2166	987
	米国	べいこく	America	

北 R-612		ホク		480
	北海道	ほっかいどう	Hokkaidō (Japanese island)	

脈 R-613		ミャク		2000
	動脈	どうみゃく	artery	

滅 R-614		メツ		390
	滅亡	めつぼう	downfall; destruction	

勿論 R-615		モチ		1128
		ロン	R-1002	1961
	勿論	もちろん	obvious; beyond dispute	
物 R-616		モツ	R-1111	1129
	食物	しょくもつ	foodstuffs	
辣 R-617		ラツ		1798
	辣腕	らつわん	shrewdness	
力 R-618		リキ	R-1200	922
	馬力	ばりき	horsepower	
陸 R-619		リク		1631
	陸上	りくじょう	on shore	
律 R-620		リチ	R-1815	1814
	律義	りちぎ	honesty; integrity	
略 R-621		リャク	R-1473	314
	略語	りゃくご	abbreviation	
賄 R-622		ワイ		84
	収賄	しゅうわい	accepting a bribe	
惑 R-623		ワク		661
	迷惑	めいわく	trouble; inconvenience	

CHAPTER 4

Characters with No Chinese Readings

THE KANJI that make up this chapter are presented more for recognition than for memorization. As the title indicates, their common point is that they are assigned no Chinese reading in this book.

In the case of those that belong to the general-use kanji, this means that no reading has been assigned them in the official list, though many of them do have traditional readings. In the case of those that fall outside the general-use list, this means that no Chinese reading they may have is useful enough to bear learning at this stage.

Look over this list carefully before you go on to the next chapter, making sure that you recognize all the characters from your study of VOL. 1. In some cases, you will no doubt recognize signal primitives used in CHAPTER 2. Here, of course, the primitives do not come into the picture at all—even though some of the kanji given here will themselves serve as signal primitives in the course of this book.

The cross-reference numbers in bold print under the number of the kanji refer only to the frame in VOL. 1 in which the character in question first appeared.

Finally, you will notice that 8 of the kanji have numbers followed by an asterisk (*). This sets them off as homemade kanji or 国字 (こくじ) which the Japanese did not inherit from Chinese but invented on their own. These characters have only one reading, which is almost always a Japanese reading. In this regard they differ from several of the others below, which do in fact have assigned Chinese readings but are not given here because they fall outside the rules of the general-use kanji.

昌	旭	亙	肘	只
R-624	R-625	R-626	R-627	R-628
25	27	32	46	55

貝 R-629 **56**	唄 R-630 **57**	頁 R-631 **64**	肌 R-632 **70**	汐 R-633 **115**
埼 R-634 **164**	垣 R-635 **165**	畑 R-636* **178**	鯉 R-637 **188**	柏 R-638 **211**
枠 R-639* **212**	梢 R-640 **213**	棚 R-641 **214**	杏 R-642 **215**	柿 R-643 **441**
株 R-644 **236**	荻 R-645 **257**	辻 R-646 **297**	幌 R-647 **438**	ヒ R-648 **476**
勺 R-649* **478**	頃 R-650 **479**	乞 R-651 **501**	茨 R-652 **513**	栃 R-653* **553**
虹 R-654 **559**	滝 R-655 **576**	誰 R-656 **598**	曰 R-657 **620**	串 R-658 **649**

掛 R-659 727	扱 R-660 745	又 R-661 752	爪 R-662 784	峠 R-663* 835
嵐 R-664 839	崎 R-665 840	込 R-666* 843	姫 R-667 912	脇 R-668 935
桁 R-669 956	梨 R-670 973	謎 R-671 994	膝 R-672 1002	笠 R-673 1009
笹 R-674* 1010	箱 R-675 1013	但 R-676 1026	俺 R-677 1091	畝 R-678 1093
勿 R-679* 1104	塚 R-680 1117	尻 R-681 1134	堀 R-682 1142	据 R-683 1144
裾 R-684 1145	届 R-685 1191	岬 R-686 1196	廿 R-687 1274	芝 R-688 1301

弥 R-689 1322	箸 R-690 1348	渚 R-691 1353	頬 R-692 1358	釜 R-693 1367
鍋 R-694 1388	窪 R-695 1421	繰 R-696 1469	卸 R-697 1499	酉 R-698 1534
皿 R-699 1555	娘 R-700 1581	坪 R-701 1598	刈 R-702 1600	梓 R-703 1614
菱 R-704 1635	亥 R-705 1637	漬 R-706 1665	椿 R-707 1691	鎌 R-708 1725
栗 R-709 1735	楠 R-710 1741	闇 R-711 1748	芋 R-712 1784	瀬 R-713 1795
杉 R-714 1849	彦 R-715 1852	蚊 R-716 1864	井 R-717 1947	浦 R-718 1980

蒲	枕	鶴	蔦	鳩
R-719	R-720	R-721	R-722	R-723
1981	2034	2093	2095	2096
岡	駒	虞	鹿	熊
R-724	R-725	R-726	R-727	R-728
2112	2133	2150	2154	2159
寅	咲	且	潟	丑
R-729	R-730	R-731	R-732	R-733
2162	2174	2190	2195	2197
卯	巳			
R-734	R-735			
2199	2200			

5

Semi-Pure Groups

THE KANJI treated in this chapter differ from those of CHAPTER 2 only in one significant detail: the signal primitive bears a uniform reading for all but *one* of the characters in which it appears. Here again, secondary or tertiary readings for the kanji do not necessarily follow the rule. The point is only that one of the assigned readings of the character is not affected at all by the semi-pure group to which it belongs by virtue of its signal primitive.

Let us take a group of 6 kanji, the first 5 of which show a common reading based on the lead character which serves as a signal primitive for the others:

次		シ	R-1749	512
R-736	次第	しだい	gradually; little by little	
姿		シ		515
R-737	姿勢	しせい	posture	
資		シ		514
R-738	資本	しほん	capital; funds	
恣		シ		641
R-739	恣意	しい	arbitrariness; whim	
諮		シ		516
R-740	諮問	しもん	consultation	

There is one more kanji in the list of those treated in this book that bears the same signal primitive but a completely unrelated reading. This character characterizes the group as "semi-pure":

盗		トウ		1559
R-741	窃盗	せっとう	larceny; theft	

In some of these groups the exceptional reading has already been learned in one of the previous chapters. In other cases a new reading has to be learned. To facilitate recognition of the odd character, the frame shall be slightly indented. These groups may be as large as 8 kanji and as small as 3. As we did in CHAPTER 2, we begin with the larger groups first.

交		コウ		1368
R-742	社交	しゃこう	social life; socializing	
校		コウ		1371
R-743	校歌	こうか	school song	
効		コウ		1369
R-744	効力	こうりょく	efficacy; validity	
郊		コウ		1987
R-745	郊外	こうがい	(outlying) suburbs	
絞		コウ		1448
R-746	絞殺	こうさつ	death by strangulation	
較		カク		1370
R-747	比較	ひかく	comparison	

召 R-748	召喚	ショウ しょうかん	summons	90
昭 R-749	昭和	ショウ しょうわ	name of Japanese era, 1926–1989	91
照 R-750	照明	ショウ しょうめい	illumination; lighting	182
招 R-751	招請	ショウ しょうせい	invitation	702
紹 R-752	紹介	ショウ しょうかい	introduction	1459
沼 R-753	湖沼	ショウ こしょう	lakes and marshes	145
詔 R-754	詔書	ショウ しょうしょ	imperial rescript or edict	366
超 R-755	超過	チョウ ちょうか	excess	411
令 R-756	令嬢	レイ れいじょう	young lady	1503
冷 R-757	冷却	レイ れいきゃく	refrigeration; cooling	1506

零		レイ		1504
R-758	零時	れいじ	12:00 (midnight)	
鈴		レイ	R-2025	1508
R-759	電鈴	でんれい	an electric bell	
齢		レイ		1505
R-760	高齢	こうれい	advanced age	
領		リョウ		1507
R-761	領土	りょうど	territory; dominion	
作	乍	サク	R-2184	1224
R-762	作文	さくぶん	(written) composition	
昨		サク		1222
R-763	昨年	さくねん	last year	
酢		サク		1542
R-764	酢酸	さくさん	acetic acid	
搾		サク		1422
R-765	搾取	さくしゅ	exploitation; squeezing	
詐		サ		1223
R-766	詐欺	さぎ	fraud; swindle	
墓	莫	ボ		246
R-767	墓地	ぼち	cemetery	

暮 R-768		ボ		**247**
	歳暮	せいぼ	end-of-the-year present	
模 R-769		ボ	R-2141	**244**
	規模	きぼ	scale; size	
募 R-770		ボ		**925**
	募集	ぼしゅう	recruiting	
慕 R-771		ボ		**683**
	思慕	しぼ	longing; yearning	
膜 R-772		マク		**248**
	膜状	まくじょう	filmy; like a membrane	
幕 R-773		バク・マク		**437**
	幕府 開幕	ばくふ かいまく	Shogunate government curtain raising	
漠 R-774		バク		**245**
	漠然	ばくぜん	vague	

The former group was included to demonstrate how more than one reading can be given for the exception in the semi-pure group. Strictly speaking, the group belongs to CHAPTER 7.

生 R-775		セイ	R-1077, 1389	**1675**
	先生	せんせい	teacher	

性 R-776	女性	セイ じょせい	R-1391 woman	1679
星 R-777	星座	セイ せいざ	R-1392 a "sign" of the zodiac	1676
醒 R-778	覚醒剤	セイ かくせいざい	stimulant drug	1677
姓 R-779	姓名	セイ せいめい	R-1390 one's full name	1678
牲 R-780	犠牲	セイ ぎせい	R-1394 sacrifice	1680
産 R-781	不動産	サン ふどうさん	R-1393 real estate	1681
復 R-782	复 復習	フク ふくしゅう	review (of one's lessons)	940
複 R-783	複雑	フク ふくざつ	complicated	504
腹 R-784	空腹	フク くうふく	empty stomach	503
覆 R-785	覆面	フク ふくめん	mask; disguise	1738

履	リ		1137
R-786	履歴　りれき		one's personal history

奇	キ		133
R-787	奇数　きすう		an odd number

寄	キ		204
R-788	寄付　きふ		donation

騎	キ		2135
R-789	騎士　きし		knight

椅	イ		218
R-790	椅子　いす		chair

旦	タン	R-1036	30
R-791	元旦　がんたん		New Year's Day

胆	タン		31
R-792	大胆　だいたん		bold; daring

担	タン		721
R-793	担架　たんか		a stretcher

壇	タン	R-2301	631
R-794	土壇場　どたんば		place of execution

Note the mixture of *on* and *kun* readings.

昼 R-795		チユウ		1156
	昼食	ちゅうしょく	lunch; noon meal	

経 R-796	圣	ケイ	R-2396	1460
	経験	けいけん	experience	

軽 R-797		ケイ	774
	軽食	けいしょく	snack; light meal

茎 R-798		ケイ	772
	花茎	かけい	flowering stem

径 R-799		ケイ	947
	径路	けいろ	route; course

怪 R-800		カイ	773
	奇怪	きかい	strange; weird

肖 R-801		ショウ	119
	肖像画	しょうぞうが	a portrait (painting)

消 R-802		ショウ	155
	消化	しょうか	digestion

硝 R-803		ショウ	120
	硝煙	しょうえん	gunpowder smoke

宵 R-804		ショウ		201
	徹宵	てっしょう	all through the night	

削 R-805		サク		124
	削減	さくげん	reduction; curtailment	

In the following group of characters, the signal primitive is immediately evident as the first member of the group. Be careful to note that earlier (FRAMES 477–478) this same signal primitive was itself part of another signal primitive with an entirely different reading.

辰 R-806		シン		2164
	辰宿	しんしゅく	house of the Dragon (in the Sino-Japanese zodiac)	

震 R-807		シン		2166
	震動	しんどう	quake; shock	

娠 R-808		シン		2168
	妊娠	にんしん	pregnancy	

振 R-809		シン		2167
	三振	さんしん	3 strikes (in baseball)	

唇 R-810		シン		2169
	口唇	こうしん	lips	

辱 R-811		ジョク	R-591	2165
	屈辱	くつじょく	humiliation; disgrace	

裁 R-812	戈	サイ		424
	裁縫	さいほう	sewing; needlework	

載 R-813		サイ		383
	記載	きさい	mention (in the press)	

栽 R-814		サイ		382
	栽培	さいばい	cultivation; growing	

繊 R-815		セン		1929
	繊維	せんい	fiber; textiles	

併 R-816	并	ヘイ		1107
	併用	へいよう	joint use	

塀 R-817		ヘイ		1136
	塀	へい	fence	

餅 R-818		ヘイ		1590
	煎餅	せんべい	rice crackers	

The reading of the first kanji in the word above will be introduced later in this chapter (FRAME 1106).

瓶 R-819		ビン		1109
	花瓶	かびん	flower vase	

票 R-820		ヒョウ		1732
	投票	とうひょう	casting a vote	

漂 R-821		ヒョウ	**1733**
	漂白	ひょうはく	bleaching
標 R-822		ヒョウ	**1734**
	目標	もくひょう	target; aim
慄 R-823		リツ	**1736**
	戦慄	せんりつ	shivering; trembling
福 R-824	畐	フク	**1171**
	福祉	ふくし	(social) welfare
副 R-825		フク	**93**
	副詞	ふくし	adverb
幅 R-826		フク	**435**
	全幅	ぜんぷく	full extent; all
富 R-827		フ	R-2347	**205**
	富士山	ふじさん	Mt. Fuji
億 R-828	(意)	オク	**1058**
	一億円	いちおくえん	100 million yen
憶 R-829		オク	**679**
	記憶	きおく	memory (of something)
臆 R-830		オク	**655**
	臆病	おくびょう	cowardice

意	イ		654
R-831	用意	30い	preparation; arrangements

旨	シ		493
R-832	要旨	ようし	the gist; essentials

指	シ		711
R-833	指導	しどう	guidance

脂	シ		494
R-834	脂肪	しぼう	fat

詣	ケイ		495
R-835	参詣	さんけい	visit a Shinto shrine

固	コ		622
R-836	頑固	がんこ	stubborn; persistent

個	コ		1047
R-837	個人	こじん	an individual

錮	コ		623
R-838	錮疾	こしつ	chronic disease

箇	カ		2185
R-839	一箇月	いっかげつ	one month

This character is commonly abbreviated to the *katakana* ケ, as in FRAME 590, which uses the same exemplary compound with that writing.

観 R-840	隹	カン		614
	観察	かんさつ	observation	

勧 R-841		カン		928
	勧奨	かんしょう	encouragement; stimulation	

歓 R-842		カン		612
	交歓	こうかん	exchange of courtesies	

権 R-843		ケン・ゴン		613
	権利	けんり	rights	
	権現	ごんげん	avatar	

果 R-844		カ		1202
	果汁	かじゅう	fruit juice	

課 R-845		カ		1204
	課長	かちょう	section head	

菓 R-846		カ		1203
	菓子	かし	confectionery	

裸 R-847		ラ		1205
	裸身	らしん	naked body	

責 R-848		セキ		1661
	責任	せきにん	responsibility	

積		セキ	1663
R-849	積善	せきぜん	accumulation of good deeds
績		セキ	1662
R-850	成績	せいせき	results; showing
債		サイ	1664
R-851	公債	こうさい	public bonds
列		レツ	875
R-852	列車	れっしゃ	train
烈		レツ	877
R-853	壮烈	そうれつ	heroic; sublime
裂		レツ	876
R-854	分裂	ぶんれつ	dissolution; disruption
例		レイ	1046
R-855	例外	れいがい	an exception
更		コウ	749
R-856	更生	こうせい	rebirth
梗		コウ	751
R-857	梗概	こうがい	outline; resume

硬 R-858		コウ		750
	硬貨	こうか	coin (solid money)	

便 R-859		ビン・ベン		1066
	郵便	ゆうびん	post; mail	
	便利	べんり	convenient	

壁 R-860	辟	ヘキ		1616
	壁画	へきが	a mural (painting)	

璧 R-861		ヘキ		1617
	完璧	かんぺき	perfect; impeccable	

癖 R-862		ヘキ		1826
	病癖	びょうへき	(personal) weakness; bad habit	

避 R-863		ヒ		1618
	不可避	ふかひ	unavoidable	

謄 R-864	朕	トウ		1296
	謄本	とうほん	transcript; certified copy	

騰 R-865		トウ		2144
	沸騰	ふっとう	boiling	

藤 R-866		トウ		1295
	葛藤	かっとう	feud; discord	

The first character in the compound above was not treated in VOL. 1, but the exemplary compound given above is useful to know. When the phonetic group to which this character belongs appears again in CHAPTER 7 (FRAMES 1307–1312), you will see how easy it is to learn.

勝 R-867	勝利	ショウ しょうり	victory	1294
偶 R-868	禺 偶像	グウ ぐうぞう	idol; image	2105
遇 R-869	遭遇	グウ そうぐう	encounter	2106
隅 R-870	一隅	グウ いちぐう	one corner	2108
愚 R-871	愚痴	グ ぐち	grumbling	2107
苑 R-872	夗 御苑	エン ぎょえん	Emperor's Garden	1523
怨 R-873	怨声	エン えんせい	R-2285 complaint; grudging	1524
宛 R-874	宛転	エン えんてん	smooth; fair (of face)	1521
腕 R-875	腕力	ワン わんりょく	physical strength	1522

牙 R-876		ガ	R-1839	2053
	牙城	がじょう	stronghold (of conservatism)	

芽 R-877		ガ		2054
	発芽	はつが	germination; sprout	

雅 R-878		ガ		2056
	優雅	ゆうが	graceful	

邪 R-879		ジャ		2055
	邪魔	じゃま	intrusion	

因 R-880		イン		626
	原因	げんいん	source; cause	

咽 R-881		イン		628
	咽喉	いんこう	throat	

姻 R-882		イン		627
	婚姻	こんいん	matrimony	

恩 R-883		オン		652
	謝恩	しゃおん	expression of gratitude	

兼 R-884		ケン		1723
	兼任	けんにん	double post or appointment	

謙 R-885		ケン		1726
	謙譲	けんじょう	modesty	

嫌 R-886		ケン・ゲン		1724
	嫌疑	けんぎ	suspicion	
	機嫌	きげん	mood; disposition	

廉 R-887		レン		1727
	廉売	れんばい	bargain; sale	

奉 R-888		ホウ	R-2270	1695
	奉仕	ほうし	service	

俸 R-889		ホウ		1696
	年俸	ねんぽう	annual salary	

棒 R-890		ボウ		1697
	鉄棒	てつぼう	iron bar or staff	

加 R-891		カ	R-25	932
	加入	かにゅう	admission; subscription	

架 R-892		カ		934
	架空	かくう	fiction; make-believe	

賀 R-893		ガ		933
	祝賀会	しゅくがかい	commemorative celebration	

定 R-894		ジョウ	R-1236	408
	定紋	じょうもん	family crest	

錠 R-895	錠	ジョウ じょう	lock	409
綻 R-896	破綻	タン はたん	bankrupcy	1439
綱 R-897	岡 綱領	コウ こうりょう	general plan; main point	2114
鋼 R-898	鋼鉄	コウ こうてつ	steel	2113
剛 R-899	剛健	ゴウ ごうけん	strong; robust	2115
般 R-900	一般	ハン いっぱん	general; average	2015
搬 R-901	運搬	ハン うんぱん	conveyance; transport	2018
盤 R-902	円盤	バン えんばん	disc; discus	2017
毛 R-903	毛布	モウ　R-50 もうふ	blanket	2062

耗 R-904	消耗	モウ しょうもう	R-2318 consumption; use	2063
尾 R-905	尾行	ビ びこう	following; tailing	2064
某 R-906	某氏	ボウ ぼうし	a certain person	1896
謀 R-907	陰謀	ボウ いんぼう	R-2239 conspiracy; plot	1897
媒 R-908	媒介	バイ ばいかい	mediation	1898
栓 R-909	消火栓	セン しょうかせん	fire hydrant	282
詮 R-910	詮議	セン せんぎ	deliberations	360
全 R-911	安全	ゼン あんぜん	safety	281
概 R-912	概念	既 ガイ がいねん	concept; general notion	1594

慨 R-913	憤慨	ふんがい	ガイ indignation; resentment	1595
既 R-914	既製	きせい	キ manufactured; ready-made	1593
原 R-915	高原	こうげん	ゲン plateau	142
源 R-916	源泉	げんせん	ゲン fountainhead; wellspring	153
願 R-917	志願	しがん	ガン volunteering	143
疑 R-918	容疑	ようぎ	ギ suspicion	1513
擬 R-919	模擬	もぎ	ギ imitation; sham	1514
凝 R-920	凝固	ぎょうこ	ギョウ coagulation	1515
屯 R-921	駐屯	ちゅうとん	トン being stationed (somewhere)	2189

頓		トン	1610
R-922	頓死	とんし	sudden death

鈍		ドン	1611
R-923	鈍物	どんぶつ	dimwit

布		フ	433
R-924	毛布	もうふ	blanket

怖		フ	670
R-925	恐怖	きょうふ	fear

希		キ	1602
R-926	希望	きぼう	hope

沿	公	エン		858
R-927	沿線	えんせん	along a railway line	

鉛		エン		857
R-928	鉛管	えんかん	lead pipe	

船		セン	2019
R-929	船長	せんちょう	(ship's) captain

馬		バ	2132
R-930	馬車	ばしゃ	horse-drawn carriage

罵 R-931		バ		**2143**
	嘲罵	ちょうば	taunt	

篤 R-932		トク		**2142**
	危篤	きとく	dangerously ill	

夫 R-933		フ	R-1693	**901**
	夫人	ふじん	(married) lady	

扶 R-934		フ		**902**
	扶養	ふよう	support; maintenance	

規 R-935		キ		**904**
	規則	きそく	rule; regulation	

英 R-936	央	エイ		**1878**
	英語	えいご	English language	

映 R-937		エイ		**1879**
	映画	えいが	film; movie	

央 R-938		オウ		**1877**
	中央	ちゅうおう	center; central	

広 R-939		コウ		**799**
	広義	こうぎ	broad sense (of a term)	

鉱 R-940		コウ		802
	鉱山	こうざん	a mine	

拡 R-941		カク		801
	拡大	かくだい	expansion; enlargement	

浄 R-942	争	ジョウ		1239
	清浄	せいじょう	purity	

静 R-943		ジョウ	R-82, 1650	1660
	静脈	じょうみゃく	a vein	

争 R-944		ソウ		1238
	争議	そうぎ	dispute	

孤 R-945	瓜	コ		2024
	孤独	こどく	loneliness; solitude	

弧 R-946		コ		2023
	円弧	えんこ	circular arc	

瓜 R-947		カ		2022
	西瓜	すいか	watermelon	

The use of the first character is an example of what Japanese call 当て字 (あてじ), a character chosen to accompany a reading that does not strictly belong to it. Since the exemplary compound is a common word, it has been included here.

員		イン		59
R-948	船員	せんいん	sailor; member of the crew	

韻		イン	R-1415	522
R-949	音韻	おんいん	phoneme; vocal sound	

損		ソン		719
R-950	損失	そんしつ	loss	

堪	甚	カン		1907
R-951	堪忍	かんにん	forgiveness; tolerance	

勘		カン		1906
R-952	勘定	かんじょう	payment of a bill	

甚		ジン		1905
R-953	甚大	じんだい	enormous	

群	君	グン		1247
R-954	大群	たいぐん	large crowd	

郡		グン		1986
R-955	郡会	ぐんかい	a county assembly	

君		クン		1246
R-956	君主	くんしゅ	monarch	

市		シ		440
R-957	市長	しちょう	mayor	

姉		シ		442
R-958	姉妹	しまい	sisters	

肺		ハイ		443
R-959	肺病	はいびょう	pulmonary disease	

景		ケイ		336
R-960	景気	けいき	(economic) boom	

憬		ケイ		682
R-961	憧憬	しょうけい	hanker for; aspire after	

影		エイ		1848
R-962	影響	えいきょう	influence	

獲	蒦	カク		757
R-963	捕獲	ほかく	capture	

穫		カク		974
R-964	収穫	しゅうかく	harvest	

護		ゴ		756
R-965	保護	ほご	protection; patronage	

| 文 R-966 | | モン | R-1991 | 1861 |
| | 文句 | もんく | expression; complaint | |

| 紋 R-967 | | モン | | 1863 |
| | 指紋 | しもん | fingerprint | |

対 R-968		タイ・ツイ		1862
	反対	はんたい	opposite	
	一対	いっつい	a pair	

| 凶 R-969 | | キョウ | | 1603 |
| | 凶悪 | きょうあく | fiendish; satanic | |

| 胸 R-970 | | キョウ | | 1604 |
| | 度胸 | どきょう | pluck; mettle | |

| 離 R-971 | | リ | R-361 | 1605 |
| | 離陸 | りりく | take off (e.g., an airplane) | |

| 孝 R-972 | | コウ | | 1342 |
| | 孝行 | こうこう | filial duty; filial piety | |

| 酵 R-973 | | コウ | | 1538 |
| | 酵母 | こうぼ | yeast | |

| 教 R-974 | | キョウ | | 1343 |
| | 教授 | きょうじゅ | professor | |

系 R-975	ケイ		1492
	系列 けいれつ	succession; order	

係 R-976	ケイ		1493
	係争 けいそう	dispute; contention	

孫 R-977	ソン		1494
	子孫 しそん	descendants	

遜 R-978	ソン		1496
	謙遜 けんそん	humility	

吉 R-979	キツ	R-581	342
	不吉 ふきつ	unlucky	

詰 R-980	キツ		367
	詰問 きつもん	cross-examination	

結 R-981	ケツ		1451
	結論 けつろん	conclusion (of an argument)	

割 R-982	害 カツ		1673
	割礼 かつれい	circumcision	

轄 R-983	カツ		1672
	管轄 かんかつ	jurisdiction	

害 R-984	ガイ		1671
	損害 そんがい	damage	

敬 R-985	敬意	ケイ けいい	homage; respect	356
警 R-986	警察	ケイ けいさつ	police	358
驚 R-987	驚異	キョウ きょうい	wonder; astonishment	2141

粋 R-988	卆 粋人	スイ すいじん	romantic fellow; dandy	993
酔 R-989	泥酔	スイ でいすい	plastered; stewed to the gills	1543
砕 R-990	砕石	サイ さいせき	rubble; macadam	121

朗 R-991	良 朗読	ロウ ろうどく	reading aloud or in public	1579
浪 R-992	流浪	ロウ るろう	vagrancy; wandering	1580
良 R-993	良心	リョウ りょうしん R-46	conscience	1578

慮 R-994	慮 遠慮	リョ えんりょ		2151 sense of reserve
虜 R-995	捕虜	リョ ほりょ		2146 prisoner; captive
膚 R-996	皮膚	フ ひふ		2147 skin
左 R-997	左右	サ さゆう	(R-5)	81 left and right; both sides
佐 R-998	補佐	サ ほさ		1024 assistant
惰 R-999	惰気	ダ だき		676 sluggishness
倫 R-1000	侖 倫理学	リン りんりがく		1962 ethics; moral philosophy
輪 R-1001	五輪	リン ごりん		1963 the Olympic Games
論 R-1002	勿論	ロン もちろん	R-615	1961 of course

| 任 R-1003 | 壬 | ニン | | 1078 |
| | 責任 | せきにん | responsibility | |

| 妊 R-1004 | | ニン | | 546 |
| | 妊娠 | にんしん | pregnancy | |

| 賃 R-1005 | | チン | | 1079 |
| | 運賃 | うんちん | fare (for transportation) | |

| 史 R-1006 | | シ | | 747 |
| | 歴史 | れきし | history | |

| 使 R-1007 | | シ | | 1065 |
| | 大使 | たいし | ambassador | |

| 吏 R-1008 | | リ | | 748 |
| | 官吏 | かんり | government official | |

| 舎 R-1009 | | シャ | | 338 |
| | 宿舎 | しゅくしゃ | hostel; residence | |

| 捨 R-1010 | | シャ | | 707 |
| | 取捨 | しゅしゃ | adoption or rejection | |

| 舗 R-1011 | | ホ | R-61 | 1982 |
| | 店舗 | てんぽ | shop | |

Note how 2 signal primitives appear in the same kanji.

氏		シ		1970
R-1012	氏名	しめい	full name	

紙		シ		1971
R-1013	紙幣	しへい	paper money	

婚		コン		1972
R-1014	婚姻	こんいん	matrimony	

充		ジュウ		823
R-1015	補充	ほじゅう	supplement	

銃		ジュウ		824
R-1016	銃砲	じゅうほう	firearms	

統		トウ		1447
R-1017	大統領	だいとうりょう	president of a country	

通	甬	ツウ	R-1970	1511
R-1018	交通	こうつう	traffic	

痛		ツウ		1825
R-1019	腹痛	ふくつう	stomachache	

踊		ヨウ		1512
R-1020	舞踊	ぶよう	dance (classical)	

告 R-1021		コク	R-1119	262
	広告	こうこく	advertising	
酷 R-1022		コク		1539
	残酷	ざんこく	cruel	
造 R-1023		ゾウ		299
	構造	こうぞう	structure	

We conclude this chapter with three characters related by a common primitive element but sharing Chinese pronunciations unevenly.

識 R-1024	戠	シキ		523
	知識	ちしき	knowledge; intelligence	
職 R-1025		ショク		887
	職員	しょくいん	an employee	
織 R-1026		シキ・ショク		1432
	組織	そしき	organization; formation	
	織機	しょっき	loom	

CHAPTER 6

Readings from Everyday Words

BY THE TIME you pick up this book you will have already learned at least the rudiments of Japanese grammar and in the process have learned some of the most useful words of everyday spoken Japanese. Taking advantage of this fact, as well as the fact that you already know the meanings of all the characters treated here, you can enlarge your knowledge of the *on-yomi* by seeing how those everyday words, in fact, look when set to kanji.

Take, for example, the ordinary Japanese word for a medical "doctor," which is いしゃ. The two kanji with which it is written mean respectively "to doctor" and "someone." This allows us to add two new readings to those we already know:

医		イ		1829
R-1027	医療	いりょう	medical care	
者		シャ	R-1475	1345
R-1028	医者	いしゃ	doctor	

The names of well-known places can be used in much the same way, as in the following two frames:

東		トウ	R-1442	543
R-1029	東北	とうほく	the northeast	

京		キョウ	R-1962		334
R-1030	東京	とうきょう	Tokyo		

We can also make use of well-known company names or other popular proper names. For example, what student of Japanese has not thumbed through the dictionaries of Japan's foremost Japanese-English lexicographers, Kenkyūsha? By learning what the name, in fact, means, you will have learned three more Chinese readings:

研		ケン			729
R-1031	研学	けんがく	study; investigation		
究		キュウ			1417
R-1032	研究	けんきゅう	research		
社		シャ			1173
R-1033	会社	かいしゃ	company		

Without making any particular effort to keep these various sorts of "everyday words" separate from one another, let us see how far they take us into the second half of this book.

As before, readings and compounds that have appeared earlier will be drawn on as much as possible to lighten the burden. Occasionally, if only rarely, a common everyday word will lead us to a character that falls outside the compass of these pages. In such cases, it is enough to learn the *on-yomi* being practiced without stopping to learn a new kanji and its reading. For example, the word for "neat" or "pretty," one of the first you learn in studying Japanese, is きれい. It is made up of the character for "figured cloth" and that for "lovely." Normally, the word is not written in characters at all, but since it is an easy way to learn the otherwise difficult reading of the latter kanji, restoring its original kanji writing is helpful:

麗		レイ		**2158**
R-1034	綺麗	きれい	neat; clean; pretty	

In still other cases, both readings of a known compound will be new. In this case, we will combine both kanji into a single frame, like this:

御飯		ゴ	R-2090	**1500**
		ハン	R-1336	**1583**
R-1035	御飯	ごはん	rice; meal; dinner	

With that, we may carry on for another 222 frames. Incidentally, if you find that you do not know a particular word chosen for the exemplary compound, you might as well take the trouble to learn it. After all, the words *are* common everyday words.

旦那		ダン	R-791	**30**
		ナ		**1992**
R-1036	旦那	だんな	husband; master	
内		ナイ	R-2150	**1095**
R-1037	案内	あんない	guidance; information	
自分		ジ	R-1059	**36**
		ブン	R-1180, 1235, 1343	**844**
R-1038	自分	じぶん	oneself	

心 R-1039		シン		639
	安心	あんしん	peace of mind	
電話 R-1040		デン		574
		ワ	R-1624	368
	電話	でんわ	telephone	
番号 R-1041		バン		2058
		ゴウ		1330
	電話番号	でんわばんごう	telephone number	
晩 R-1042		バン		2128
	晩御飯	ばんごはん	supper	
男 R-1043		ダン	R-2180	923
	男性	だんせい	a man; male	
女 R-1044		ジョ	(R-3), 2179, 2315	102
	女性	じょせい	a woman; female	
勉強 R-1045		ベン		2129
		キョウ	R-1739	1321
	勉強	べんきょう	study	
弁当 R-1046		ベン		803
		トウ		1236
	弁当	べんとう	lunch (carry-along, picnic-style)	

瞳		ドウ		**469**
R-1047	瞳孔	どうこう	the pupil of the eye	
車		シャ		**304**
R-1048	電車	でんしゃ	(electric) train	
地図		チ	R-1100, 1395	**554**
		ズ	R-1054	**1264**
R-1049	地図	ちず	map	
団		ダン	R-1177	**625**
R-1050	団地	だんち	housing development	
下鉄		カ	R-1921	**51**
		テツ	R-1492	**909**
R-1051	地下鉄	ちかてつ	subway; metro	
挨拶		アイ		**1310**
		サツ		**713**
R-1052	挨拶	あいさつ	greetings; salutation	
沙汰		サ	R-1531	**151**
		タ		**149**
R-1053	無沙汰	ぶさた	failure to keep in touch (commonly used as an apology)	
図書		ト	R-1049	**1264**
		ショ		**349**
R-1054	図書館	としょかん	library	

大学		ダイ	R-1171	112
		ガク		346
R-1055	大学	だいがく	university	

| 丈 | | ジョウ | | 746 |
| R-1056 | 大丈夫 | だいじょうぶ | all right; okay | |

As an exception, we include 3 kanji in the next frame, all of them no doubt very familiar to you already.

外国人		ガイ	R-1752	116
		コク		624
		ジン	R-1064	1023
R-1057	外国人	がいこくじん	foreigner	

料理		リョウ		1262
		リ		283
R-1058	料理	りょうり	cooking; food	

自然		シ	R-1038	36
		ゼン	R-469	256
R-1059	自然	しぜん	nature	

| 一 | | イチ | R-1061 | 1 |
| R-1060 | 一日 | いちにち | one day | |

一緒		イツ	R-1060	1
		ショ	R-1482	1444
R-1061	一緒	いっしょ	together	

四月		シ		4
		ガツ	R-586	13
R-1062	四月	しがつ	April	

| 七 | | シチ | | 7 |
| R-1063 | 七月 | しちがつ | July | |

九人		キュウ	R-1065	9
		ニン	R-1057	1023
R-1064	九人	きゅうにん	9 people	

九時		ク	R-1064	9
		ジ	R-1557	171
R-1065	九時	くじ	9 o'clock	

十六		ジュウ	R-1252	10
		ロク		6
R-1066	十六	じゅうろく	sixteen	

千円		セン	(R-4)	40
		エン		1952
R-1067	千円	せんえん	¥1,000	

壱万 R-1068	壱万円	イチ マン いちまんえん	R-1696	496 68 ¥10,000 (in formal receipts)
銀行 R-1069	銀行	ギン コウ ぎんこう	R-1518 R-1744, 2404	1569 938 bank
旅 R-1070	旅行	リョ りょこう		1127 voyage; trip
火曜 R-1071	火曜日	カ ヨウ かようび		173 618 Tuesday

The third kanji in the compound has a *kun-yomi*.

乳 R-1072	牛乳	ニュウ ぎゅうにゅう		786 (cow's) milk
瓦 R-1073	瓦解	ガ がかい		1108 collapse; debacle
水 R-1074	水曜日	スイ すいようび		137 Wednesday
木 R-1075	木曜日	モク もくようび	R-2322	207 Thursday

午 後 R-1076		ゴ		610
		ゴ	R-1966	1479
	午後	ごご	afternoon	
生 命 R-1077		ショウ	R-775, 1389	1675
		メイ	R-2266	1502
	一生懸命	いっしょうけんめい	with all one's might	
戚 R-1078		セキ		385
	親戚	しんせき	relatives	
非 常 R-1079		ヒ	R-1550	1760
		ジョウ	R-1457	862
	非常	ひじょう	emergency; extraordinary	
金 R-1080		キン	R-2177	289
	金曜日	きんようび	Friday	
山 R-1081		サン		830
	富士山	ふじさん	Mt. Fuji	
本 R-1082		ホン		224
	日本	にほん	Japan	
土 R-1083		ド	R-1684	161
	土曜日	どようび	Saturday	

辞典		ジ	R-1625	**1613**
		テン		**1969**
R-1084	英和辞典	えいわじてん	English-Japanese dictionary	
完		カン		**199**
R-1085	完全	かんぜん	complete	
都		ト	R-1172, 1483	**1989**
R-1086	京都	きょうと	Kyoto	
報		ホウ		**1625**
R-1087	電報	でんぽう	telegraph	
元		ゲン	R-339	**63**
R-1088	元気	げんき	lively; alive and well	
漢字		カン		**1701**
		ジ		**197**
R-1089	漢字	かんじ	kanji	
冗談		ジョウ		**321**
		ダン		**374**
R-1090	冗談	じょうだん	joke	
住所		ジュウ	R-1451	**1027**
		ショ		**1208**
R-1091	住所	じゅうしょ	address	

関 R-1092		カン		2173
	玄関	げんかん	main entrance; front porch	

主 R-1093		シュ	R-1450	284
	主人	しゅじん	husband	

秘 R-1094		ヒ	R-1400	970
	秘密	ひみつ	secret	

必 R-1095		ヒツ	R-1402	685
	必要	ひつよう	necessity; need	

単 R-1096		タン		2078
	簡単	かんたん	simple; uncomplicated	

段 R-1097		ダン		2003
	階段	かいだん	stairway	

信 R-1098		シン		1043
	自信	じしん	self-confidence	

飛 R-1099		ヒ		2032
	飛行機	ひこうき	airplane	

地 R-1100		ジ	R-1049, 1395	554
	地震	じしん	earthquake	

転 R-1101		テン		449
	自転車	じてんしゃ	bicycle	

酎		チュウ		**1537**
R-1102	焼酎	しょうちゅう	ordinary distilled spirits	

由		ユウ	R-14, 1460, 2316	**1186**
R-1103	自由	じゆう	free; freedom	

柔		ジュウ	R-1342	**1312**
R-1104	柔道	じゅうどう	judo	

去年		キョ	R-1122	**812**
		ネン		**1114**
R-1105	去年	きょねん	last year	

聞		ブン	R-2251	**1754**
R-1106	新聞	しんぶん	newspaper	

商店		ショウ		**471**
		テン		**632**
R-1107	商店	しょうてん	store; shop	

慶応		ケイ		**2157**
		オウ		**653**
R-1108	慶応大学	けいおうだいがく	Keiō University	

前		ゼン		**309**
R-1109	午前	ごぜん	morning	

煎		セン		310
R-1110	煎餅	せんべい	rice crackers	

見 物		ケン		61
		ブツ	R-616	1129
R-1111	見物	けんぶつ	sightseeing; a visit	

近		キン		1210
R-1112	付近	ふきん	vicinity	

中		ジュウ	R-57	39
R-1113	一日中	いちにちじゅう	all day long	

煙		エン		1739
R-1114	禁煙	きんえん	No Smoking!	

喫 茶		キツ		1670
		サ	R-597	267
R-1115	喫茶店	きっさてん	coffee shop	

今 週		コン	R-2250	1711
		シュウ	R-1655	340
R-1116	今週	こんしゅう	this week	

度		ド	R-495, 2262	1278
R-1117	今度	こんど	this time	

場		ジョウ	R-1490	584
R-1118	工場	こうじょう	factory	

告 R-1119	広告	コク こうこく	R-1021	262 advertisement
音楽 R-1120	音楽	オン ガク おんがく	R-1416 R-1967	520 1872 music
速 R-1121	高速道路	ソク こうそくどうろ	R-1597	1799 expressway; superhighway
去 R-1122	過去	コ かこ	R-1105	812 the past
室 R-1123	教室	シツ きょうしつ		816 classroom
営業 R-1124	営業中	エイ ギョウ えいぎょうちゅう	R-2395	1111 1931 "Open for Business"
掃除 R-1125	掃除	ソウ ジ そうじ	R-1631	1235 1787 cleaning; housecleaning
写 R-1126	写真	シャ しゃしん		1336 photograph
急 R-1127	急行	キュウ きゅうこう		1229 express (train)

給 R-1128	給料	キュツ きゅうりょう		1449
			salary	
毎 R-1129	毎日	マイ まいにち	R-1420	497
			every day	
形 R-1130	人形	ギョウ にんぎょう	R-1717	1847
			doll	
来 R-1131	来年	ライ らいねん		2029
			next year	
待 R-1132	招待	タイ しょうたい	R-1559	944
			invitation	
小 R-1133	小学校	ショウ しょうがっこう		110
			primary school	
売 R-1134	商売	バイ しょうばい		345
			business	
質 問 R-1135	質問	シツ モン しつもん	R-2045, 2360	1219 1744
			question	
題 R-1136	問題	ダイ もんだい	R-1609	415
			problem	

油 R-1137		ユ	R-1461	1188
	醤油	しょうゆ	soy sauce	
	The first kanji in the compound is not in the general-use list, but can be found on most every dinner table in Japan.			

食堂 R-1138		ショク	R-1711	1582
		ドウ	R-1458	861
	食堂	しょくどう	dining room; refectory	

拳 R-1139		ケン		1290
	拳銃	けんじゅう	handgun	

券 R-1140		ケン		1291
	食券	しょっけん	meal ticket	

聖 R-1141		セイ		888
	聖書	せいしょ	Holy Writ; the Bible	

庫 R-1142		コ	R-2390	633
	冷蔵庫	れいぞうこ	refrigerator	

練習 R-1143		レン	R-1444	1443
		シュウ		616
	練習	れんしゅう	practice	

乱暴 R-1144		ラン		76
		ボウ	R-355	1941
	乱暴	らんぼう	wild; unruly; rebellious	

財 R-1145		リイ	R-1638	737
	財布	さいふ	wallet	
西洋 R-1146		セイ	R-1677	1728
		ヨウ	R-1571	588
	西洋	せいよう	the West; Occident	
劇 R-1147		ゲキ		2152
	劇場	げきじょう	theater	
政 R-1148		セイ	R-1301	407
	政府	せいふ	the government	
専門 R-1149		セン		47
		モン		1743
	専門家	せんもんか	a specialist	
選手 R-1150		セン		1944
		シュ		687
	選手	せんしゅ	athlete	
終点 R-1151		シュウ		1452
		テン		181
	終点	しゅうてん	end of the line; terminal	
活 R-1152		カツ	R-1621	154
	生活	せいかつ	life; livelihood	

徒		ト		943
R-1153	生徒	せいと	student	

挙		キョ		2088
R-1154	選挙	せんきょ	elections	

戦		セン		2079
R-1155	戦争	せんそう	war	

説		セツ	R-1509	538
R-1156	説明	せつめい	explanation	

試		シ		378
R-1157	試験	しけん	text; exam	

幹		カン	R-1373	1783
R-1158	新幹線	しんかんせん	the "Bullet Train"	

失敗		シツ	R-1494	908
		ハイ		353
R-1159	失敗	しっぱい	failure	

沢		タク		1153
R-1160	沢山	たくさん	a lot	

誕		タン		420
R-1161	誕生日	たんじょうび	birthday	
	Note the phonetic change in the second kanji.			

丁 R-1162	丁寧	テイ ていねい	R-1579 politeness; courtesy	95
特別 R-1163	特別	トク ベツ とくべつ	R-1561 special	261 94
有 R-1164	有名	ユウ ゆうめい	R-2263 famous	83
運 R-1165	運動	ウン うんどう	R-1644 exercise; sports	325
約束 R-1166	約束	ヤク ソク やくそく	R-1596 promise	1462 1793
訳 R-1167	翻訳	ヤク ほんやく	translation	1154
台風 R-1168	台風	タイ フウ たいふう	R-1186, 1367 R-1169 typhoon	805 563
風 R-1169	風呂	フ ふろ	R-1168 Japanese bath	563
駅 R-1170	駅長	エキ えきちょう	stationmaster	2138

大変		タイ	R-1055	112
		ヘン		1882
R-1171	大変	たいへん	very much; awfully; awful	
都合		ツ	R-1086, 1483	1989
		ゴウ	R-2230	269
R-1172	都合	つごう	conditions; "things"	
芸		ゲイ		450
R-1173	芸者	げいしゃ	geisha	
服		フク		1501
R-1174	洋服	ようふく	Western clothes	
子		シ	R-2178	99
R-1175	帽子	ぼうし	a cap; hat	
薬局		ヤク		1873
		キョク		1147
R-1176	薬局	やっきょく	pharmacy	
団		トン	R-1050	625
R-1177	布団	ふとん	Japanese quilt or mattress	
部		ブ	(R-13)	1988
R-1178	全部	ぜんぶ	all; everything	
頭		ズ	R-1566	1549
R-1179	頭痛	ずつう	headache	

分		ブ	R-1038, 1235, 1343	844
R-1180	大分	だいぶ	fairly; considerably	
仏		ブツ		1037
R-1181	大仏	だいぶつ	Great Buddha (statue)	
体		タイ	R-2254	1030
R-1182	大体	だいたい	generally; on the whole	
杯		ハイ		1304
R-1183	一杯	いっぱい	full; one cupful	
三画		サン	R-2	3
		カク	R-1241	1254
R-1184	三画	さんかく	3 strokes (as in a kanji)	

The next 5 frames present the characters used for some of the more common "counters" for which Japanese is notorious.

回		カイ	R-2398	630
R-1185	一回	いっかい	one time	
台		ダイ	R-1168, 1367	805
R-1186	三台	さんだい	3 (vehicles)	
枚		マイ		354
R-1187	二枚	にまい	2 (sheets of …)	

軒 R-1188	五軒	ケン ごけん	R-1377 5 (houses)	1781
冊 R-1189	二冊	サツ にさつ	R-453 2 (volumes of …)	1967

仙 R-1190	仙台	セン せんだい	(city of) Sendai	1061
歳 R-1191	十二歳	サイ じゅうにさい	R-2162 12 years old	551
才 R-1192	天才	サイ てんさい	R-1639 genius	736

In the exemplary compounds given in the next two frames, note how pronunciation of the first syllable of the second kanji is changed from アイ to ワイ because of the clumsiness of having two "a" sounds back to back.

哀 R-1193	可哀そう	アイ かわいそう	pitiable; pathetic	428
客 R-1194	客	キャク きゃく	R-1469 a guest	315
治代 R-1195	明治時代	ジ ダイ めいじじだい	R-1370 R-283 Meiji Era (1866–1912)	807 1080

光 R-1196	日光	コウ にっこう	(city of) Nikkō; sunlight	125
海 R-1197	北海道	カイ ほっかいどう	R-1418 Hokkaidō	500
湾 R-1198	台湾	ワン たいわん	Taiwan	1886
筆 R-1199	鉛筆	ヒツ えんぴつ	lead pencil	1014
力 R-1200	協力	リョク きょうりょく	R-618 cooperation	922
読 R-1201	読本	ドク どくほん	R-1973, 2361 a reader	372
媛 R-1202	才媛	エン さいえん	talented, accomplished woman	2100
事 R-1203	火事	ジ かじ	R-2359 a fire	1240
父 R-1204	祖父	フ そふ	grandfather	1366
母 R-1205	祖母	ボ そぼ	grandmother	105

神		ジン	R-146	1200
R-1206	神社	じんじゃ	Shinto shrine	

美		ビ	R-45, 1578	587
R-1207	美人	びじん	a beauty; beautiful woman	

労		ロウ		924
R-1208	苦労	くろう	trouble; ordeal	

王		オウ		271
R-1209	王子	おうじ	prince	

残		ザン	R-1366	871
R-1210	残念	ざんねん	"Too bad!" "What a shame!"	

守		ス	R-539	198
R-1211	留守	るす	absence (from home or post)	

第		ダイ	R-1537	1327
R-1212	第一	だいいち	No. 1	

免		メン		2126
R-1213	ご免	ごめん	"I beg your pardon."	

禅		ゼン		2080
R-1214	坐禅	ざぜん	sitting in Zen meditation	

Observe that the first character is a variant of the general-use character 座. It is used typically for sitting in Zen.

覧		ラン		919
R-1215	ご覧	ごらん	"Do have a look!"	

送		ソウ		2172
R-1216	放送	ほうそう	broadcasting	

温		オン		1560
R-1217	温泉	おんせん	hot springs; spa	

科		カ		1263
R-1218	科学	かがく	science	

無		ム	R-365	1913
R-1219	無理	むり	unreasonable; too difficult	

具		グ		78
R-1220	家具	かぐ	furniture	

省		ショウ	R-1529	131
R-1221	文科省	もんかしょう	Ministry of Science and Education	

毒		ドク		1651
R-1222	お気の毒	おきのどく	"I am very sorry for you!"	

歩		ホ	R-1534	397
R-1223	歩道	ほどう	sidewalk	

注 R-1224		チュウ	R-1447	**285**
	注意	ちゅうい	taking care; watching out	
目 的 R-1225		モク	R-2070	**15**
		テキ		**73**
	目的	もくてき	aim; goal	
色 R-1226		シキ	R-2097	**1890**
	色紙	しきし	square piece of paper for writing a poem or signature on	
囲 碁 R-1227		イ		**1948**
		ゴ	R-1355	**1903**
	囲碁	いご	Go; Japanese checkers	
他 R-1228		タ	R-1399	**1034**
	他人	たにん	outsider; stranger	
予 R-1229		ヨ	R-1627	**1719**
	天気予報	てんきよほう	weather forecast	
灯 R-1230		トウ	R-1584	**177**
	電灯	でんとう	electric light	
現 在 R-1231		ゲン		**275**
		ザイ		**740**
	現在	げんざい	modern times; the present	

宣伝	セン		**200**
	デン	R-1765	**1036**
R-1232	宣伝 せんでん	propaganda	

貿易	ボウ		**1529**
	エキ	R-1836	**1130**
R-1233	貿易会社 ぼうえきがいしゃ	trading company	

族	ゾク		**1307**
R-1234	家族 かぞく	the family	

秒分	ビョウ	R-1532	**965**
	フン	R-1038, 1180, 1343	**844**
R-1235	五分五秒 ごふんごびょう	5 min., 5 sec.	

定席	テイ	R-894	**408**
	セキ		**1277**
R-1236	指定席 していせき	reserved seat	

鉢	バチ	R-2406	**289**
R-1237	火鉢 ひばち	(charcoal) brazier	

拝	ハイ		**1686**
R-1238	拝見 はいけん	to look at (honorific)	

俗	ゾク	R-1613	**1042**
R-1239	俗語 ぞくご	vulgarism; slang	

武 R-1240	武士	ブ ぶし	R-22	403
				(samurai) warrior
画 R-1241	映画	ガ えいが	R-1184	1254
				a movie; film
老 R-1242	老人	ロウ ろうじん		1340
				old person
岸 R-1243	海岸	ガン かいがん	R-1378	1782
				seashore
両 R-1244	両親	リョウ りょうしん		1252
				one's parents
康 R-1245	健康	コウ けんこう		1243
				health; physical condition
太 陽 R-1246	太陽	タイ ヨウ たいよう	R-19 R-1485	126 1397
				the sun
華 R-1247	中華料理	カ ちゅうかりょうり	R-2396	1704
				Chinese food
刺 R-1248	名刺	シ めいし		446
				calling card

豆 R-1249	豆腐	トウ とうふ	R-1562 bean curd; tofu	1548
危 R-1250	危険	キ きけん	Danger!	1520
乾 R-1251	乾杯	カン かんぱい	"Bottoms up!" "Cheers!"	502
十 R-1252	十本	ジッ じっぽん	R-1066 10 (long, straight objects)	10
貧 乏 R-1253	貧乏	ビン ボウ びんぼう	R-1348 poor; destitute	845 1300
病 院 R-1254	病院	ビョウ イン びょういん	R-288 hospital	1813 1401

The following two frames show characters learned in VOL. 1 directly with their Sino-Japanese readings because there was no good English equivalent. All you need to do is see how they work in compounds.

尺 R-1255	尺八	シャク しゃくはち	*shakuhachi* flute 1151

里		リ		185
R-1256	七里	しちり	*7 ri*	

厘		リン		190
R-1257	一厘	いちりん	the slightest jot	

CHAPTER 7

Mixed Groups

AFTER THE RELAXING detour into everyday words, we must return to the work that remains with signal primitives. From here on, the work will be more complicated than it was in CHAPTERS 2 and 5 because of the increasing number of exceptions. In spite of that, I am sure you will find that it does provide considerable help with what would otherwise be a hodgepodge of disconnected readings.

Unlike the "semi-pure" groups, which (except for the group in FRAMES 767–774 and 975–978) had only *one* exception, these "mixed" groups are composed of at least 4 kanji sharing a common signal primitive that assigns the same reading to at least 2 members of the group, but which has more than 1 exception. The definition will get clearer as we go along.

The chapter divides mixed groups into three subgroupings of ascending difficulty. We begin with the easiest: groups of kanji in which a signal primitive has 2 readings that apply to 2 or more kanji each. At times, you will notice, a character will be assigned *both* readings.

A. MIXED GROUPS OF 2 READINGS ONLY

同		ドウ		192
R-1258	同時	どうじ	simultaneous	
銅		ドウ		290
R-1259	青銅	せいどう	bronze	
胴		ドウ		194
R-1260	胴体	どうたい	trunk of the body	

洞 R-1261	ドウ		193
	洞察	どうさつ	insight

筒 R-1262	トウ		1015
	水筒	すいとう	canteen; water flask

桐 R-1263	トウ		216
	桐油	とうゆ	(Chinese) wood oil

兆 R-1264	チョウ		250
	兆候	ちょうこう	sign; symptom

跳 R-1265	チョウ		1378
	跳躍板	ちょうやくばん	springboard; jumping board

挑 R-1266	チョウ		710
	挑戦	ちょうせん	challenge

眺 R-1267	チョウ		252
	眺望	ちょうぼう	outlook; prospects

桃 R-1268	トウ		251
	桃源郷	とうげんきょう	heaven-on-earth; Shangri-la

逃 R-1269	トウ		301
	逃走	とうそう	desertion; escape

The remaining frames of SECTION A are not as confusing as they look, if you take the time to study them. The two readings of the signal primitive overlap in some kanji and not in others.

Some of the readings you have learned already (refer to the cross-reference number), but they are all repeated here for the sake of completeness.

成 R-1270		セイ・ジョウ		**386**
	成功	せいこう	success	
	成仏	じょうぶつ	achieving "Buddhahood"	
盛 R-1271		セイ・ジョウ		**1567**
	全盛	ぜんせい	in its prime; full splendor	
	繁盛	はんじょう	flourishing	
誠 R-1272		セイ		**388**
	忠誠	ちゅうせい	loyalty	
城 R-1273		ジョウ		**387**
	城内	じょうない	inside the castle walls	
判 R-1274	半	ハン・バン	R-168	**1289**
	判定	はんてい	judgment	
	裁判	さいばん	trial; hearing	
伴 R-1275		ハン・バン	R-170	**1287**
	同伴	どうはん	company; companion	
	伴奏	ばんそう	(musical) accompaniment	
半 R-1276		ハン	R-167	**1286**
	半分	はんぶん	half	

畔 R-1277		ハン	R-169	1288
	湖畔	こはん	lakeside	

未 R-1278		ミ		229
	未知	みち	unknown	

味 R-1279		ミ		233
	薬味	やくみ	spices; seasoning	

魅 R-1280		ミ		2179
	魅力	みりょく	fascination; charm	

妹 R-1281		マイ		234
	義妹	ぎまい	(younger) sister-in-law	

昧 R-1282		マイ		231
	三昧	さんまい	*samādhi*; deep concentration	

亡 R-1283		ボウ・モウ		524
	死亡	しぼう	death	
	亡者	もうじゃ	the dead	

望 R-1284		ボウ・モウ		528
	希望	きぼう	hope	
	本望	ほんもう	long-cherished desire	

忘 R-1285		ボウ		640
	忘年会	ぼうねんかい	end-of-the-year party	

忙 R-1286		ボウ		665
	多忙	たぼう	very, very busy	

網 R-1287		モウ		1473
	放送網	ほうそうもう	broadcasting network	

盲 R-1288		モウ		525
	盲目	もうもく	blindness	

曽 R-1289		ソ	R-48, 594	540
	中曽根	なかそね	Nakasone (surname)	

層 R-1290		ソウ		1146
	知識層	ちしきそう	intelligentsia	

僧 R-1291		ソウ		1057
	禅僧	ぜんそう	Zen priest	

増 R-1292		ゾウ		541
	増加	ぞうか	augmentation; increase	

憎 R-1293		ゾウ		673
	憎心	ぞうしん	hatred; spite	

贈 R-1294		ソウ・ゾウ		542
	寄贈	きそう	donation	
	贈呈	ぞうてい	offering; present	

共 R-1295		キョウ		1934
	共産主義	きょうさんしゅぎ	Communism	

As with many other signal primitives we have met, this one carries a reading only when it occupies a prominent place (above or to the right) in the character.

恭 R-1296		キョウ		1943
	恭敬	きょうけい	deference; respect	

供 R-1297		キョウ・ク		1935
	供給	きょうきゅう	supply	
	供養	くよう	Buddhist "mass"	

港 R-1298		コウ		1940
	空港	くうこう	airport	

洪 R-1299		コウ		1939
	洪水	こうずい	flood	

正 R-1300		ショウ・セイ		405
	正月	しょうがつ	January; New Year's	
	正義	せいぎ	justice	

政 R-1301		セイ・ショウ	R-1148	407
	政府	せいふ	government	
	摂政	せっしょう	regency; regent	

整 R-1302		セイ	R-1598	1800
	調整	ちょうせい	adjustment	

征		セイ	946
R-1303	征伐	せいばつ	subjugating; conquest
証		ショウ	406
R-1304	保証	ほしょう	guarantee
症		ショウ	1816
R-1305	病症	びょうしょう	nature of a disease

B. MIXED GROUPS WITH 2 EXCEPTIONS ONLY

Unlike the mixed groups in SECTION A, those that follow share two characteristics: (1) they contain at least 3 kanji with a common reading; and (2) only 2 members of the group have readings different from the others. Let us begin with an example:

喝	曷	カツ	491
R-1306	一喝	いっかつ	thundering cry
葛		カツ	492
R-1307	葛藤	かっとう	complication; entanglement
褐		カツ	490
R-1308	褐色	かっしょく	brown
渇		カツ	488
R-1309	渇水	かっすい	drought

謁		エツ		489
R-1310	謁見	えっけん	interview; audience	
揭		ケイ		726
R-1311	掲示板	けいじばん	notice board	

It may have crossed your mind to ask why we should bother to classify these characters into groups at all—or it certainly will by the time the groups get smaller and smaller.

The answer is twofold. On the one hand, if we did not, you would find yourself adrift in a massive sea of disconnected readings far earlier than you need to be. On the other, since we have learned nearly 1,000 readings up to this point by means of the signal primitives, to ignore them in cases where there are exceptions would be to cut short our understanding of how these signal primitives work in the Japanese writing system. Without some experience in the mixed groups treated in these chapters, you will not appreciate the complex blend of consistency and inconsistency that characterize the *on-yomi*.

古		コ		16
R-1312	古語	こご	archaic word; old adage	
湖		コ		159
R-1313	湖畔	こはん	lakeside; along a lake	
故		コ		355
R-1314	事故	じこ	accident	
枯		コ		219
R-1315	枯淡	こたん	elegance; simplicity	

苦		ク	**239**
R-1316	苦悩	くのう	distress; suffering
居		キョ	**1143**
R-1317	居住	きょじゅう	residence

違	韋	イ	**1773**
R-1318	相違	そうい	difference
偉		イ	**1772**
R-1319	偉大	いだい	majestic; magnificent
緯		イ	**1774**
R-1320	経緯	けいい	longitude and latitude

衛		エイ	**1775**
R-1321	防衛	ぼうえい	defense
韓		カン	**1776**
R-1322	韓国	かんこく	South Korea

己		キ・コ	R-24	**564**
R-1323	知己	ちき		acquaintance
	自己	じこ		oneself
記		キ		**568**
R-1324	記者	きしゃ		journalist; reporter

起 R-1325		キ	565
	起原	きげん	source

紀 R-1326		キ	1454
	世紀	せいき	century

忌 R-1327		キ	644
	忌中	きちゅう	mourning

妃 R-1328		ヒ	566
	王妃	おうひ	queen

配 R-1329		ハイ	1544
	心配	しんぱい	worry; concern

坂 R-1330	反	ハン	780
	急坂	きゅうはん	steep hill

反 R-1331		ハン・ホン・タン	779
	反感	はんかん	animosity; antipathy
	謀反	むほん	conspiracy; rebellion
	反物	たんもの	cloth; textile

The second reading is rare. The compound in the final reading combines an *on-yomi* and a *kun-yomi*.

板 R-1332		ハン・バン	781
	鉄板	てっぱん	griddle; grill
	掲示板	けいじばん	notice board

販 R-1333		ハン		783
	販売	はんばい	selling	

版 R-1334		ハン		1298
	出版社	しゅっぱんしゃ	publishing company	

阪 R-1335		ハン		1390
	阪神	はんしん	Osaka and Kobe	

The Japanese commonly take one character from the name of two places or organizations and then turn the result into an *on-yomi* compound which then represents the two original words. In this example, the result is the name of a large corporation that runs a railway, a department-store chain, and a baseball team.

飯 R-1336		ハン	R-1035	1583
	ご飯	ごはん	rice; meal; dinner	

返 R-1337		ヘン		782
	返事	へんじ	reply; answer	

仮 R-1338		カ	R-2313	1039
	仮面	かめん	mask	

矛 R-1339		ム		1311
	矛盾	むじゅん	contradiction	

務 R-1340		ム		1313
	事務	じむ	office work	

霧 R-1341		ム	1314
	霧散	むさん	dispersion; dissipation

柔 R-1342		ジュウ・ニュウ	R-1104	1312
	柔道	じゅうどう		judo
	柔和	にゅうわ		gentleness; mildness

分 R-1343		フン・ブン・ブ	R-1038, 1180, 1235	844
	五分	ごふん		5 minutes
	自分	じぶん		oneself
	大分	だいぶ		greatly; considerably

粉 R-1344		フン	1458
	粉末	ふんまつ	powder

紛 R-1345		フン	988
	紛議	ふんぎ	dissension; controversy

雰 R-1346		フン	2184
	雰囲気	ふんいき	atmosphere; ambience

盆 R-1347		ボン	1557
	盆栽	ぼんさい	dwarfed "bonsai" plants

貧 R-1348		ビン・ヒン	R-1253	845
	貧乏	びんぼう		destitute; poor
	貧富	ひんぷ		rich and poor

頒 R-1349		ハン	846
	頒布	はんぷ	distribution

旗 R-1350	其 国旗	キ こっき	national flag	1901
棋 R-1351	 将棋	キ しょうぎ	Japanese chess	1900
基 R-1352	 基本	キ きほん	fundamental	1904
期 R-1353	 学期	キ がっき	R-2311 academic term	1902
欺 R-1354	 詐欺	ギ さぎ	fraud	1899
碁 R-1355	 囲碁	ゴ いご	R-1227 Japanese checkers	1903
垂 R-1356	 懸垂	スイ けんすい	chinning (exercises)	1705
睡 R-1357	 睡眠	スイ すいみん	sleep	1707
錘 R-1358	 紡錘	スイ ぼうすい	spindle	1708
郵 R-1359	 郵便	ユウ ゆうびん	mail; post	1990

唾 R-1360		ダ		1706
	唾液	だえき	saliva	

浅 R-1361		セン		395
	浅学	せんがく	shallow or superficial learning	

箋 R-1362		セン		1011
	便箋	びんせん	stationery; writing paper	

銭 R-1363		セン		394
	金銭	きんせん	cash; money	

践 R-1364		セン		1380
	実践	じっせん	praxis; practical	

桟 R-1365		サン		393
	桟橋	さんばし	pier; landing-wharf	
	The exemplary compound includes a *kun-yomi*.			

残 R-1366		ザン	R-1210	871
	残念	ざんねん	"What a pity!"	

台 R-1367		タイ・ダイ	R-1168, 1186	805
	台湾	たいわん	Taiwan	
	三台	さんだい	3 (vehicles)	

怠 R-1368		タイ		806
	怠業	たいぎょう	sloth; indolence	

胎 R-1369		タイ		810
	母胎	ぼたい	matrix	

治 R-1370		ジ・チ	R-1195	807
	明治時代	めいじじだい	Meiji Era (1868–1912)	
	治安	ちあん	law and order	

始 R-1371		シ		809
	原始的	げんしてき	primitive	

干 R-1372		カン		1777
	干潮	かんちょう	low tide; ebb tide	

幹 R-1373		カン	R-1158	1783
	新幹線	しんかんせん	Japan's superexpress "Bullet Train"	

刊 R-1374		カン		1779
	週刊	しゅうかん	weekly (magazine)	

汗 R-1375		カン		1780
	汗顔	かんがん	perspiration	

肝 R-1376		カン		1778
	肝要	かんよう	essential	

軒 R-1377		ケン	R-1188	1781
	五軒	ごけん	5 (houses, buildings)	

岸 R-1378		ガン	R-1243	1782
	海岸	かいがん	seashore	

監 R-1379	臣	カン		1562
	総監	そうかん	inspector general	

艦 R-1380		カン		2020
	艦長	かんちょう	captain (of a ship)	

鑑 R-1381		カン		1564
	年鑑	ねんかん	yearbook; annual report	

濫 R-1382		ラン		1563
	氾濫	はんらん	deluge	

藍 R-1383		ラン		1565
	出藍	しゅつらん	outshine; outdo	

兄 R-1384		ケイ・キョウ		107
	父兄	ふけい	father and elder brother(s)	
	兄弟	きょうだい	brothers (and sisters)	

Note that the primitive element 兑 does not figure as a member of this group, but is used later as a signal primitive from FRAME 1509.

競 R-1385		ケイ・キョウ		465
	競馬	けいば	horse racing	
	競争	きょうそう	competition	

況		キョウ			156
R-1386	概況	がいきょう	general conditions		

祝		シュク・シュウ			1170
R-1387	祝福	しゅくふく	blessing		
	祝儀	しゅうぎ	celebration		

克		コク			109
R-1388	克己	こっき	self-denial		

The final six frames of SECTION B merit careful study. Some of the readings were learned earlier. A few of them will be met with only rarely. In any event, the complete list is presented here.

生		セイ・ショウ	R-775, 1077	1675
R-1389	先生	せんせい	teacher	
	一生	いっしょう	one's life; lifetime	

姓		セイ・ショウ	R-779	1678
R-1390	姓名	せいめい	one's full name	
	百姓	ひゃくしょう	farmer; peasant	

性		セイ・ショウ	R-776	1679
R-1391	女性	じょせい	woman	
	性分	しょうぶん	nature; disposition	

星		セイ・ショウ	R-777	1676
R-1392	星座	せいざ	a "sign" of the zodiac	
	明星	みょうじょう	Venus; morning star	

産 R-1393		サン	R-781	**1681**
	不動産	ふどうさん	real estate	
牲 R-1394		セイ	R-780	**1691**
	犠牲	ぎせい	sacrifice	

C. REMAINING MIXED GROUPS

As indicated earlier, this final class of mixed groups is by far the most diffi-cult and—unfortunately—the most numerous. Despite the many exceptions, it pays to learn these characters in their respective groups. Fortunately, a good number of the characters included for the sake of completeness have already been learned under another rubric.

As before, characters that have more than one standard reading are treated in full here with exemplary compounds provided for each of their readings.

地 R-1395	也	チ・ジ	R-1049, 1100	**554**
	地図	ちず	map	
	地震	じしん	earthquake	
池 R-1396		チ		**555**
	電池	でんち	battery	
施 R-1397		シ・セ		**1124**
	施行	しこう	enforcement; excecution	
	布施	ふせ	alms; offering (to a priest)	
也 R-1398		ヤ	R-38	**2236**
	也寸志	やすし	Yasushi (personal name for a man)	

他 R-1399		タ	R-1228	1034
	他人	たにん	outsider; stranger	

秘 R-1400	必	ヒ	R-1094	970
	秘密	ひみつ	secret	

泌 R-1401		ヒ・ヒツ		686
	泌尿 分泌	ひにょう ぶんぴつ	urination; urinary secretion	

必 R-1402		ヒツ	R-1095	685
	必要	ひつよう	necessary; need	

堅 R-1403	臤	ケン		917
	中堅	ちゅうけん	mainstay; "backbone"	

賢 R-1404		ケン		915
	賢明	けんめい	sagacious; wise	

緊 R-1405		キン		1474
	緊張	きんちょう	tension; str	

腎 R-1406		ジン		916
	腎臓	じんぞう	kidney	

真 R-1407		シン		79
	真実	しんじつ	truth	

慎 R-1408	シン			677
	謹慎	きんしん	penitence; good behavior	

鎮 R-1409	チン			294
	鎮圧	ちんあつ	quelling (of a disturbance)	

填 R-1410	テン			166
	填補	てんぽ	filling up	

叔 R-1411	シュク			775
	叔父	しゅくふ	uncle	
	The example compound is normally read おじ.			

淑 R-1412	シュク			778
	貞淑	ていしゅく	chastity	

督 R-1413	トク			776
	監督	かんとく	coach; director	

寂 R-1414	ジャク・セキ			777
	静寂	せいじゃく	retreat into silence	
	寂静	せきせい	retreat into silence	

韻 R-1415	音	イン	R-949	520
	音韻	おんいん	phoneme	

音 R-1416		オン・イン	R-1120	518
	音楽	おんがく	music	
	福音	ふくいん	Gospel	

暗 R-1417		アン 暗記	あんき	memorization	519

海 R-1418	毎 海岸	カイ かいがん	R-1197 seashore		500
悔 R-1419		カイ 後悔	こうかい	remorse	672

毎 R-1420		マイ 毎日	まいにち	R-1129 every day	497
梅 R-1421		バイ 梅花	ばいか	plum blossoms	499
侮 R-1422		ブ 侮辱	ぶじょく	humiliation; disgrace	1064
敏 R-1423		ビン 敏速	びんそく	brisk; prompt	498
繁 R-1424		ハン 繁栄	はんえい	prosperity	1435

Pay special attention to the following group of 12 kanji, made up of 2 readings and 2 exceptions. This is a unique group whose mastery now will save you much confusion later. Be careful not to include FRAMES 535–536, where the present signal primitive figured as part of a larger signal primitive.

防 R-1425	方	ボウ		1399
	防衛	ぼうえい	defense	

紡 R-1426		ボウ		1457
	紡績	ぼうせき	spinning (cloth)	

坊 R-1427		ボウ・ボッ		531
	坊主	ぼうず	Buddhist priest; bonze	
	坊ちゃん	ぼっちゃん	young master; greenhorn	

妨 R-1428		ボウ		530
	妨害	ぼうがい	interference; obstruction	

肪 R-1429		ボウ		533
	脂肪	しぼう	fat	

傍 R-1430		ボウ		1090
	傍線	ぼうせん	marks indicating emphasis, similar to italics in Western typesetting	

房 R-1431		ボウ		1159
	官房長	かんぼうちょう	secretary general	

方 R-1432		ホウ		529
	方面	ほうめん	direction	

芳 R-1433		ホウ		532
	芳志	ほうし	your kind offer	

訪		ホウ		534
R-1434	訪問	ほうもん	formal visit	

激		ゲキ		536
R-1435	感激	かんげき	deeply felt emotion	

敷		フ		2028
R-1436	敷設	ふせつ	laying out (e.g., rails)	

値	直	チ		1052
R-1437	価値	かち	value; worth	

置		チ		895
R-1438	放置	ほうち	neglect; leaving unattended	

殖		ショク		874
R-1439	生殖	せいしょく	procreation	

植		ショク		217
R-1440	植物園	しょくぶつえん	botanical garden	

直		チョク・ジキ		77
R-1441	直面	ちょくめん	confrontation	
	正直	しょうじき	honest; frank	

東		トウ	R-1029	543
R-1442	東京	とうきょう	Tokyo	

凍 R-1443	凍結	トウ とうけつ		545 freezing
練 R-1444	練習	レン れんしゅう	R-1143	1443 practice
錬 R-1445	錬金術	レン れんきんじゅつ		2186 alchemy
陳 R-1446	陳列	チン ちんれつ		1398 display; exhibit
注 R-1447	主 注射	チュウ ちゅうしゃ	R-1224	285 injection
柱 R-1448	電柱	チュウ でんちゅう		286 telephone pole
駐 R-1449	駐車場	チュウ ちゅうしゃじょう		2136 parking lot
主 R-1450	主人 坊主	シュ・ス しゅじん ぼうず	R-1093	284 one's husband Buddhist priest
住 R-1451	住所	ジュウ じゅうしょ	R-1091	1027 address; residence

往 R-1452		オウ		945
	往復	おうふく	round trip	

裳 R-1453	尚	ショウ		863
	衣裳	いしょう	dress; costume [rare]	

賞 R-1454		ショウ		859
	懸賞	けんしょう	reward or prize	

償 R-1455		ショウ		1060
	賠償	ばいしょう	indemnity; compensation	

掌 R-1456		ショウ		864
	車掌	しゃしょう	conductor (on a bus or train)	

常 R-1457		ジョウ	R-1079	862
	非常	ひじょう	extraordinary; emergency	

堂 R-1458		ドウ	R-1138	861
	食堂	しょくどう	dining hall	

党 R-1459		トウ		860
	与党	よとう	ruling political party	

由 R-1460		ユ・ユウ	R-14, 1103, 2316	1186
	由来	ゆらい	reason; origin	
	自由	じゆう	freedom; free	

油 R-1461		ユ	R-1137	1188
	石油	せきゆ	oil	

宙 R-1462		チュウ		1190
	宇宙	うちゅう	universe; space	

抽 R-1463		チュウ		1187
	抽象	ちゅうしょう	abstraction	

軸 R-1464		ジク	R-589	1193
	車軸	しゃじく	axle; wheel	

袖 R-1465		シュウ		1189
	袖手	しゅうしゅ	hands-in-one's-sleeves	

各 R-1466		カク		311
	各自	かくじ	each one; each person	

格 R-1467		カク	R-2312	312
	性格	せいかく	character; nature	

閣 R-1468		カク		1752
	内閣	ないかく	(government) cabinet	

客 R-1469		キャク・カク	R-1194	315
	お客さん	おきゃくさん	guest	
	旅客	りょかく	passenger; tourist	

絡 R-1470		ラク		1450
	脈絡	みゃくらく	(logical) coherence	

落 R-1471		ラク		320
	落語	らくご	comic storytelling	

酪 R-1472		ラク		1541
	酪農	らくのう	dairy farming	

略 R-1473		リャク	R-621	314
	略語	りゃくご	abbreviation	

額 R-1474		ガク		316
	全額	ぜんがく	sum total	

者 R-1475		シャ	R-1028	1345
	医者	いしゃ	doctor	

煮 R-1476		シャ		1346
	煮沸	しゃふつ	boiling	

署 R-1477		ショ		1349
	警察署	けいさつしょ	police station	

暑 R-1478		ショ		1350
	残暑	ざんしょ	"Indian summer"	

諸 R-1479	ショ		1351
	諸国	しょこく	(various) countries

著 R-1480	チョ		1347
	著者	ちょしゃ	author

猪 R-1481	チョ		1352
	猪勇	ちょゆう	foolhardy courage

緒 R-1482	ショ・チョ	R-1061	1444
	一緒	いっしょ	together
	情緒	じょうちょ	heartstrings; emotionalism

都 R-1483	ト・ツ	R-1086, 1172	1989
	京都	きょうと	Kyoto
	都合	つごう	conditions

賭 R-1484	ト		1354
	賭博	とばく	gambling

陽 R-1485	昜 ヨウ	R-1246, 2071	1397
	太陽	たいよう	sun

The signal primitive at play in this and the following frames has its own reading, as was learned back in FRAME 1229.

揚 R-1486	ヨウ		717
	掲揚	けいよう	hoisting; raising

瘍 R-1487		ヨウ		1817
	潰瘍	かいよう	ulcer	

腸 R-1488		チョウ		583
	大腸	だいちょう	colon; large intestine	

湯 R-1489		トウ		585
	熱湯	ねっとう	boiling water	

場 R-1490		ジョウ	R-1118	584
	工場	こうじょう	factory	

傷 R-1491		ショウ		1071
	傷害	しょうがい	wound; injury	

鉄 R-1492	失	テツ	R-1051	909
	地下鉄	ちかてつ	subway train	

迭 R-1493		テツ		910
	更迭	こうてつ	change; shakeup	

失 R-1494		シツ	R-1159	908
	失礼	しつれい	discourtesy	

秩 R-1495		チツ		969
	秩序	ちつじょ	order; discipline	

博 R-1496	専	ハク・バク		48
	博愛	はくあい	philanthropy	
	賭博	とばく	gambling	

薄 R-1497		ハク		242
	薄荷	はっか	peppermint	

縛 R-1498		バク		1476
	束縛	そくばく	restraint; restriction	

簿 R-1499		ボ		1020
	簿記	ぼき	bookkeeping	

街 R-1500		ガイ・カイ		955
	商店街	しょうてんがい	shopping street	
	街道	かいどう	thoroughfare; highroad	

涯 R-1501	圭	ガイ		169
	生涯	しょうがい	lifetime; one's life	

崖 R-1502		ガイ		841
	断崖	だんがい	precipice	

圭 R-1503		ケイ		167
	圭子	けいこ	Keiko (personal name of a woman)	

桂 R-1504		ケイ		210
	桂皮	けいひ	cinnamon	

佳		カ		1044
R-1505	佳作	かさく	excellent piece of work	

封		フウ・ホウ		168
R-1506	封筒	ふうとう	envelope	
	封建	ほうけん	feudalism	

閲		兌 エツ		1745
R-1507	閲覧室	えつらんしつ	reading room	

悦		エツ		666
R-1508	満悦	まんえつ	delighted; satisfied	

説		セツ・ゼイ	R-1156	538
R-1509	説明	せつめい	explanation	
	遊説	ゆうぜい	campaigning; stumping	

税		ゼイ		961
R-1510	税金	ぜいきん	taxes	

鋭		エイ		539
R-1511	鋭敏	えいびん	acute; sharp-witted	

脱		ダツ		537
R-1512	脱税	だつぜい	tax evasion	

根		艮 コン		1571
R-1513	大根	だいこん	large garden radish	

痕 R-1514	痕跡	コン こんせき	vestiges	1822
恨 R-1515	悔恨	コン かいこん	regret; remorse	1570
限 R-1516	無限	ゲン むげん	infinity	1576
眼 R-1517	眼球 開眼	ガン・ゲン がんきゅう かいげん	eyeball Buddhist ceremony for consecrating a new image	1577
銀 R-1518	銀行	ギン ぎんこう	R-1069 bank	1569
退 R-1519	撤退	タイ てったい	withdrawal; retreat	1575
支 R-1520	支店	シ してん	branch office or store	768
枝 R-1521	枝葉	シ しよう	branch and leaf; nonessentials	770
肢 R-1522	肢体	シ したい	limbs; members	771

伎 R-1523	歌舞伎	キ かぶき	kabuki	1040
岐 R-1524	岐路	キ きろ	forked road	834
技 R-1525	技能	ギ ぎのう	technical skill	769

少 R-1526	少年	ショウ しょうねん	child; juvenile	111
渉 R-1527	交渉	ショウ こうしょう	negotiations	398
抄 R-1528	抄録	ショウ しょうろく	selection; excerpt	699
省 R-1529	文科省 反省	ショウ・セイ もんかしょう はんせい	R-1221 Ministry of Science and Education reflection; consideration	131
砂 R-1530	砂糖	サ さとう	R-2306 sugar	122
沙 R-1531	沙汰	サ さた	R-1053 news; information	151

秒		ビョウ	R-1235	965
R-1532	五秒	ごびょう	5 seconds	

妙		ミョウ		130
R-1533	奇妙	きみょう	queer; curious	

歩		ホ・ブ・フ	R-1223	396
R-1534	歩道	ほどう	sidewalk	
	歩合	ぶあい	rate; ratio	
	歩	ふ	a pawn (in Japanese chess)	

捗		チョク		728
R-1535	進捗	しんちょく	progress	

劣		レツ		926
R-1536	劣等感	れっとうかん	inferiority complex	

第	弟	ダイ	R-1212	1327
R-1537	第一	だいいち	No. 1	

弟		デ・デイ・ダイ	R-598	1328
R-1538	弟子	でし	disciple	
	子弟	してい	young people	
	兄弟	きょうだい	brothers (and sisters)	

皮		ヒ		865
R-1539	皮肉	ひにく	sarcasm	

被 R-1540		ヒ		870
	被害	ひがい	damage; harm; injury	

彼 R-1541		ヒ		948
	彼岸	ひがん	equinox	

疲 R-1542		ヒ		1823
	疲労	ひろう	fatigue	

披 R-1543		ヒ		868
	披露宴	ひろうえん	wedding reception	

破 R-1544		ハ		869
	破産	はさん	bankruptcy	

波 R-1545		ハ	R-18	866
	電波	でんぱ	radio waves; air waves	

婆 R-1546		バ		867
	老婆	ろうば	old woman	

俳 R-1547	非	ハイ		1761
	俳句	はいく	haiku poem	

輩 R-1548		ハイ		1765
	先輩	せんぱい	one's senior	

排 R-1549		ハイ		1762
	排水管	はいすいかん	water pipe; conduit	

非		ヒ	R-1079	1782
R-1550	非常	ひじょう	emergency; extraordinary	

悲		ヒ		1763
R-1551	悲観	ひかん	pessimism	

扉		ヒ		1766
R-1552	門扉	もんぴ	doors (of a gate)	

罪		ザイ		1764
R-1553	有罪	ゆうざい	guilty	

寺		ジ		170
R-1554	寺内	じない	within the temple precincts	

持		ジ		712
R-1555	支持	しじ	backup; support	

侍		ジ		1050
R-1556	侍従	じじゅう	chamberlain	

時		ジ	R-1065	171
R-1557	時間	じかん	time	

詩		シ		370
R-1558	詩人	しじん	poet	

待 R-1559		タイ	R-1132	**944**
	招待	しょうたい	invitation	
等 R-1560		トウ		**1016**
	劣等	れっとう	inferior	
特 R-1561		トク	R-1163	**261**
	特別	とくべつ	special	
豆 R-1562		トウ・ズ	R-1249	**1548**
	豆腐 大豆	とうふ だいず	bean curd; tofu soybeans	
痘 R-1563		トウ		**1815**
	天然痘	てんねんとう	smallpox	
闘 R-1564		トウ		**1757**
	戦闘	せんとう	battle	
登 R-1565		トウ・ト		**1838**
	登録 登山	とうろく とざん	registration mountain climbing	
頭 R-1566		トウ・ト・ズ	R-1179	**1549**
	先頭 音頭 頭痛	せんとう おんど ずつう	forefront; van leading (in singing) headache	
豊 R-1567		ホウ		**1551**
	豊年	ほうねん	bumper year	

澄		チョウ		1839
R-1568	清澄	せいちょう	limpid; clear	

短		タン		1550
R-1569	短気	たんき	short temper	

羊		ヨウ		586
R-1570	羊毛	ようもう	wool	

洋		ヨウ	R-1146	588
R-1571	西洋	せいよう	the West; Occident	

様		ヨウ		1003
R-1572	様相	ようそう	aspect; phase	

養		ヨウ		1591
R-1573	休養	きゅうよう	rest and recuperation	

窯		ヨウ		1423
R-1574	窯業	ようぎょう	ceramics manufacturing	

祥		ショウ		1169
R-1575	発祥地	はっしょうち	cradle; birthplace	

詳		ショウ		589
R-1576	詳細	しょうさい	details; particulars	

鮮		セン		590
R-1577	新鮮	しんせん	fresh	

美		ビ	R-45, 1207	587
R-1578	美人	びじん	beautiful woman	

丁		テイ・チョウ	R-1162	95
R-1579	丁寧	ていねい	civility; courtesy	
	二丁目	にちょうめ	city block no. 2	

町		チョウ		96
R-1580	町人	ちょうにん	merchant (class)	

頂		チョウ		98
R-1581	頂点	ちょうてん	apex; summit	

庁		チョウ		635
R-1582	県庁	けんちょう	prefectural office	

貯		チョ		206
R-1583	貯金	ちょきん	(bank) savings	

灯		トウ	R-1230	177
R-1584	電灯	でんとう	electric light	

訂		テイ		362
R-1585	訂正	ていせい	correction; revision	

打		ダ		705
R-1586	打倒	だとう	a fall (from power)	

取 R-1587		シュ		**882**
	取捨	しゅしゃ	adoption or rejection	
趣 R-1588		シュ		**883**
	趣味	しゅみ	hobby; pastime	
最 R-1589		サイ		**884**
	最新	さいしん	latest; newest	
撮 R-1590		サツ		**885**
	撮影	さつえい	photographing	
区 R-1591		ク		**1831**
	地区	ちく	region	
駆 R-1592		ク		**2137**
	先駆	せんく	harbinger; forerunner	
欧 R-1593		オウ		**1834**
	欧州	おうしゅう	Europe	
殴 R-1594		オウ		**1833**
	殴打	おうだ	blow; assault	
枢 R-1595		スウ		**1832**
	枢軸	すうじく	pivot	
束 R-1596		ソク	R-1166	**1793**
	約束	やくそく	promise	

速		ソク	R-1121	1799
R-1597	高速道路	こうそくどうろ	highway; expressway	

整		セイ	R-1302	1800
R-1598	調整	ちょうせい	adjustment	

勅		チョク		1796
R-1599	詔勅	しょうちょく	imperial proclamation	

疎		ソ		1797
R-1600	疎外	そがい	alienation	

頼		ライ		1794
R-1601	信頼	しんらい	reliance; trust	

松	公	ショウ		848
R-1602	松竹梅	しょうちくばい	pine, bamboo, and plum	

A word of explanation about the explanatory compound in this frame: because of their resistance to the winter cold, the pine, bamboo, and plum often appear together in end-of-the year decorations. From there, they have come to be associated with festive occasions in general.

訟		ショウ		850
R-1603	訴訟	そしょう	legal suit	

公		コウ		847
R-1604	公園	こうえん	public park	

翁 R-1605	老翁	オウ ろうおう		849 venerable old man

提 R-1606	是 提案	テイ ていあん		718 proposal; proposition

堤 R-1607	堤防	テイ ていぼう		416 dike

是 R-1608	是非	ゼ ぜひ	R-592	414 absolutely; by all means

題 R-1609	問題	ダイ もんだい	R-1136	415 problem

欲 R-1610	谷 欲望	ヨク よくぼう		855 craving; appetite; ambition

浴 R-1611	浴室	ヨク よくしつ		852 bathing room

谷 R-1612	幽谷	コク ゆうこく		851 deep ravine; glen

俗 R-1613	俗語	ゾク ぞくご	R-1239	1042 slang; vulgarism

裕 R-1614	余裕	ユウ よゆう	856 surplus; breathing room

昔 R-1615	昔日 今昔	セキ・シャク せきじつ こんじゃく	1268 bygone days past and present

籍 R-1616	戸籍	セキ こせき	1689 census registration

惜 R-1617	惜敗	セキ せきはい	1271 narrow defeat

錯 R-1618	錯誤	サク さくご	1269 mix-up; mistake

借 R-1619	借金	シャク しゃっきん	1270 debt; liability

措 R-1620	措置	ソ そち	1272 measures; steps

活 R-1621	舌 生活	カツ せいかつ	R-1152 154 life; livelihood

括 R-1622	包括	カツ ほうかつ	714 all-embracing; comprehensive

舌		ゼツ		41
R-1623	弁舌	べんぜつ	eloquence	

話		ワ	R-1040	368
R-1624	電話	でんわ	telephone	

辞		ジ	R-1084	1613
R-1625	辞典	じてん	dictionary	

憩		ケイ		658
R-1626	休憩	きゅうけい	recess; rest	

予		ヨ	R-1229	1719
R-1627	予約	よやく	reservation	

預		ヨ		1721
R-1628	預金	よきん	deposit (in a bank)	

序		ジョ		1720
R-1629	序文	じょぶん	preface (to a book)	

野		ヤ		722
R-1630	野球	やきゅう	baseball	

除	余	ジョ・ジ	R-1125	1787
R-1631	除外	じょがい	exception; exclusion	
	掃除	そうじ	cleaning	

叙 R-1632		ジョ	1789
	叙事詩	じょじし	epic
徐 R-1633		ジョ	1788
	徐行	じょこう	"Go Slowly!"
塗 R-1634		ト	1792
	塗装	とそう	painting; coating
途 R-1635		ト	1790
	途中	とちゅう	halfway; on the way
余 R-1636		ヨ	1786
	余白	よはく	empty space (in a painting)
材 R-1637	オ	ザイ	738
	取材	しゅざい	gathering data or material
財 R-1638		ザイ・サイ R-1145	737
	財産 財布	ざいさん さいふ	one's possessions or wealth wallet
才 R-1639		サイ R-1192	736
	天才	てんさい	genius
閉 R-1640		ヘイ	1751
	閉店	へいてん	closing time (of a shop)

揮 R-1641	軍	キ		715
	指揮者	しきしゃ	conductor (of an orchestra)	

輝 R-1642		キ		324
	光輝	こうき	splendor; dazzling brilliance	

軍 R-1643		グン		323
	海軍	かいぐん	navy	

運 R-1644		ウン	R-1165	325
	運動	うんどう	exercise; sports	

青 R-1645		セイ・ショウ	R-78	1654
	青年	せいねん	youth	
	緑青	ろくしょう	verdigris; green rust	

精 R-1646		セイ・ショウ	R-79	1655
	精神	せいしん	mind; psyche	
	不精	ぶしょう	indolence; sloth	

清 R-1647		セイ・ショウ	R-80	1659
	清潔	せいけつ	clean	
	清浄	しょうじょう	purity; innocence	

請 R-1648		セイ・シン	R-83	1656
	申請	しんせい	application; petition	
	普請	ふしん	building; construction	

晴 R-1649		セイ	R-81	1658
	晴天	せいてん	clear skies	

静 R-1650		セイ	R-82, 943	1660
	静止	せいし	standstill; stationary	

	情 R-1651	ジョウ	R-84	1657
	感情	かんじょう	feelings; emotions	

調 R-1652	周	チョウ		373
	調子	ちょうし	condition; state	

彫 R-1653		チョウ		1846
	彫像	ちょうぞう	sculpture; statue	

	周 R-1654	シュウ		339
	円周	えんしゅう	circumference	

	週 R-1655	シュウ	R-1116	340
	週間	しゅうかん	week	

該 R-1656	亥	ガイ		1640
	該当	がいとう	pertinent; relevant	

The signal primitive above has no Chinese reading, as we learned back in FRAME 707.

劾 R-1657		ガイ		1642
	弾劾	だんがい	impeachment	

骸 R-1658		ガイ		1641
	骸骨	がいこつ	skeleton	

核 R-1659		カク		1638
	核心	かくしん	nucleus	

刻 R-1660		コク		1639
	時刻表	じこくひょう	timetable	

済 R-1661	斉	サイ		1868
	経済	けいざい	economy; economics	

斎 R-1662		サイ		1869
	書斎	しょさい	private study; library	

斉 R-1663		セイ		1866
	斉唱	せいしょう	homophony	

剤 R-1664		ザイ		1867
	洗剤	せんざい	cleanser; laundry soap	

Pay attention to the overlaps of multiple Chinese readings in the final set of mixed groups.

殺 R-1665	柔	サツ	R-1667, 1669	1607
	自殺	じさつ	suicide	

刹 R-1666		サツ	R-1668	1601
	刹	さつ	central pillar in a Buddhist pagoda	

殺 R-1667		セツ	R-1665, 1669	1607
	殺生戒	せっしょうかい	injunction against taking life	
刹 R-1668		セツ	R-1666	1601
	刹鬼	せっき	destructive demon	
殺 R-1669		サイ	R-1665, 1667	1607
	相殺	そうさい	mutual offsetting or canceling out	

CHAPTER 8

Readings from Useful Compounds

WE HAVE done everything we can with the signal primitives but are still left with 701 frames to complete our study of the Chinese readings. Now we return to the procedure followed in CHAPTER 6, focusing on the exemplary compounds. Many of the words that appear in the following 237 frames are not common to everyday conversation, but they are all words that you will meet frequently in everyday reading materials such as newspapers, magazines, billboards, street signs, and menus. If you have studied the language formally for a half a year or more, you will probably know at least a third of them already.

能		ノウ		2160
R-1670	芸能界	げいのうかい	entertainment world	

発		ホッ	R-1672	1840
R-1671	発足	ほっそく	inauguration; start-up	

発		ハツ	R-1671	1840
R-1672	発音	はつおん	pronunciation	

工		ク	R-115	80
R-1673	大工	だいく	carpenter	

雨		ウ		451
R-1674	梅雨	ばいう	Japan's "rainy season"	

考		コウ		1341
R-1675	考案	こうあん		plan; idea being considered

憲		ケン		1674
R-1676	憲法	けんぽう		(national) constitution

西		サイ	R-1146	1728
R-1677	関西	かんさい		the "Kansai" district

豚		トン		577
R-1678	豚カツ	とんかつ		pork cutlets

迷		メイ		992
R-1679	迷惑	めいわく		trouble; inconvenience

審		シン		2059
R-1680	陪審	ばいしん		jury

買 収		バイ		894
		シュウ		1628
R-1681	買収	ばいしゅう		bribery; buying off

独 立		ドク		561
		リツ	R-2255	462
R-1682	独立	どくりつ		independence

廃 止		ハイ		1841
		シ	(R-20)	396
R-1683	廃止	はいし		repeal; abolition

土 R-1684	土地 とち	ト とち	R-1083 tract of land	161
口 R-1685	人口 じんこう	コウ じんこう	R-2249 population	11
皇 R-1686	天皇 てんのう	オウ てんのう	R-1762 (Japanese) emperor	279
援 助 R-1687	援助 えんじょ	エン ジョ えんじょ	assistance; financial aid	2101 1921
互 恵 R-1688	互恵 ごけい	ゴ ケイ ごけい	R-31 reciprocal	819 659
派 遣 R-1689	派遣 はけん	ハ ケン はけん	dispatching (e.g., a delegate)	1999 1910
入 R-1690	入院 にゅういん	ニュウ にゅういん	admittance into a hospital	842
明 R-1691	明日 みょうにち	ミョウ みょうにち	R-465 the morrow	20

化粧 R-1692		ケ	R-111	1083
		ショウ		991
	化粧室	けしょうしつ	"powder room"	
夫婦 R-1693		フウ	R-933	901
		フ		1234
	夫婦	ふうふ	man and wife; couple	
首相 R-1694		シュ		74
		ショウ	R-277	222
	首相	しゅしょう	prime minister	
衣類 R-1695		イ	R-23	423
		ルイ		1000
	衣類	いるい	clothing (generic term)	
万 R-1696		バン	R-1068	68
	万歳	ばんざい	"Hip, hip, hurray!"	
思 R-1697		シ		651
	思想	しそう	thought; ideas	
妬 R-1698		ト		123
	嫉妬	しっと	jealousy; envy	
迅 R-1699		ジン		298
	迅速	じんそく	speedy; prompt	

平均		ヘイ	R-2183	**1596**
		キン		**172**
R-1700	平均	へいきん	an average	
児童		ジ	R-2186	**62**
		ドウ		**468**
R-1701	児童	じどう	child; juvenile	
解釈		カイ	R-2397	**1955**
		シャク		**2057**
R-1702	解釈	かいしゃく	interpretation	
句		ク		**69**
R-1703	文句	もんく	complaint	
休日		キュウ		**1038**
		ジツ	R-603	**12**
R-1704	休日	きゅうじつ	holiday; day off	
役		ヤク	R-2309	**949**
R-1705	市役所	しやくしょ	city hall	
集		シュウ		**601**
R-1706	募集	ぼしゅう	recruiting	
罰		バツ	R-596	**896**
R-1707	罰金	ばっきん	fine; penalty	

位		イ		1028
R-1708	地位	ちい		position; status

接		セツ		725
R-1709	直接	ちょくせつ		direct; immediate

間		ケン	R-425	1747
R-1710	世間	せけん		public world; society

断		ダン		1218
食		ジキ	R-1138	1582
R-1711	断食	だんじき		fasting

品		ヒン		23
R-1712	事務用品	じむようひん		office supplies

世		セイ	R-7	28
R-1713	二世	にせい		second generation

島		トウ		2098
R-1714	半島	はんとう		peninsula

瞬		シュン		880
R-1715	瞬間	しゅんかん		instant; blink of the eye

進		シン		603
R-1716	進行	しんこう		advance; progress

形式 R-1717		ケイ	R-1130	**1847**
		シキ		**377**
	形式	けいしき	form; formality	
宗 R-1718		シュウ	R-2261	**1181**
	宗教	しゅうきょう	religion	
査 R-1719		サ		**1920**
	調査	ちょうさ	investigation; research	
聴 R-1720		チョウ		**890**
	公聴会	こうちょうかい	public hearing	
村 R-1721		ソン		**221**
	町村	ちょうそん	towns and villages	
継 R-1722		ケイ		**1470**
	中継	ちゅうけい	(television or radio) relay	
臣 R-1723		ジン	R-2362	**911**
	大臣	だいじん	cabinet minister	
開 R-1724		カイ		**1750**
	打開	だかい	break (in a deadlock)	
延 R-1725		エン		**419**
	延期	えんき	postponement; adjournment	

演 R-1726	演説	エン えんぜつ		address; speech	2163
興 R-1727	復興	コウ ふっこう	R-1735	revival; rehabilitation	1533
言 R-1728	言明	ゲン げんめい	R-1895	(press) statement	357
範 R-1729	範囲	ハン はんい		sphere; range	1516
氾 R-1730	氾濫	ハン はんらん		deluge	1518
潰 R-1731	潰瘍	カイ かいよう		ulcer	
了 R-1732	終了	リョウ しゅうりょう		conclusion; ending	101
決 R-1733	決勝	ケツ けっしょう		decision (of a contest)	1770
黒 R-1734	黒板	コク こくばん		blackboard	186
興 R-1735	興味	キョウ きょうみ	R-1727	interest; appeal	1533

旧 R-1736	復旧	キュウ ふっきゅう	restoration; restitution	35
負 R-1737	負担	フ ふたん	charge; burden; responsibility	67
減 R-1738	削減	ゲン さくげん	reduction; curtailment	391
強 R-1739	強盗	ゴウ ごうとう	R-1045 armed robbery	1321
勢 R-1740	姿勢	セイ しせい	position (on an issue)	1633
漁 R-1741	漁業	ギョ ぎょぎょう	R-2267 fishing industry	184
納 R-1742	収納	ノウ しゅうのう	R-601, 2185, 2321, 2323 receipts; harvest (of crops)	1456
樹 R-1743	樹立	ジュ じゅりつ	establishment; creation	1554
行 R-1744	行政	ギョウ ぎょうせい	R-1069, 2404 (governmental) administration	938
犯 R-1745	犯人	ハン はんにん	criminal; offender	1517

設 R-1746	建設	セツ けんせつ		765 large-scale construction
築 R-1747	建築	チク けんちく		1021 small-scale construction
肥 R-1748	肥料	ヒ ひりょう		1893 fertilizer
次 R-1749	次元	ジ じげん	R-736	512 dimension
身 R-1750	自身	シン じしん		1337 oneself; personally
展 R-1751	発展	テン はってん		2075 development; expansion
外 R-1752	外科	ゲ げか	R-1057	116 surgery
得 R-1753	所得	トク しょとく		941 income; earnings
貪 R-1754	貪欲	ドン どんよく		1713 avarice
重 R-1755	重要	ジュウ じゅうよう	R-1851	1805 important; weighty

評 R-1756		ヒョウ		**1599**
	評論家	ひょうろんか	critic; commentator	
依 R-1757		イ	R-2393	**1045**
	依頼	いらい	dependency	
否 R-1758		ヒ		**1303**
	否定	ひてい	denial; negation	
実 R-1759		ジツ		**1694**
	事実	じじつ	fact	
維 R-1760		イ		**1441**
	明治維新	めいじいしん	Meiji Restoration	
改革 R-1761		カイ		**567**
		カク		**2041**
	改革	かいかく	reform; reformation	
皇 R-1762		コウ	R-1686	**279**
	皇居	こうきょ	Imperial Palace	
折衝 R-1763		セツ		**1211**
		ショウ		**1811**
	折衝	せっしょう	negotiations	
礎 R-1764		ソ		**421**
	基礎	きそ	foundation; basis	

伝 R-1765		デン	R-1232	1036
	宣伝	せんでん	publicity; propaganda	
満 R-1766		マン		1253
	満開	まんかい	in full bloom	
幼 稚 R-1767		ヨウ		1478
		チ		962
	幼稚園	ようちえん	kindergarten	
恒 久 R-1768		コウ		667
		キュウ	R-43, 2310	1092
	恒久	こうきゅう	permanence; perpetuity	
卓 塩 R-1769		タク		52
		エン		1568
	食卓塩	しょくたくえん	table salt	
撃 R-1770		ゲキ		766
	攻撃	こうげき	attack	
益 R-1771		エキ	R-2391	2026
	利益	りえき	profit; gains	
追 R-1772		ツイ		1359
	追求	ついきゅう	pursuit	

費用		ヒ		1265
		ヨウ		1326
R-1773	費用	ひよう	expenses	
拓		タク		703
R-1774	開拓	かいたく	reclamation (of wasteland)	
携		ケイ		742
R-1775	携帯	けいたい	portable	
象		ショウ	R-513	2130
R-1776	気象	きしょう	weather	
混		コン		487
R-1777	混乱	こんらん	disorder; confusion	
条		ジョウ		319
R-1778	条約	じょうやく	treaty	
件		ケン		1032
R-1779	事件	じけん	affair; matter	
向		コウ		195
R-1780	意向	いこう	intention; inclination	
答		トウ		1018
R-1781	回答	かいとう	reply; answer	

契		ケイ		1669
R-1782	契約	けいやく	contract; agreement	

訴		ソ		1221
R-1783	起訴	きそ	indictment	

許		キョ		611
R-1784	許可	きょか	permission	

討		トウ		364
R-1785	討議	とうぎ	debate; discussion	

診		シン		1860
R-1786	診察	しんさつ	medical examination	

上		ジョウ	R-2389	50
R-1787	以上	いじょう	above; more than	

種		シュ		1810
R-1788	種類	しゅるい	kind; type	

腫		シュ		1807
R-1789	腫瘍	しゅよう	tumor	

棄		キ		820
R-1790	棄権	きけん	abstention (from voting)	

扇		セン		1160
R-1791	扇風機	せんぷうき	electric fan	

酒 R-1792		シュ		1535
	日本酒	にほんしゅ	Japanese saké	
私 R-1793		シ		968
	私立	しりつ	privately owned and run	
数 R-1794		スウ	R-2248	998
	数学	すうがく	mathematics	
催 R-1795		サイ		1062
	主催	しゅさい	sponsorship; promotion	
価 R-1796		カ		1729
	定価	ていか	fixed price	
融 R-1797		ユウ		1123
	金融	きんゆう	monetary circulation; credit	
季 R-1798		キ		978
	四季	しき	the four seasons	
蚕 R-1799		サン		562
	養蚕	ようさん	sericulture; raising silkworms	
算 R-1800		サン		1017
	予算	よさん	budget	
索 R-1801		サク		1465
	捜索	そうさく	manhunt; search	

着 R-1802	到着	チャク とうちゃく	R-2281 arrival (of a plane, train, etc.)	594
連邦 R-1803	連邦	レン ホウ れんぽう	union; federate state	305 1991
困難 R-1804	困難	コン ナン こんなん	distress; difficulty	621 1703
森林 R-1805	森林	シン リン しんりん	woods and forests	209 208
突 R-1806	突破	トツ とっぱ	breakthrough; surmounting	1416
汚染 R-1807	汚染	オ セン おせん	pollution	1334 548
累 R-1808	累増	ルイ るいぞう	spiraling; continuous increase	1464
投 R-1809	投票	トウ とうひょう	voting; poll	762

玩 R-1810	玩具	ガン がんぐ		276 toys
逮 R-1811	逮捕	タイ たいほ		1244 arrest; apprehension
率 R-1812	能率	リツ のうりつ	R-548	1874 efficiency
焼 R-1813	全焼	ショウ ぜんしょう		1284 entirely destroyed by fire
災 R-1814	災害	サイ さいがい		179 calamity; disaster
律 R-1815	法律	リツ ほうりつ	R-620	939 the law
再 R-1816	再開	サイ さいかい	R-1903	1956 reopening; resumption
犬 R-1817	愛犬	ケン あいけん		253 pet dog
魚 R-1818	金魚鉢	ギョ きんぎょばち		183 goldfish bowl
極 R-1819	積極	キョク せっきょく	R-1937	2052 positive

絶		ゼツ		1891
R-1820	絶対	ぜったい	absolute; unconditional	
態		タイ		2161
R-1821	態度	たいど	attitude; manner	
留		リュウ	R-17	1527
R-1822	留学	りゅうがく	studying abroad	
初		ショ		431
R-1823	最初	さいしょ	first; initial	
押		オウ		1195
R-1824	押収	おうしゅう	confiscation; forfeiture	
節		セツ	R-593	1574
R-1825	季節	きせつ	season	
策		サク		1019
R-1826	政策	せいさく	(government) policy	
幸		コウ		1622
R-1827	幸福	こうふく	happiness	
欠		ケツ		507
R-1828	欠点	けってん	defect; negative point	
厚		コウ		132
R-1829	厚生	こうせい	public welfare	

栄		エイ		348
R-1830	光栄	こうえい	glory; honor	

臨		リン		918
R-1831	臨時	りんじ	special; extraordinary	

逆		ギャク		2109
R-1832	逆転	ぎゃくてん	reversal; turnabout	

視		シ		1174
R-1833	視察	しさつ	inspection	

牧		ボク		351
R-1834	牧師	ぼくし	(Protestant) pastor	

悪		アク	R-2259	1951
R-1835	悪魔	あくま	devil	

易		イ	R-1233	1130
R-1836	容易	ようい	easy; facile	

委		イ		979
R-1837	委員会	いいんかい	committee	

井		ショウ	R-44, 2091	1946
R-1838	天井	てんじょう	ceiling	

牙		ゲ	R-876	2053
R-1839	象牙	ぞうげ	ivory	

畳 R-1840	八畳	ジョウ はちじょう		1923 8 tatami mats in size
占 R-1841	独占	セン どくせん		49 monopoly
札 R-1842	改札口	サツ かいさつぐち		225 ticket checking or punching
恋 R-1843	失恋	レン しつれん		1885 lovelorn; unrequited love
看 R-1844	看護婦	カン かんごふ		688 nurse
香 R-1845	線香	コウ せんこう	R-2246	977 incense
哲 R-1846	哲学	テツ てつがく		1212 (Western) philosophy
迎 R-1847	歓迎	ゲイ かんげい		1837 welcome
隻 R-1848	一隻	セキ いっせき		755 one vessel (counter for ships)
啓 R-1849	拝啓	ケイ はいけい		1166 Dear Sir/Madam: (formal letter salutation)

患 R-1850		カン		650
	患者	かんじゃ	a patient	
尊 重 R-1851		ソン		1547
		チョウ	R-1755	1805
	尊重	そんちょう	esteem; respect	
獄 R-1852		ゴク		361
	地獄	じごく	hell	
霊 R-1853		レイ	R-2285	1930
	聖霊	せいれい	Holy Spirit	
宴 R-1854		エン		203
	宴会	えんかい	banquet	
孔 R-1855		コウ		100
	孔子	こうし	Confucius	
針 R-1856		シン		292
	方針	ほうしん	course of action; policy	
墨 R-1857		ボク		187
	白墨	はくぼく	chalk	
沈 黙 R-1858		チン		2033
		モク		255
	沈黙	ちんもく	silence	

猫		リョウ		2090
R-1859	狩猟	しゅりょう	game hunting	
隷		レイ		2192
R-1860	奴隷	どれい	slave	
猛		モウ		1566
R-1861	猛犬	もうけん	"Beware the Dog!"	
印刷		イン		1530
		サツ		1150
R-1862	印刷	いんさつ	printing	
岩石		ガン		832
		セキ	R-2164, 2352	118
R-1863	岩石	がんせき	crags; rocks	
暖		ダン		2099
R-1864	暖房	だんぼう	heating	
寒		カン		1645
R-1865	寒風	かんぷう	cold wind	
炭		タン		833
R-1866	石炭	せきたん	coal	
湿気		シツ		1927
		ケ	R-437	2030
R-1867	湿気	しっけ	humidity	

道 R-1868	神道	トウ しんとう	R-375 Shinto	295
確 R-1869	確実	カク かくじつ	certitude	609
企 R-1870	企業	キ きぎょう	(business) enterprise	401
賛 R-1871	賛成	サン さんせい	approval; agreement	906
声 R-1872	声明	セイ せいめい	R-2260 declaration; communiqué	2044
款 R-1873	借款	カン しゃっかん	loan	1178
死 R-1874	死亡	シ しぼう	death	878
示 R-1875	指示	ジ しじ	R-2168 indications	1167
執 R-1876	執行	シツ しっこう	R-2241 enforcement; carrying out	1623
処 R-1877	処分	ショ しょぶん	taking care of; disposal	318

承 R-1878	承認	ショウ しょうにん	acknowledgement; recognition	2050
属 R-1879	所属	ゾク しょぞく	attached to; belonging to	2103
巾 R-1880	布巾	キン ふきん	dishcloth	432
衆 R-1881	大衆	シュウ たいしゅう	R-2405 the masses	2001
祉 R-1882	福祉	シ ふくし	(social) welfare	1172
推 薦 R-1883	推薦	スイ セン すいせん	recommendation	716 2156
誘 拐 R-1884	誘拐	ユウ カイ ゆうかい	kidnapping	982 708
右 翼 R-1885	右翼	ウ ヨク うよく	R-2074 right wing	82 1937
続 R-1886	連続	ゾク れんぞく	continuation	1445

傾 R-1887		ケイ		1086
	傾向	けいこう	tendency; inclination	
呪 R-1888		ジュ		108
	呪術	じゅじゅつ	magic spell	
滑 走 R-1889		カツ	R-450	1384
		ソウ		410
	滑走路	かっそうろ	a runway	
覇 R-1890		ハ		2043
	覇権	はけん	hegemony; championship	
諾 R-1891		ダク		375
	承諾	しょうだく	consent	
斥 R-1892		セキ		1220
	排斥	はいせき	ostracizing; boycott; exclusion	
素 R-1893		ス	R-2113	1652
	素敵	すてき	splendid; swell; neat	
襲 R-1894		シュウ		2181
	襲撃	しゅうげき	raid; assault	
遺 言 R-1895		ユイ	R-1953	1909
		ゴン	R-1728	357
	遺言	ゆいごん、いごん	last will and testament	

探 R-1896	探偵	タン たんてい		1425 detective
肯 R-1897	肯定	コウ こうてい		400 affirmation
勾 R-1898	勾引状	コウ こういんじょう		800 arrest warrant
稽 R-1899	稽古	ケイ けいこ		983 training; practice
準 備 R-1900	準備	ジュン ビ じゅんび		606 1267 preparations
修 R-1901	修理	シュウ しゅうり	R-2400	1858 repairs
蓋 R-1902	頭蓋	ガイ ずがい		1561 cranium; skull
再 R-1903	再来年	サ さらいねん	R-1816	1956 the year after next
細 R-1904	詳細	サイ しょうさい		1463 details

訓 R-1905	訓練	クン くんれん	drill; training	365
帰 R-1906	帰国	キ きこく	returning to one's country	1316
彙 R-1907	語彙	イ ごい	lexicon	1237
兵 隊 R-1908	兵隊	ヘイ R-2256 タイ へいたい	soldiers; army	1429 1403
友 R-1909	友人	ユウ ゆうじん	friend	760
隙 R-1910	間隙	ゲキ かんげき	gap; aperture	1394
移 R-1911	移民	イ いみん	emigrants; immigrants	964
畏 R-1912	畏敬	イ いけい	awe and respect	2069
萎 R-1913	萎縮	イ いしゅく	shriveling up	986

淫		イン		788
R-1914	淫欲	いんよく	lust	

妥		ダ		785
R-1915	妥当	だとう	proper; suitable	

仰		コウ	R-2302	1836
R-1916	信仰	しんこう	faith	

囚		シュウ		1094
R-1917	囚人	しゅうじん	prisoner	

旺		オウ		279
R-1918	旺盛	おうせい	in excellent condition	

CHAPTER 9

A Potpourri of Readings

THE MAIN THING the kanji of this chapter have in common is that they do not fit the previous categories and are a bit too common to leave for the final chapter. It is arguable that a few of the compounds might have been included in the last chapter, and some left for the next. But there is no getting around the fact that we have come to the point where we must enlist the full assistance of brute memory.

To make the leftovers a little less formidable, I have cooked up a potpourri of exemplary compounds that I hope you find interesting or instructive enough to hold your attention while you are learning them. In some cases this has meant choosing an unusual compound; the readings, in any event, are commonly used.

The ages of 25, 42, and 62 for men and 19, 33, and 37 for women have traditionally been regarded as bad-luck years in Japan. Though not all the numbers are remembered by people today, no one is likely to forget 42, and no woman 33, especially as those years draw close. (Note that the second character is read with its *kun-yomi*.)

厄		ヤク		1519
R-1919	厄年	やくどし	bad-luck year	

There are two words among all the *on-yomi* that are virtually identical to English in sound and meaning. One of them we learned already in FRAME 931. Here is the other.

缶		カン		2116
R-1920	缶	かん	can	

The peculiarly Japanese wooden clogs worn for festive occasions and occasionally still in everyday use have been assigned characters meaning "below" and "pack horse." The more common reading of the latter character appears in the second exemplary compound.

下	ゲ	R-1051	51
駄	タ・ダ		2140

R-1921	下駄	げた	wooden clogs
	無駄	むだ	useless; in vain

The same character 体 is used to form the words for solid (固体,こたい), gas (気体,きたい), and liquid.

液	エキ	1116

R-1922	液体	えきたい	liquid

The Darwinian principle of the survival of the fittest comes out in Japanese as "the weak, the meat; the strong, the eaters."

弱	ジャク	1323

R-1923	弱肉強食	じゃくにくきょうしょく	survival of the fittest

Appropriately, the word for smile is drawn in kanji as a "delicate laugh."

微	ビ	954
笑	ショウ	1008

R-1924	微笑	びしょう	smile

A common English expression for a close resemblance is "a spitting image." No less odd is the Japanese equivalent, which reads literally "a cruel remembrance."

似	ジ	1106

R-1925	酷似	こくじ	close resemblance

Though it is a perfect homonym for the Japanese kanji for U.S.A. (米国), this compound means rice.

穀　　　　　コク　　　　　　　　　　　　　　984

R-1926　　米穀　　べいこく　　　rice (as a grain)

The standard reading of the compound in this frame has fallen into disuse in favor of the imported word for barley brew: ビール.

麦　　　　　バク　　　　　　　　　　　　　　1654

R-1927　　麦酒　　ばくしゅ　　　beer

You will often see public signs strictly prohibiting one thing or another. They usually contain the following compound.

厳　　　　　ゲン　　　　R-2396　　　　　2086

R-1928　　厳禁　　げんきん　　　"Strictly Prohibited!"

The term used in chemistry for acids of all sorts is this compound.

酸　　　　　サン　　　　　　　　　　　　　　1545

R-1929　　硫酸　　りゅうさん　　sulfuric acid

Like the English word iceberg, which brings together two Norwegian words meaning "mountain of ice," the Japanese gives a precise equivalent by using two Chinese characters.

氷　　　　　ヒョウ　　　　　　　　　　　　　138

R-1930　　氷山　　ひょうざん　　iceberg

The counter for volumes in a collection of books can use either the Japanese reading (まき, as in 巻一) or, more commonly today, the Chinese.

巻　　　　　カン　　　　　　　　　　　　　　1292

R-1931　　第一巻　だいいっかん　Vol. 1

The full and proper name for Christmas—long since yielding to the more popular *katakana* word クリスマス—is given here.

降　　　　コウ　　　　　　　　　　　　　1405

R-1932　　降誕祭　こうたんさい　　Christmas

The long and famous Edo Period, which ran from 1603 until 1867, is also named after the longest of the shogunates.

徳　　　　トク　　　　　　　　　　　　　950

R-1933　　徳川時代　とくがわじだい　　Tokugawa Period

The common Japanese euphemism for prostitution is "selling spring." In fact, the word spring is used in a number of expressions related to the world of erotic pleasures and favors.

春　　　　シュン　　　　　　　　　　　1690

R-1934　　売春　ばいしゅん　　prostitution

Among the many traditional phrases Japanese has for ladies who "sell spring" (see the frame above) is the following, which literally means "playgirl."

遊　　　　ユウ　　　　R-2258　　　　1126

R-1935　　遊女　ゆうじょ　　harlot

Those who are brought up in strict controls are referred to in Japanese as having been "kept in a box" or—as in the following example— raised in a "secluded inner room."

深　　　　シン　　　　　　　　　　　1426

R-1936　　深窓　しんそう　　strict upbringing

Whereas English thinks in vertical terms to classify something as "top secret," Japanese moves horizontally with the image of a polar extreme.

極		ゴク	R-1819	2052
R-1937	極秘	ごくひ	of utmost secrecy	

The generic term for aristocracy or peerage is expressed in the following term.

貴		キ		1908
R-1938	貴族	きぞく	nobility	

Like most Western languages, Japanese thinks of innocence and goodness as something "white." Since the white race was alien—even "barbarian"—to the Japanese, "white" was completely devoid of radical connotations.

潔		ケツ		1668
R-1939	潔白	けっぱく	integrity; innocence	

Like the English word "twang," the pronunciation of the compound for a nasal sound almost seems to reinforce the meaning.

鼻		ビ		733
R-1940	鼻音	びおん	nasal sound	

The Japanese term for a "breather" has one literally "resting one's breath."

息		ソク		657
R-1941	休息	きゅうそく	rest; recess	

As is often the case, an opaque English word is perfectly obvious in Japanese. If you meet the English word rayon for the first time, you need a dictionary to find out that it means "artificial silk." The Japanese is clear from the first time one sees it.

絹		ケン		1468
R-1942	人絹	じんけん	rayon	

Here is another example. Until you learned something of Latin etymology, you would have no idea from simply looking at the term "hibernation" what it might possibly mean. The Japanese is crystal clear, even to a young child.

冬 トウ 456

R-1943　　冬眠　　とうみん　　hibernation

One more example. If you look at the characters of the compound below before looking at the meaning, you should be able to understand its meaning precisely, even though you don't know how to read it. The more familiar you get with the way Chinese compounds work in Japanese, the easier you will find it to read complex material containing terms you have not learned before and understand it the way the Japanese themselves do—without constantly having to pull out your dictionary.

顔 ガン 1853

R-1944　　童顔　　どうがん　　boyish face

The Japanese compound for troglodyte presents still another example of the transparency of Japanese. The English reader would have to be a Greek scholar to know from the first what the word means.

穴 ケツ 1413

R-1945　　穴居人　　けっきょじん　　troglodyte; cave dweller

The term for attraction means literally "pulling power."

引 イン 1318

R-1946　　引力　　いんりょく　　attraction

The compound in this frame is not one you are likely ever to use in conversation, though you will find it written occasionally. In typical Japanese fashion, it brings together a number of kanji associated with the major rituals of life (coming of age, marriage, burial, and ancestral veneration) and arranges them into a single compound.

| 冠 | カン | 326 |
| 葬 | ソウ | 879 |

R-1947 　冠婚葬祭　かんこんそうさい　ceremonial occasions

The sense of excitement is communicated aptly in Japanese by the kanji you learned for "entertainment" and "stirred up."

| 奮 | フン | 607 |

R-1948 　興奮　こうふん　　　　　excitement

Japanese frequently creates generic terms by picking two members of the class of things that belong to it. An example is the combination of the characters for "stomach" and "intestines" to create the term for bowels.

| 胃 | イ | 29 |

R-1949 　胃腸　いちょう　　　　　bowels

In the same way that the kanji 活 adds a sense of vitality to 活動 (かつどう, activity) and 生活 (せいかつ, life), it also enlivens the kanji for cheerfulness.

| 快 | カイ | 1771 |

R-1950 　快活　かいかつ　　　　　joviality

The very sound of the word shriek conjures up the piercing, shrill cry of an animal. When Japanese speaks of the sound we humans make when our voice tightens in fear, it uses the kanji for the cry of a bird in pain.

| 鳴 | メイ | 2092 |

R-1951 　悲鳴　ひめい　　　　　shriek; scream

Japanese often combines kanji of nearly the same meaning to produce a compound word of greater force. For example, "bending" and "folding" join to create crookedness.

曲		キョク		1256
R-1952	曲折	きょくせつ	crookedness	

A compound can also reflect the various stages of a process that are hidden in the English term. For instance, the word gleanings involves a "picking up" and "passing on."

拾		シュウ	R-2233	720
遺		イ	R-1895	1909
R-1953	拾遺	しゅうい	gleanings	

Like the English word "unusual," the Japanese compound in this frame is ambiguous—used for praise, pity, and criticism.

異		イ		1936
R-1954	異常	いじょう	abnormal; exceptional	

In the same way that the English word discriminating can indicate a vice or a virtue, depending on its context, the Japanese term in this frame carries both meanings as well (though the former is the more common nowadays).

差		サ		593
R-1955	差別	さべつ	discrimination	

The compound in this frame is composed of two nouns, the first modifying the second. This procedure, which is common also in English, was inherited from the Chinese.

好		コウ		103
R-1956	好評	こうひょう	favorable criticism	

Another example of the same sort combines two kanji meaning "too much" and "spare time" to create a term for leisure.

| 暇 | カ | | | 2027 |
| R-1957 | 余暇 | よか | leisure | |

Although modern Japanese writes the names of most countries outside the "kanji belt" with *katakana*, it is still common to see abbreviations of the older names, especially in newspaper headlines. This frame gives two of them.

泰	タイ			1692
亜	ア			1950
R-1958	泰国	たいこく	Thailand	
	東亜	とうあ	East Asia	

The two kanji in the compound shown below were learned in VOL. 1 as signifying respectively "artisan" and "expert." Together they combine to mean one who has attained a high level of skill in a particular trade and has consequently become a teacher of it.

師	シ			1361
匠	ショウ			1828
R-1959	師匠	ししょう	master-teacher	

Literally the expression in this frame refers to "building a roof atop a roof."

| 屋 | オク | | | 1138 |
| R-1960 | 屋上屋を架する | おくじょうおくをかする | 5th wheel | |

There are any number of Chinese characters that have come to be used on their own, without combining to form a compound. No attempt has been made to single these out in the course of this book, since they are better learned through direct experience of the language. One of them, a very common one, appears in this frame.

| 辺 | ヘン | | | 302 |
| R-1961 | 辺 | へん | environs; neighborhood | |

As we noted earlier in frame 1238, Japanese likes to link the names of two places by taking one character from each and forming a new compound. Sometimes this involves putting an *on-yomi* where the original names use a *kun-yomi*, or sometimes an *on-yomi*. The following example shows both of these procedures at work.

京	ケイ	R-1030	**334**
浜	ヒン		**1430**

R-1962 　京浜線　　けいひんせん　　Tokyo-Yokohama (railway) Line

Another example of the same usage links the names 青森 (あおもり) and 函館 (はこだて) to identify the tunnel that links the two cities.

函	カン	**2051**

R-1963 　青函　　せいかん　　Aomori-Hakodate (Tunnel)

The everyday Japanese expression for the conjunction in any case or anyhow has been assigned kanji that mean literally "horns on the rabbit." The word for "rabbit" appeared in a note to frame 1972 of VOL. 1.

角	カク	**1953**

R-1964 　兎に角　　とにかく　　in any case; anyhow

For festive occasions the Japanese serve a steamed glutinous rice with red beans.

赤	セキ	R-2264	**1880**

R-1965 　赤飯　　せきはん　　rice with red beans

English refers to the two halves of a game as "first" and "second," but Japanese speaks of "before" and "after."

後	コウ	R-1076	**1479**

R-1966 　後半　　こうはん　　the second half

The opposite of pessimism (see FRAME 1430) is given here. The last two characters, incidentally, are the usual way of denoting an "ism."

楽   ラク   R-1120   1872

R-1967   楽観主義   らっかんしゅぎ   optimism

While we are at it, let us take the time to learn the terms for two more "isms" in Japanese.

宜   ギ   1922

享   キョウ   330

R-1968   便宜主義   べんぎしゅぎ   opportunism
             享楽主義   きょうらくしゅぎ   hedonism

Another way of describing an "ism" is with the suffix 論, which carries the particular connotation of an intellectual system of thought. Here is an example of that usage.

唯   ユイ   R-2317   595

R-1969   唯物論   ゆいぶつろん   materialism

Like the English term "wake," the Japanese carries the sense of staying up through the night.

通   ツ   R-1018   1511

夜   ヤ   1115

R-1970   通夜   つや   wake; vigil

Here we learn the name for the famous Japanese sword, world-renowned for its strength and precise craftsmanship.

刀   トウ   87

R-1971   日本刀   にほんとう   Japanese sword

Standing alongside a flowing river one day, it occurred to Confucius—as it had to his Greek contemporary, Heraclitus—that such was the state of all things: in constant flux, never stopping. This is captured in the following phrase, literally meaning "the cry of the river."

川	セン	134
嘆	タン	1702

R-1972　川上の嘆　せんじょうのたん　"All things are in flux."

English refers to an over-avid devotee as a "fanatic" (literally, one possessed of a temple god or demon) or, more colloquially, as a "freak." Here is an example of how Japanese achieves the same effect.

読	ドク	R-1201, 2361	372
狂	キョウ		277

R-1973　読書狂　どくしょきょう　book freak; bookworm

While Mark Antony was content to ask for the ears of his audience, Japanese asks for their eyes as well.

耳	ジ	881

R-1974　耳目　じもく　one's attention

While English associated the center of a target with the eye of a bull, Japanese refers to the eye of a snake. The reading combines a Chinese reading with a Japanese one, something we have met previously.

蛇	ジャ	R-2386	558

R-1975　蛇の目　じゃのめ　bull's eye

Now watch this! The repetition of two primitive-related characters takes the same meaning, except that one is for more general use and the other for a "quick" closing to a letter.

早		ソウ	R-587	26
草		ソウ		238
R-1976	早々	そうそう	in a hurry; rushed
	草々	そうそう	"Hurriedly yours, …"

Japanese refer to someone who doesn't drink—or drinks very little—as being "under the door." The tippler, logically enough, becomes "over the door."

戸		コ		1157
R-1977	下戸	げこ	teetotaler
	上戸	じょうご	tippler

The Japanese write the kanji for swan as simple "white bird."

| 鳥 | | チョウ | | 2091 |
| R-1978 | 白鳥 | はくちょう | swan |

The fall colors, to the Japanese, are either "red leaves" (more common) or "yellow leaves." The pronunciation is the same.

黄		コウ	R-431	1887
葉		ヨウ		243
R-1979	黄葉	こうよう	fall colors

The anti-Buddhist movement in the Meiji period that led to the destructions of temples is referred to as "discarding the Buddha dharma, destroying the teaching of the Buddha," the abbreviation for which has become a fixed phrase in Japanese.

| 毀 | | キ | | 1532 |
| R-1980 | 廃仏毀釈 | はいぶつきしゃく | anti-Buddhist movement |

The order that English uses for expressing things in pairs is often reversed in Japanese. For instance, we say "food and drink," but Japanese says:

飲　　　　イン　　　　　　　　　　　　　　　　1584

R-1981　　飲食　　いんしょく　　food and drink

Or again, we say "north and south," but Japanese says:

南　　　　ナン　　　R-2401　　　　　　　　1740

R-1982　　南北　　なんぼく　　north and south

The Buddhist monk who wanders homelessly in search of the truth is likened to the "clouds" and "water" that move ceaselessly.

雲　　　　ウン　　　　　　　　　　　　　　　452

R-1983　　雲水　　うんすい　　novice (Zen) monk

The character 自 can be used as a prefix to indicate either the sense of the English prefix "auto-" or to refer to oneself. An example of the former was seen earlier (frame 1005). Here we see the latter usage.

炊　　　　スイ　　　　　　　　　　　　　　　509

R-1984　　自炊　　じすい　　fixing one's own meal

We sometimes meet Japanese words that can only be used with negative endings, even though the meaning in English is entirely positive.

如　　　　ジョ　　　R-2403　　　　　　　　104

R-1985　　如才　　じょさい　　slick; smooth

The terms for high (and low) blood pressure are constructed exactly as in English.

血　　　　ケツ　　　　　　　　　　　　　　　1556

R-1986　　高血圧　　こうけつあつ　　high blood pressure

Japanese uses the same character for the wick of a candle, the plastic refill of a ballpen, and the stamen of a flower (from which its writing is derived).

芯	シン		647
R-1987	芯	しん	wick

The character 義 is used commonly in Japanese as a prefix to indicate in-laws. A similar, curious usage appears in this frame.

歯	シ		1255
R-1988	義歯	ぎし	false tooth

The idea of falling into one's own trap is expressed in Japanese as "tying oneself up with one's own rope."

縄	ジョウ		1477
R-1989	自縄自縛	じじょうじばく	falling into one's own trap

This frame should give you an idea how helpful the signal primitives can be. The second kanji in the exemplary compound will be new to you, but you should be able to guess its reading from what you learned earlier (FRAMES 704–706).

覚	カク		347
R-1990	覚醒剤	かくせいざい	stimulants; narcotics

Japanese speaks of grammar as the laws governing letters.

文	ブン	R-966	1861
法	ホウ	R-2073, 2407	813
R-1991	文法	ブンポウ	grammar

The Japanese phrase for a slowdown strike is closer to the British term "work-to-rule." The full word for strike is ストライキ, but it is commonly abbreviated to its first two syllables.

順	ジュン		136
R-1992	順法	じゅんぽう	a slowdown strike

Japanese also has a word for a walkout strike:

罷	ヒ		2188
R-1993	罷業	ひぎょう	walkout; strike

The names you see on Japanese tombstones commonly end with the character for family, the custom being for a family to share a grave site. The Chinese reading of the kanji differs from that already learned.

家	ケ	R-307	580
R-1994	福田家	ふくだけ	the Fukuda family

Where English speaks of getting "off the ground," Japanese speaks of "getting on the tracks."

軌	キ		306
R-1995	軌道に乗る	きどうにのる	getting started; inaugurating

The piracy which has moved from the seas into the world of illegal copies and clones has made the same linguistic shift in Japanese.

賊	ゾク		381
R-1996	海賊版	かいぞくばん	pirated edition

The Japanese term in this frame is a nearly literal rendering of the French phrase raison d'être, which has found its way into English.

存	ソン	R-595	739
R-1997	存在理由	そんざいりゆう	raison d'être

The first two kanji of the compound below mean "empress" and the last two are a term of respect. The term is reserved for the wife of the emperor of Japan.

后	コウ	2005
陛	ヘイ	1407

R-1998   皇后陛下   こうごうへいか   Her Highness the Empress

The Japanese equivalent of our Christmas cards are the postcards bearing New Year's greetings, all of which are supposed to be delivered on January 1st.

状	ジョウ	254

R-1999   賀状   がじょう   New Year's card

Because the abbreviated character for "happiness" is written in the form of three 七's (㐂), the Japanese call the 77th birthday the "rejoicing age."

喜	キ	1553
寿	ジュ	1687

R-2000   喜寿   きじゅ   one's 77th birthday

Notice how Japanese uses an image nearly identical to the English in the following compound.

背	ハイ	481

R-2001   背景   はいけい   background; backdrop

Although the Japanese now refer to their famous high-speed "bullet train" as the "new trunk line" (see FRAME 1269), the English term had its origin in a precise Japanese equivalent, given here.

弾	ダン	2081
丸	ガン	44

R-2002   弾丸列車   だんがんれっしゃ bullet train

Paddy fields under water are called simply:

田   デン   **14**

R-2003 水田 すいでん rice-paddy fields

All-absorbing enthusiasm is expressed in Japanese as an "interest anchoring in every port."

津   シン   **350**

R-2004 興味津々 きょうみしんしん bubbling with enthusiasm

Like the English word "contact," the Japanese equivalent connotes a sense of touching directly.

触   ショク   **1954**

R-2005 接触 せっしょく contact

We express the idea of rising in the morning in terms of "getting up" or "turning out," but for the Japanese who sleep on the floor, the equivalent term is "rising from the floor."

床   ショウ   **636**

R-2006 起床 きしょう getting out of bed; rising

The Japanese term for a roll call is a "point call."

呼   コ   **1597**

R-2007 点呼 てんこ roll call

One of the ways Japanese expresses the suffix "-able" is by the use of the kanji for "power," as we see in the following example.

浮   フ   **787**

R-2008 浮力 ふりょく buoyancy

In the same way that the etymology of the English word excellent suggests something that rises above the rest of the pack, the Japanese compound in this frame suggests something that "excels" by "deviating" from the norm.

| 秀 | シュウ | 980 |
| 逸 | イツ | 2127 |

R-2009　秀逸　しゅういつ　excellent

"Precious stones" become "treasured stones" in Japanese.

| 宝 | ホウ | 273 |

R-2010　宝石　ほうせき　precious stones

Here is another example of a compound whose meaning you can decipher by recalling the key-word meanings assigned the kanji in VOL. 1.

| 威 | イ | 389 |

R-2011　威圧的　いあつてき　overpowering

In English, children have to learn where cotton comes from; in Japanese, it is clear from the kanji.

| 綿 | メン | 1467 |

R-2012　綿花　めんか　raw cotton

The colorful Japanese phrase for giving one's seal of approval has one "banging out one's judgment on a drum."

| 鼓 | コ | 1552 |

R-2013　太鼓判　たいこばん　seal of approval

The two compounds in this frame offer a typical example of what a big difference the long vowel can make in Japanese: a slight slip of the vocal cords and a handshake turns into a foul smell.

| 握 | アク | 1139 |
| 臭 | シュウ | 128 |

| R-2014 | 握手 | あくしゅ | handshake |
| | 悪臭 | あくしゅう | stench; bad odor |

At Japanese funeral services there is often a public reading of a number of telegrams of condolence, which it is the custom to send in Japan on such occasions if one cannot be present.

| 弔 | チョウ | 1319 |

| R-2015 | 弔電 | ちょうでん | telegram of condolence |

Japanese fire alarms were traditionally described as a "half bell."

| 鐘 | ショウ | 470 |

| R-2016 | 半鐘 | はんしょう | fire alarm; alarm bell |

The Japanese expression for a skyscraper takes over the English image precisely.

| 楼 | ロウ | 999 |

| R-2017 | 摩天楼 | まてんろう | skyscraper |

The title of "professor emeritus" in Japan bestows a "name of repute."

| 誉 | ヨ | 2089 |

| R-2018 | 名誉教授 | めいよきょうじゅ | professor emeritus |

The compound in this frame is a good example of how the same term can be used for exactly opposite meanings.

| 傑 | ケツ | 1074 |

| R-2019 | 傑作 | けっさく | masterpiece; gross blunder |

You will often see the following sign on a small clinic. Here again, the meaning should be obvious even before you learn how to pronounce it.

獣　　　　ジュウ　　　　　　　　　　　　　　　2083

R-2020　　獣医　　じゅうい　　　veterinarian

Like English, Japanese uses the craft of tempering metals as a metaphor for spiritual and physical disciplines as well.

鍛　　　　タン　　　　　　　　　　　　　　　2004

R-2021　　鍛錬　　たんれん　　　temper; discipline

The character 未 is frequently used in Japanese as a negative prefix close to the English "un-" but often carrying the additional sense of "not yet."

遂　　　　スイ　　　　　　　　　　　　　　　579

R-2022　　自殺未遂　じさつみすい　　　attempted suicide

The Japanese term for something of an ashen color comes out as "ash-white."

灰　　　　カイ　　　　　　　　　　　　　　　180

R-2023　　灰白色　　かいはくしょく　　　ashen colored

One of the expressions Japanese has for going on a spree or "painting the town red" is "powerful play."

豪　　　　ゴウ　　　　　　　　　　　　　　　582

R-2024　　豪遊　　ごうゆう　　　merrymaking; a spree

The Japanese expression for a wind-bell is almost an onomatopoeia: fuuuuu for the wind and rinnnnn for the tinkle of the bell.

鈴　　　　リン　　　　　　R-759　　　　　1508

R-2025　　風鈴　　ふうりん　　　wind-bell

Japanese abounds in reduplicated sounds, a number of which we have met already. Here are four more, beginning with the word for butterfly.

蝶 チョウ **560**

R-2026 　　　蝶々婦人 　　ちょうちょうふじん 　Madame Butterfly

Next, a word denoting tardiness or procrastination.

遅 チ **1148**

R-2027 　　　遅々 　　ちち 　　late; slow

Taking a mishap with quiet reserve—or "philosophically" as the English idiom goes—is expressed in Japanese by reduplicating the character for "faint."

淡 タン **176**

R-2028 　　　淡々 　　たんたん 　　even-tempered

And finally, a curious phrase for meticulous attention, meaning literally "grain-by-grain."

粒 リュウ **990**

R-2029 　　　粒々 　　りゅうりゅう 　　assiduously

The "voicing" of a *kana* syllable which Japanese indicates by two small lines is referred to as the "muddying" of a sound.

濁 ダク **898**

R-2030 　　　濁音 　　だくおん 　　voiced sound

Japan's version of the limerick—a short, witty poem—is called a "river willow" and comprises three lines of 5, 7, and 5 syllables respectively.

柳 リュウ **1525**

R-2031 　　　川柳 　　せんりゅう 　　satirical poem

Although the baseball world has taken over numerous American terms, after adjusting them to suit Japanese tastes and sounds, there are still several expressions that retain their older form. Here is one of them.

塁　　　ルイ　　　　　　　　　　　　　　1871

R-2032　　盗塁　　とうるい　　　　stolen base

Combining the characters for "old man" and "decayed" gives us a suitable compound for decrepit.

朽　　　キュウ　　　　　　　　　　　　1331

R-2033　　老朽　　ろうきゅう　　　decrepit

Not unlike the English expression "Spit it out!" is the Japanese expression for speaking one's mind.

吐　　　ト　　　　　　　　　　　　　　162

R-2034　　吐露　　とろ　　　　　　speaking one's mind

If you look at the carton of milk on your breakfast table, you will probably find the following compound written on it some where, perhaps giving you a better idea of what pasteurization means than you had before.

菌　　　キン　　　　　　　　　　　　　985

R-2035　　殺菌　　さっきん　　　　pasteurization; sterilization

This character is generally used all on its own and refers to the deep blue that you see in so many of the traditional blue-and-white Japanese fabric designs.

紺　　　コン　　　　　　　　　　　　　1895

R-2036　　紫紺　　しこん　　　　　navy blue

Oddly, the Japanese refer to a lightning bolt as "falling thunder."

雷　　　ライ　　　　　　　　　　　　　454

R-2037　　落雷　　らくらい　　　　bolt of lightning

Since we have already learned most of the set, let us complete the listing of the first four of the old calendar signs still used to enumerate things.

甲　　　　コウ　　　　R-2279　　　　**1194**

R-2038　　甲乙丙丁　こうおつへいてい　A, B, C, D

The Old West spoke of "roping the herd with one throw," while the Japanese speak of "catching something with one cast of the net."

尽　　　　ジン　　　　**1152**

R-2039　　一網打尽　いちもうだじん　catching all at once

While English speaks of "manual labor" (as distinct from "clerical labor"), Japanese speaks of "muscle labor."

筋　　　　キン　　　　**1012**

R-2040　　筋肉労働　きんにくろうどう　manual labor

Like the straw that breaks the camel's back or the spark that sets off a fire, here is an explosion ticked off by a single brush of the hand.

即　　　　ソク　　　　**1572**

R-2041　　一触即発　いっしょくそくはつ explosive situation

A colorful expression for "ranking favorably with" someone has one "standing up to the shoulders of" that person.

肩　　　　ケン　　　　**1158**

R-2042　　比肩　ひけん　　　　rank with

Christian scriptural imagery has given us the expression "to sweat blood." Japanese has an equally graphic image: "crying blood."

涙　　　　ルイ　　　　**1163**

R-2043　　血涙　けつるい　　　　bitter tears

Japanese is more direct than the English when it comes to "henpecking." Note how the word for "house" is often used to refer to an individual.

恐　　　キョウ　　　　　　　　　　　　　660

妻　　　サイ　　　　　　　　　　　　　2035

R-2044　　恐妻家　　きょうさいか　　henpecked husband

In place of the three large golden balls that mark the pawn shops of the West, Japan uses a kanji in a circle, the full compound for which is given here. (Note that the second character uses a Japanese reading.)

質　　　シチ　　　R-1135, 2360　　1219

R-2045　　質屋　　しちや　　pawnshop

The character featured in this frame is often used as a prefix to carry the sense of the English suffix "-resistant."

耐　　　タイ　　　　　　　　　　　　　1248

R-2046　　耐水　　たいすい　　water-resistant

By making use of an outdated word for plagiarism, Japanese has the following phrase for adapting something to new use: stealing the matrix and changing the bones.

奪　　　ダツ　　　　　　　　　　　　　608

R-2047　　換骨奪胎　　かんこつだったい　　recasting; remodeling

In English we speak of something that is deep black as "jet black," a term that takes its name from the hard lignite called "jet." Japanese uses the idiom "lacquer black."

漆　　　シツ　　　　　　　　　　　　　1001

R-2048　　漆黒　　しっこく　　deep black

Japanese distinguishes between rice plants: those that grow in dry fields from those that grow in cultivated paddies.

稲	トウ		976
R-2049	水稲	すいとう	rice plant in a paddy

Traditional Japanese cookery reckons five basic tastes, captured here in an uncommon compound. The first two characters give us "sweet-and-sour"; the second and third characters refer metaphorically to the "bitter-and-sour" disappointments of life. (The last character, by the way, is rare.)

甘	カン	1894
辛	シン	1612

R-2050	甘酸辛苦鹹	かんさんしんくかん	sweet, sour, hot, bitter, salty

Though often a monotonous-sounding language to the untrained ear, Japanese has definite cadences important to the language. Naturally, it also has a word for it.

抑	ヨク		1835
R-2051	抑揚	よくよう	intonation; accent

Instead of short circuits, Japanese think of electrical lines "leaking" the same way water pipes do.

漏	ロウ		1149
R-2052	漏電	ろうでん	short circuit

Most of us are used to thinking of the seven stars of the constellation Ursus Major not as the bear the ancients imagined but as the Big Dipper. Japanese agrees.

斗	ト		1261
R-2053	北斗七星	ほくとしちせい	the Big Dipper

The character featured in this frame refers to a part of town (in particular, the old "licensed quarters"). That it should be linked with the character for "public" to create the word for the cuckoo bird is due to the fact that the pronunciation of the compound is thought to approximate the sound that the bird makes, as is the English name.

郭　　　　　　カク　　　　　　　　　　　　　　1985

R-2054　　郭公　　かっこう　　cuckoo bird

"Cloak and dagger" intrigue is depicted in Japanese as a ghost hiding in the gall bladder (the seat of courage).

魂　　　　　　コン　　　　　　　　　　　　　　2177

R-2055　　魂胆　　こんたん　　underhanded scheme

Note the colorful term Japanese use for the ovary.

卵　　　　　　ラン　　　　　　　　　　　　　　1526

巣　　　　　　ソウ　　　　　　　　　　　　　　2077

R-2056　　卵巣　　らんそう　　ovary

One of the most difficult Japanese words to translate is the single kanji given in this frame. It combines the senses of fate, providence, and "karmic affinity."

縁　　　　　　エン　　　　　　　　　　　　　　1472

R-2057　　縁　　えん　　affinity; predestined connection

We speak of people who "eat like a horse" or "drink like a fish." Japanese unites the two idioms, substituting "whale" for "fish."

鯨　　　　　　ゲイ　　　　　　　　　　　　　　337

R-2058　　鯨飲馬食　げいいんばしょく　making a pig of oneself

A showdown is often described in English as "separating the men from the boys." Japanese gives its own twist in a similar idiom.

雄　　　　　　　ユウ　　　　　　　　　　　　　　804

R-2059　　雌雄を決する　　しゆうをけっする　　have a showdown

To be "big on" something or "intoxicated with" it is described in Japanese as being "pot drunk." We shall take the occasion to learn the word for pottery.

陶　　　　　　　トウ　　　　　　　　　　　　　　2117

器　　　　　　　キ　　　　　　　　　　　　　　　127

R-2060　　陶器　　とうき　　　　pottery
　　　　　陶酔　　とうすい　　　fascination

In sumō bouts and other sporting tournaments a special award is often presented to the athlete who shows the most "fighting spirit." Here is the compound that is used.

敢　　　　　　　カン　　　　　　　　　　　　　　889

R-2061　　敢闘賞　　かんとうしょう　　award for fighting spirit

Doubts that "gnaw" at us on the inside are depicted in Japanese as devils working their dark arts in one's heart.

鬼　　　　　　　キ　　　　　　　　　　　　　　　2175

R-2062　　疑心暗鬼　ぎしんあんき　　gnawing doubt

The "jaws of death" become the "tiger's mouth" in Japanese.

虎　　　　　　　コ　　　　　　　　　　　　　　　2145

R-2063　　虎口　　ここう　　　the jaws of death

The watch stem is slowly fading from everyday life, as is this colorful word for it.

竜 リュウ 575

R-2064　竜頭　りゅうず　watch stem

Although the kanji suggest someone serving as a mediator by serving drinks, the actual meaning is quite different.

酌 シャク 1536

R-2065　媒酌結婚　ばいしゃくけっこん　arranged marriage

Japanese expresses the idea of "running here, there, and everywhere" by characters meaning "running east, fleeing west."

奔 ホン 1280

R-2066　東奔西走　とうほんせいそう　run helter-skelter

Japanese depicts a shining example of something as a "turtle pattern." The image comes from the fact that the character for "turtle" once referred to a kind of tool used for making official seals.

亀 キ 573

R-2067　亀鑑　きかん　paradigm; shining example

The lights that English likens to the opening of a flower, Japanese likens to the glow of a lightning bug.

蛍 ケイ 557

R-2068　蛍光電灯　けいこうでんとう　fluorescent light bulb

The darkish, brown tea you are often served at Chinese restaurants in Japan, as throughout the Orient, comes from Taiwan, where it got its name as "crow and dragon tea." In order to give a "Chinese" flavor to the sound, the on-yomi for "crow" is lengthened and that for "dragon" given a reading approximating the original.

烏 ウ 2094

R-2069　烏竜茶　うーろんちゃ　dark Chinese (oolong) tea

The "face" that Asians are said to want to save and to avoid losing is written in Japanese like this.

目		ボク	R-1225		**15**
R-2070	面目	めんぼく		face; honor	

Japanese contrasts temperaments that are cheerful and bright with those that are dark and gloomy by using kanji that the Chinese used to distinguish light from darkness, sun from shade. These are none other than the words popularly known in the West as *yang* and *yin* respectively.

陰		イン			**1718**
陽		ヨウ	R-145		**1704**
R-2071	陰気	いんき		gloomy	
	陽気	ようき		cheerful	

CHAPTER 10

Supplementary Readings

THE FINAL CHAPTER dealing with the Chinese readings falls into two parts of roughly equal length. In the first part I have included what seem to me the most useful of the remaining readings to know—or at least, those least unusual. The second half of the chapter picks up all the leftovers, uncommon and close to obsolescence as some of them may be. Without wishing to slight the reasons which the Ministry of Education and Science has for deciding that all of these readings belong to the general-use kanji, the fact remains: if there is one part of the book you would be justified in skimming over lightly and not cracking your skull to master at this stage of your language study, it is this last section.

A. COMMON SUPPLEMENTARY READINGS

璽		ジ		2194
R-2072	国璽	こくじ	great seal of the state	
法		ハッ	R-1991, 2407	71
R-2073	法度	はっと	ordinance; prohibition	
右		ユウ	R-1885	82
R-2074	左右	さゆう	right and left; both sides	
欄		ラン		1756
R-2075	欄外	らんがい	margin (of a printed page)	

裏		リ		426
R-2076	表裏	ひょうり	front side and back	

猶		ユウ		1546
R-2077	猶予	ゆうよ	postponement	

並		ヘイ		1924
R-2078	並行	へいこう	parallel	

献		ケン	R-2320	1742
R-2079	献身	けんしん	devotion; commitment	

珍		チン		1859
R-2080	珍味	ちんみ	delicacy (food)	

虚 偽		キョ	R-2294	2148
		ギ		2068
R-2081	虚偽	きょぎ	falsehood; untruth	

鎖		サ		2087
R-2082	鎖国	さこく	national isolation	

片		ヘン		1297
R-2083	断片	だんぺん	piece; fragment	

頻		ヒン		399
R-2084	頻度	ひんど	frequency	

挿 R-2085	挿入	ソウ そうにゅう		1197
			insertion	
陵 R-2086	陵墓	リョウ りょうぼ		1636
			imperial mausoleum	
至 R-2087	至当	シ しとう		815
			propriety; reasonableness	
巡 R-2088	巡回	ジュン じゅんかい		303
			patrol; rounds	
飾 R-2089	装飾	ショク そうしょく		1587
			ornamentation	
御 R-2090	制御	ギョ せいぎょ	R-1035	1500
			regulation; controls	
井 R-2091	油井	セイ ゆせい	R-44, 1838	1946
			oil well	
妄 R-2092	妄想	モウ もうそう	R-2341	528
			fantasy; delusion	
羅 R-2093	羅列	ラ られつ		1442
			enumerate	
耕 R-2094	農耕	コウ のうこう		1949
			agriculture	

拘 R-2095	拘束	コウ こうそく		constraint; restraint	706
拠 R-2096	根拠	キョ こんきょ	R-2149	basis; foundation	722
色 R-2097	特色	ショク とくしょく	R-1226	characteristic; distinctive feature	1890
悠 R-2098	悠然	ユウ ゆうぜん		perfect composure	1031
棟 R-2099	病棟	トウ びょうとう		hospital ward	544
准 R-2100	批准	ジュン ひじゅん		ratification	602
若 R-2101	若干	ジャク じゃっかん	R-604	few; small number	237
遮 R-2102	遮断	シャ しゃだん		quarantine	1276
蒸 R-2103	蒸発	ジョウ じょうはつ		evaporation	2049
凡 R-2104	平凡	ボン へいぼん	R-328	commonplace; ordinary	66

膨 R-2105	膨張	ボウ ぼうちょう	**1855** inflation; bloating
端 R-2106	極端	タン きょくたん	**1251** radical; extreme
粘 R-2107	粘土	ネン ねんど	**989** clay
旋 R-2108	旋回	セン せんかい	**1125** circling
穏 R-2109	穏和	オン おんわ	**1230** moderate (as in politics)
衡 R-2110	均衡	コウ きんこう	**957** balance
賓 R-2111	賓客	ヒン ひんきゃく	**550** guest of honor
越 R-2112	超越	エツ ちょうえつ	**413** transcendence
素 R-2113	質素	ソ しっそ	R-1893　　　**1652** simple; unadorned
渋 R-2114	渋滞	ジュウ じゅうたい	**1875** (traffic) jam; delay

醜		シュウ		2176
R-2115	美醜	びしゅう	beauty or ugliness; personal appearance	

誇		コ		1332
R-2116	誇張	こちょう	bombast; exaggeration	

陣		ジン		1402
R-2117	出陣	しゅつじん	advance into battle	

崇		スウ		1182
R-2118	崇拝	すうはい	worship; veneration	

隣		リン		1408
R-2119	隣人	りんじん	one's neighbor	

誓		セイ		1214
R-2120	宣誓	せんせい	vow; oath	

帥		スイ		1362
R-2121	統帥	とうすい	supreme command	

擁		ヨウ		1488
R-2122	抱擁	ほうよう	hug; embrace	

隔		カク		1409
R-2123	隔年	かくねん	every other year	

尿		ニョウ		1132
R-2124	糖尿病	とうにょうびょう	diabetes	

顕		ケン	1928
R-2125	顕微鏡	けんびきょう	microscope

塊		カイ	2180
R-2126	塊状	かいじょう	mass (of something)

控		コウ	1415
R-2127	控訴	こうそ	(legal) appeal

添		テン	684
R-2128	添付	てんぷ	appendix; addition

奏		ソウ	1693
R-2129	伴奏	ばんそう	(musical) accompaniment

純		ジュン	1609
R-2130	純金	じゅんきん	solid gold

See also the signal primitive in FRAMES 921–3.

叫		キョウ	1626
R-2131	叫喚	きょうかん	scream; holler

騒		ソウ	2139
R-2132	騒動	そうどう	row; agitation

拷		ゴウ	1344
R-2133	拷問	ごうもん	torture

埋		マイ	191
R-2134	埋葬	まいそう	interment; burial in the ground

択		タク		1155
R-2135	選択	せんたく	choice; option	

致		チ		818
R-2136	一致	いっち	unity	

祈		キ		1209
R-2137	祈願	きがん	prayer; petition	

透		トウ		981
R-2138	透明	とうめい	transparent	

圏		ケン		1293
R-2139	圏内	けんない	within the sphere of	

寛		カン		241
R-2140	寛容	かんよう	tolerance	

模		モ	R-769	244
R-2141	模範	もはん	model; pattern	

踪 跡		ソウ		1382
		セキ		1883
R-2142	踪跡	そうせき	whereabouts	

潤		ジュン		1755
R-2143	潤色	じゅんしょく	embellishment; flourish	

脊 R-2144	脊髄	セキ せきずい		268 spinal marrow
赦 R-2145	赦免	シャ しゃめん		1881 pardon; amnesty
憧 R-2146	憧憬	ショウ しょうけい		681 aspire after; hanker for
凄 R-2147	凄気	セイ せいき		2036 feeling of appall or dread
恥 羞 R-2148	羞恥	チ シュウ しゅうち		886 2198 feeling of embarrassment
拠 R-2149	証拠	コ しょうこ	R-2096	722 proof; evidence
境 内 R-2150	境内	ケイ ダイ けいだい	R-461 R-1037	525 1095 precincts; grounds
叱 R-2151	叱声	シツ しっせい		477 scolding voice
髪 R-2152	金髪	ハツ きんぱつ		2074 blond

傲		ゴウ		1054
R-2153	傲岸	ごうがん	arrogant	

拭		ショク		695
R-2154	払拭	ふっしょく	sweep away; eradicate	

墜		ツイ		1404
R-2155	墜落	ついらく	(airplane) crash	

虐		ギャク		2153
R-2156	虐殺	ぎゃくさつ	massacre	

析		セキ		1207
R-2157	分析	ぶんせき	analysis	

惧		タン		680
R-2158	絶滅危惧種	ぜつめつきぐしゅ	endangered species	

賦		フ		404
R-2159	月賦	げっぷ	monthly installment	

糾		キュウ		1627
R-2160	糾弾	きゅうだん	censure; arraignment	

沸		フツ		1325
R-2161	沸騰	ふっとう	boiling	

歳		セイ	R-1191	551
R-2162	歳暮	せいぼ	end-of-the-year present	

悼 R-2163	追悼	トウ ついとう		668 mourning
石 R-2164	磁石	シャク じしゃく	R-1863, 2352	1194 magnet
麓 R-2165	山麓	ロク さんろく		2155 foot of the mountain
米 R-2166	新米	マイ しんまい	R-611	987 new rice
昆 虫 R-2167	昆虫	コン チュウ こんちゅう		483 556 insects; bugs
示 唆 R-2168	示唆	シ サ しさ	R-1875	1167 828 suggestion
宮 R-2169	神宮	グウ じんぐう	R-2192, 2257	1110 Shinto shrine
剥 R-2170	剥奪	ハク はくだつ		1227 usurp
岳 R-2171	山岳	ガク さんがく		1428 hills and mountains

逓 R-2172	逓送 ていそう	テイ		2002
			posting; sending by mail	
汁 R-2173	果汁 かじゅう	ジュウ		150
			fruit juice	
炉 R-2174	原子炉 げんしろ	ロ		1161
			nuclear reactor	
炎 R-2175	火炎 かえん	エン		174
			flames; blaze	
堕 R-2176	堕落 だらく	ダ		1411
			depravity; corruption	
金 R-2177	黄金 おうごん	コン R-1080		289
			gold	
子 R-2178	様子 ようす	ス R-1175		99
			state of affairs; circumstances	
女 R-2179	女房 にょうぼう	ニョウ R-3, 1044, 2315		102
			(one's own) wife	
男 R-2180	長男 ちょうなん	ナン R-1043		923
			oldest son	

竹 R-2181		チク		1007
	松竹梅	しょうちくばい	pine, bamboo, plum	
	See FRAME 1481 for an explanation of this term.			

不 R-2182		ブ	R-6	1302
	不用心	ぶようじん	carelessness; insecurity	

平 R-2183		ビョウ	R-1700	1596
	平等	びょうどう	equality	

作 R-2184		サ	R-762	1224
	作業	さぎょう	work; operation	

出 納 R-2185		スイ	R-590	829
		トウ	R-601, 1742, 2321, 2323	1456
	出納	すいとう	cash-accounting; receipts and expenses	

児 R-2186		ニ	R-1701	62
	小児	しょうに	infant	

椎 R-2187		ツイ		597
	椎骨	ついこつ	vertebrae	

雑 R-2188		ゾウ	R-588	604
	雑煮	ぞうに	rice cakes boiled in broth with vegetables	
	Note that the second kanji is read with its *kun-yomi*.			

羽		ウ		615
R-2189	羽毛	うもう	down (feathers)	
拍		ヒョウ	R-92	704
R-2190	拍子	ひょうし	beat; rhythm	
餌		ジ		1588
R-2191	好餌	こうじ	lure; tempting bait	
宮 殿		キュウ	R-2169, 2257	1110
		デン	R-2295	1945
R-2192	宮殿	きゅうでん	palace	
剖		ボウ		519
R-2193	解剖	かいぼう	autopsy	
阜		フ		1360
R-2194	岐阜県	ぎふけん	Gifu prefecture	
蔑		ベツ		392
R-2195	軽蔑	けいべつ	scorn; disdain	
貌		ボウ		2125
R-2196	全貌	ぜんぼう	complete picture; full story	
勃		ボツ		930
R-2197	勃発	ぼっぱつ	outbreak; sudden occurrence	

嘱 R-2198	委嘱	ショク いしょく	entrusting; commission	2104
窮 R-2199	困窮	キュウ こんきゅう	destitution; penury	1424
遷 R-2200	変遷	セン へんせん	vicissitudes; changes	1737
眉 R-2201	柳眉	ビ りゅうび	R-2202 lovely, crescent eyebrows	2045
眉 R-2202	眉間	ミ みけん	R-2201 brow; space on the forehead between the eyebrows	2045
翌 R-2203	翌日	ヨク よくじつ	the day after; morrow	617
戴 R-2204	戴冠式	タイ たいかんしき	coronation	1938
拉 R-2205	拉致	ラ らち	kidnapping; abduction	696
夢 R-2206	夢中	ム むちゅう	in a daze; enraptured	327
弓 R-2207	弓道	キュウ きゅうどう	Japanese "way of the bow"	1317

抜		バツ	**761**
R-2208	抜群	ばつぐん	exceptional
翻		ホン	**2060**
R-2209	翻訳	ほんやく	translation
仁		ジン R-32, 249	**1063**
R-2210	仁義	じんぎ	benevolence and justice
漸		ゼン	**1217**
R-2211	漸次	ぜんじ	gradually; step by step
尋		ジン	**1228**
R-2212	尋問	じんもん	cross-examining (a witness)
喪		ソウ	**2076**
R-2213	喪失	そうしつ	loss
賜		シ	**1131**
R-2214	下賜	かし	bestowal
幻		ゲン	**2006**
R-2215	幻想	げんそう	illusion; vision
緩		カン	**2102**
R-2216	緩和	かんわ	mitigation
疫		エキ R-2272	**1824**
R-2217	疫病	えきびょう	epidemic

軟 R-2218		ナン	**511**
	軟化	なんか	softening; mollifying
窒 R-2219		チツ	**1418**
	窒息	ちっそく	asphyxiation
斜 R-2220		シャ	**1791**
	斜面	しゃめん	sloped surface
励 R-2221		レイ	**931**
	奨励金	しょうれいきん	scholarship grant
陥 R-2222		カン	**1412**
	陥没	かんぼつ	cave-in
逐 R-2223		チク	**578**
	逐一	ちくいち	one-by-one; minutely
蛮 R-2224		バン	**1884**
	野蛮	やばん	barbarians
鋳 R-2225		チュウ	**1688**
	鋳鉄	ちゅうてつ	cast iron
俊 R-2226		シュン	**1089**
	俊才	しゅんさい	person of great talent
含 R-2227		ガン	**1712**
	含蓄	がんちく	connotation

躍		ヤク		1379
R-2228	飛躍	ひやく	leap	

幽		ユウ		1480
R-2229	幽玄	ゆうげん	elegance; mysteriousness	

合		カッ	R-1172	269
R-2230	合戦	かっせん	skirmish; fight	

露		ロウ	R-201	1377
R-2231	披露宴	ひろうえん	wedding reception	

称		ショウ		971
R-2232	愛称	あいしょう	pet name; name of affection	

拾		ジュウ	R-1953	720
R-2233	拾万円	じゅうまんえん	¥100,000 (in formal receipts)	

戯		ギ		2149
R-2234	遊戯	ゆうぎ	sport; game	

把		ハ		1889
R-2235	把握	はあく	grasp; grip	

惨		ザン	R-524	1857
R-2236	惨酷	ざんこく	cruel	

粛		シュク		1870
R-2237	自粛	じしゅく	self-discipline	

就 R-2238	成就	ジュ じょうじゅ	R-565 attainment; accomplishment	2121

B. UNCOMMON SUPPLEMENTARY READINGS

謀 R-2239	謀反	ム むほん	R-907 rebellion; conspiracy	1897
宰 R-2240	首宰	サイ しゅさい	supervision; presidency	1615
執 R-2241	我執	シュウ がしゅう	R-1876 egotism; self-assertion	1623
想 R-2242	愛想	ソ あいそ	R-278 civility; amiability	656
従 R-2243	従三位	ジュ じゅさんみ	R-401, 2363 third rank, second grade	942
羨 R-2244	羨望	セン せんぼう	envy	592
貢 R-2245	年貢	ク ねんぐ	R-121 annual tribute	85
香 R-2246	香車	キョウ きょうしゃ	R-1845 a "spear" in Japanese chess	977

切 R-2247	一切	サイ いっさい	R-527 all; everything	89
数 R-2248	数奇	ス すき	R-1794 refined taste	998
口 R-2249	口伝	ク くでん	R-1685 oral tradition	11
今 R-2250	今上	キン きんじょう	R-1116 reigning emperor	1711
聞 R-2251	聴聞	モン ちょうもん	R-1106 audience; audition	1754
名 R-2252	大名	ミョウ だいみょう	R-385 feudal lord	117
夏 R-2253	夏至	ゲ げし	R-511 summer solstice	317
体 R-2254	体裁	テイ ていさい	R-1182 getup; appearance	1030
建立 R-2255	建立	コン リュウ こんりゅう	R-325 R-1682 building; erection	417 462

兵 糧 R-2256		ヒョウ	R-1908	**1429**
		ロウ	R-520	**995**
	兵糧	ひょうろう	army provisions	
宮 R-2257		ク	R-2169, 2192	**1110**
	宮内庁	くないちょう	Imperial Household Agency	
遊 R-2258		ユ	R-1935	**1126**
	遊山	ゆさん	outing in the mountains	
悪 R-2259		オ	R-1835	**1951**
	憎悪	ぞうお	hatred	
声 R-2260		ショウ	R-1872	**2044**
	大音声	だいおんじょう	stentorian voice	
宗 R-2261		ソウ	R-1718	**1181**
	宗匠	そうしょう	master; teacher	
度 R-2262		タク	R-495, 1117	**1278**
	支度	したく	outfit; arrangement	
有 R-2263		ウ	R-1164	**83**
	有無	うむ	being and nothingness	
赤 R-2264		シャク	R-1965	**1880**
	赤銅	しゃくどう	alloy of gold and copper	

礼		ライ	R-51	1168
R-2265	礼賛	らいさん	high praise	
命		ミョウ	R-1077	1502
R-2266	寿命	じゅみょう	span of one's life	
漁		リョウ	R-1741	184
R-2267	漁師	りょうし	fisherman	
払		フツ		798
R-2268	払底	ふってい	shortage; scarcity	
没		ボツ		763
R-2269	埋没	まいぼつ	buried and forgotten	
奉		ブ	R-888	1695
R-2270	奉行	ぶぎょう	magistrate	
懸		ケ	R-436	1495
R-2271	懸念	けねん	anxiety; fear	
疫		ヤク	R-2217	1824
R-2272	疫病神	やくびょうがみ	god of the plague; jinx	
夕		セキ		114
R-2273	今夕	こんせき	this evening	
桜		オウ		2082
R-2274	観桜会	かんおうかい	cherry-blossom viewing party	

泣		キュウ		463
R-2275	感泣	かんきゅう	moved to tears	

矢		シ		1305
R-2276	一矢	いっし	a single arrow	

丘		キュウ		1427
R-2277	砂丘	さきゅう	dune; sandhill	

穂		スイ		975
R-2278	穂状	すいじょう	shaped like an ear of corn	

甲		カン	R-2038	1194
R-2279	甲板	かんぱん	deck (of a ship)	

吹		スイ		508
R-2280	吹奏	すいそう	playing a wind instrument	

着		ジャク	R-1802	594
R-2281	執着	しゅうじゃく	attachment; tenacity	

奥		オウ		997
R-2282	深奥	しんおう	the depths; inner mysteries	

郷		ゴウ	R-459	1993
R-2283	郷社	ごうしゃ	village shrine	

旬		シュン	R-405	71
R-2284	旬の野菜	しゅんのやさい	vegetables of the season	

怨霊		オン	R-873	1524
		リョウ	R-1853	1930
R-2285	怨霊	おんりょう	vengeful spirit	
朕		チン		2183
R-2286	朕	ちん	(a first person singular reserved for use by the emperor and not compounded with other kanji)	
替		タイ		905
R-2287	交替	こうたい	alteration; change	
装		ショウ	R-276	425
R-2288	装束	しょうぞく	costume (for an occasion)	
婿		セイ		422
R-2289	女婿	じょせい	son-in-law	
睦		ボク		1632
R-2290	親睦	しんぼく	friendship; intimacy	
錦		キン		439
R-2291	錦鶏	きんけい	golden pheasant	
殻		カク		767
R-2292	甲殻	こうかく	shell; crust; carapace	
煩		ハン	R-2394	175
R-2293	煩雑	はんざつ	complexity; trouble	

虚 R-2294	虚空	コ こくう	R-2081 empty space; "thin air"	2148
殿 R-2295	御殿	テン ごてん	R-2192 palace	1945
閑 R-2296	閑却	カン かんきゃく	negligence; oversight	1753
冥 R-2297	冥利	ミョウ みょうり	R-2298 divine favor; providence	322
冥 R-2298	冥王星	メイ めいおうせい	R-2297 Pluto	322
冶 R-2299	冶金	ヤ やきん	metallurgy	808
笛 R-2300	警笛	テキ けいてき	alarm whistle	1192
壇 R-2301	花壇	ダン かだん	R-794 flower bed	631
仰 R-2302	仰天	ギョウ ぎょうてん	R-1916 flabbergasted	1836
衰 R-2303	衰弱	スイ すいじゃく	debility	2038

琴 R-2304	キン 琴線　きんせん		**1717** "heart strings"
藩 R-2305	ハン 廃藩　はいはん		**2061** abolition of the feudal clans
砂 R-2306	シャ 土砂崩壊　どしゃほうかい	R-1530	**122** landslide (of earth and sand)
傘 R-2307	サン 傘下　さんか		**1103** under the influence of; affiliated
験 R-2308	ゲン 霊験　れいげん	R-133	**2134** miracle
役 R-2309	エキ 懲役　ちょうえき	R-1705	**949** prison with hard labor
久 R-2310	ク 久遠　くおん	R-43, 1768	**1092** eternity
期 R-2311	ゴ 最期　さいご	R-1353	**1902** one's dying moments
格 R-2312	コウ 格子　こうし	R-1467	**312** lattice
仮 R-2313	ケ 仮病　けびょう	R-1338	**1039** feigned illness

充 R-2314	イン		827
	允許 いんきょ		license; permit

女 R-2315	ニョ	R-3, 1044, 2179	102
	天女 てんにょ		heavenly maiden

由 R-2316	ユイ	R-14, 1103, 1460	1186
	由緒 ゆいしょ		pedigree; lineage

唯 R-2317	イ	R-1969	595
	唯々諾々 いいだくだく		willingly; submissively

耗 R-2318	コウ	R-904	2063
	心神耗弱 しんしんこうじゃく		fainthearted

末 R-2319	バツ	R-310	230
	末子 ばっし		youngest child

献 R-2320	コン	R-2079	1742
	一献 いっこん		a cup (of saké offered)

納 R-2321	ナ	R-601, 1742, 2185, 2323	1456
	納屋 なや		shed
	The second kanji takes a *kun-yomi*.		

木 R-2322	ボク	R-1075	207
	大木 たいぼく		towering tree

納 R-2323		ナン	R-601, 1742, 2185, 2321	1456
	納戸	なんど	wardrobe; closet	
	The second kanji takes a *kun-yomi*.			

匹 R-2324		ヒツ		1830
	匹敵	ひってき	a match for; equal to	

凸 R-2325		トツ		34
	凸面鏡	とつめんきょう	convex lens	

凹 R-2326		オウ		33
	凹面鏡	おうめんきょう	concave lens	

繭糸 R-2327		ケン		2025
		シ		1431
	繭糸	けんし	cocoon thread	

踏 R-2328		トウ		1381
	踏破	とうは	traveling on foot	

隆 R-2329		リュウ		1682
	隆起	りゅうき	protrusion; projection	

爽涼 R-2330		ソウ		1608
		リョウ		335
	爽涼	そうりょう	cool and refreshing	

塞 R-2331		ソク	R-2369	1646
	塞栓症	そくせんしょう	embolism	

曇 R-2332	曇天	ドン どんてん	cloudy skies	453
暁 R-2333	暁天	ギョウ ぎょうてん	morning skies	1285
嫡 R-2334	廃嫡	チャク はいちゃく	disinherit	472
遵 R-2335	遵法	ジュン じゅんぽう	law-abiding	2187
潜伏 R-2336	潜伏	セン フク せんぷく	hiding out	907 1035
艶 R-2337	艶聞	エン えんぶん	love affair; romance	1892
褒 R-2338	過褒	ホウ かほう	excessive praise	1073
堆 R-2339	堆積	タイ たいせき	pile; heap	596
舟 R-2340	舟艇	シュウ しゅうてい	watercraft	2012

妄 R-2341	妄言	ボウ ぼうげん	R-2092 careless, wild remarks	528
戻 R-2342	返戻	レイ へんれい	return; giving back	1162
釣 R-2343	釣艇	チョウ ちょうてい	fishing boat	291
匿 R-2344	隠匿	トク いんとく	concealment	1827
緑 R-2345	新緑	リョク しんりょく	R-338 fresh verdure	1471
貼 R-2346	貼付	チョウ ちょうふ	post (a bill)	60
富 R-2347	富貴	フウ ふうき	R-827 wealth and prestige	205
功 R-2348	功徳	ク くどく	R-116 work of charity	927
逝 R-2349	逝去	セイ せいきょ	passing away; death	1213
緻 R-2350	緻密	チ ちみつ	minuteness	1437

| 吟 R-2351 | 詩吟 | ギン しぎん | reciting (Chinese) poems | 1714 |

The following three frames contain readings of kanji related to old weights and measures which are no longer used but are still judged to be of historical importance.

石 R-2352	一石	コク いっこく	R-1863, 2164 one *koku* (of rice, about 0.18 m^3)	118
勺 R-2353	一勺	シャク いっしゃく	one *shaku* (about 1.8 cl)	72
斤 R-2354	一斤	キン いっきん	one *kin* (about 600 g)	1206
刃 R-2355	自刃	ジン じじん	death by one's own sword	88
紅 R-2356	真紅	ク しんく	R-119 crimson	1455
雪 R-2357	積雪	セツ せきせつ	piled-up snow	1225
仕 R-2358	給仕	ジ きゅうじ	R-142 office boy; page boy	1033

事 R-2359	好事家	ズ こうずか	R-1203 dilettante	1240
質 R-2360	言質	チ げんち	R-1135, 2045 pledge; commitment	1219
読 R-2361	句読点	トウ くとうてん	R-1201, 1973 punctuation and reading marks	372
臣 R-2362	臣下	シン しんか	R-1723 retainer; subject	911
従 R-2363	従容	ショウ しょうよう	R-401, 2243 tranquility; composure	942
嗅 R-2364	嗅覚	キュウ きゅうかく	sense of smell; olfactory sense	129
臼 R-2365	臼歯	キュウ きゅうし	molar (tooth)	1531
股 R-2366	股関節	コ こかんせつ	hip joint	764
顎 R-2367	顎骨	ガク がっこつ	jawbone	1333
瑠 R-2368	瑠璃	ル るり	lapis lazuli gem	1528

	Note that this character shares its Chinese reading with the readings of the root character for the hiragana る learned in FRAME 17.		

塞	サイ	R-2331	**1646**
R-2369	塞内 さいない	inside the fortress	

濯	タク		**619**
R-2370	洗濯 せんたく	laundry; washing	

摯	シ		**1624**
R-2371	摯獣 しじゅう	ferocious animal	

乃	ナイ	(R-36)	**741**
R-2372	一乃至十 いちないしじゅう	from 1 to 10	

侶	リョ		**1025**
R-2373	伴侶 はんりょ	companion; partner; spouse	

弄	ロウ		**731**
R-2374	嘲弄 ちょうろう	mockery; ridicule	

篭	ロウ		**1022**
R-2375	篭絡 ろうらく	cajolement; enveiglement	

朴	ボク		**220**
R-2376	純朴 じゅんぼく	rustic simplicity	

拙	セツ		**831**
R-2377	拙劣 せつれつ	clumsiness; ineptitude	

| 茂 | | モ | | 384 |
| R-2378 | 繁茂 | はんも | luxuriant growth (trees, etc.) | |

| 隠 | | イン | | 1410 |
| R-2379 | 楽隠居 | らくいんきょ | an easy life of retirement | |

| 衷 | | チュウ | | 2038 |
| R-2380 | 衷心 | ちゅうしん | one's innermost feeling | |

| 嚇 | | カク | | 2182 |
| R-2381 | 威嚇 | いかく | intimidation; menace | |

| 丹 | | タン | | 2195 |
| R-2382 | 丹誠 | たんせい | sincerity; purity of heart | |

| 庶 | | ショ | | 1275 |
| R-2383 | 庶民 | しょみん | common people | |

| 爵 | | シャク | | 1573 |
| R-2384 | 男爵 | だんしゃく | baron | |

| 庸 | | ヨウ | | 1266 |
| R-2385 | 中庸 | ちゅうよう | golden mean; happy medium | |

| 蛇 | | ダ | R-1975 | 558 |
| R-2386 | 蛇足 | だそく | redundancy | |

| 沃 | | ヨク | | 71 |
| R-2387 | 肥沃 | ひよく | fertility (of the soil) | |

妖		ヨウ		458
R-2388	妖精	ようせい	fairy; sprite	

We may conclude with a number of supplementary readings used for rather common Buddhist terms. Buddhism has traditionally preserved its own distinct readings for many of the kanji (see FRAME 2131). These frames should give you some idea of just how different they can be.

上		ショウ	R-1787	50
R-2389	上人	しょうにん	saint	
庫		ク	R-1142	633
R-2390	庫裏	くり	temple dining room or living quarters	
益		ヤク	R-1771	2026
R-2391	御利益	ごりやく	benefit of having one's prayers to the Buddha answered	
勤		ゴン	R-331	1700
R-2392	勤行	ごんぎょう	Buddhist religious service	
依		エ	R-1757	1045
R-2393	帰依	きえ	conversion (religious)	
煩		ボン	R-2293	175
R-2394	煩悩	ぼんのう	worldly passions	
業		ゴウ	R-1124	1931
R-2395	宿業	しゅくごう	accumulated karma	

華厳経 R-2396		ケ	R-1247	**1704**
		ゴン	R-1928	**2086**
		キョウ	R-796	**1460**
	華厳経	けごんぎょう	*Avatamsaka Sutra,* a Buddhist text treasured in particular by the Kegon (Hua-yen) sect	
解 R-2397		ゲ	R-1702	**1955**
	解脱	げだつ	liberation; salvation	
回 R-2398		エ	R-1185	**630**
	回心	えしん	conversion	
尼 R-2399		ニ		**1133**
	尼僧	にそう	Buddhist nun	
修 R-2400		シュ	R-1901	**1858**
	修行	しゅぎょう	ascetic exercises; discipline	
南阿陀 R-2401		ナ	R-1982	**1740**
		ア		**1391**
		ダ		**2952**
	南無阿弥陀仏	なむあみだぶつ	"Refuge in the name of Amida Buddha"	
和尚 R-2402		オ	R-12	**963**
		ショウ		**196**
	和尚	おしょう	title of respect for a monk	

如 R-2403	如来	ニョ にょらい	R-1985 the Tathagata or "Thus-Come" (one of the titles of the Buddha)	104
行 R-2404	行脚	アン あんぎゃ	R-1069, 1744 religious pilgrimage	938
衆 R-2405	衆生	シュ しゅじょう	R-1881 sentient beings	2001
鉢 R-2406	衣鉢	ハツ えはつ	R-1237 transmission of the robe and bowl (symbolizing the passing on of tradition from master to successor)	289
法 R-2407	法身	ホッ ほっしん	R-1991, 2073 Dharma-body (of the Buddha)	813
摂 R-2408	摂取	セツ せっしゅ	providence or protection by a buddha or bodhisattva on one's way to salvation	1876
弘 R-2409	弘法大師	コウ こうぼうだいし	posthumous title of Kūkai, founder of Japanese Shingon Buddhism	1320

PART TWO

Japanese Readings

CHAPTER 11

A Mnemonics for
the Japanese Readings

As explained in the Introduction, the *kun-yomi* or Japanese readings of
the kanji differ considerably from the *on-yomi* treated in the last ten chapters.
Kun-yomi generally stand on their own as phonetic units and not as compo-
nents of compounds, are often inflected with a *hiragana* ending, contain far
fewer homonyms than the Chinese readings, and admit of no "signal primitives" or any comparable device for associating form with pronunciation.

If anything, the Japanese readings of the characters present us with a problem much like that we faced in learning to write them, at least in these two
respects: (1) they have no relationship to Western languages; and yet (2) they
can be broken up into component or "primitive" parts. What I would like to
do in this concluding chapter is outline a method for taking advantage of the
second characteristic to weaken the force of the first.

I do not anticipate that what is written here will come as a complete surprise to anyone who has already struggled with the radical unfamiliarity of
Japanese vocabulary and toyed around with memory tricks of one sort or
another. What I hope it will do is help you think more systematically about
your mnemonic devices.

Were Japanese words transcribed phonetically after the manner of Western alphabets, it would be impossible—or at least far more trouble than it is
worth—to assign meanings to each of the individual sounds. But since Japanese divides words phonetically according to syllables, such assignation
is comparatively simple. Most of the monosyllabic sounds that make up the
syllabary are themselves already Japanese words; and those that remain can
choose a meaning from the full range of available Chinese readings studied
in the previous chapters. The main problem is to fix one meaning to one syllable. Once that is done, virtually any Japanese word can be broken up into
"primitive phonemes" much the same way as the kanji were broken up into
their primitive elements in VOL. 1.

The presence of variant *hiragana* inflections need not complicate the procedure. The forms and functions of these inflections can be left to grammati-

cal studies. For the purposes of this chapter it is enough to focus on the root-words to which they are appended. For example, when 語 is used in a Chinese compound, there are no inflections, but when the Japanese reading 語る (かたる) is used, we can generate forms like 語った and 語れば. The root-word かた remains unchanged. Should it happen that the root-word undergoes significant change or is too short or confusing on its own, you can simply learn the "dictionary form" of the word as a whole. The main thing is to find a natural, comfortable way of linking a new word to its meaning (namely, its foreign equivalent) without allowing the inflections to interfere.

When it happens that a single kanji has several root-word readings, each reading will have to be learned independently as belonging to that kanji. In fact, most of the work of linking Japanese words to kanji has already been taken care of by the key words you learned in VOL. 1, because the vast majority of the Japanese readings will bear a direct, logical relationship to the meaning of the key word assigned there. Once a Japanese word has become "second nature" and you no longer need to mediate its meaning with a foreign word, the meaning-writing associations established with foreign key words will adjust themselves as a matter of course.

There is, however, one complication which—if it is any consolation—is as much a headache and a fascination to the Japanese as it will be to you. A good number of *kun-yomi* can be written with more than one kanji, each giving a slight change in meaning. Though writers frequently extend this principle ad libitum, the official general-use list is less tolerant. An example, admittedly an extreme one, will make the point. The Japanese word とる uses at least 10 characters to capture its variety of nuances, 5 of them (marked here with a *) belonging to the general-use list, and most of them have other Japanese readings as well. By appending the inflection る to any of the kanji below, the reading とる is possible, but with a different connotation each time:

	摂	to take in; absorb; take the place of
	獲	to catch (fish or game)
	穫	to harvest (a crop from the fields)
*	採	to pluck (as fruit from a tree)
*	撮	to take (photos)
*	執	to take control of, manage
*	取	to take and hold on to (not throwing away)
	盗	to take (what belongs to another); steal
*	捕	to take hold of firmly; grasp
	録	to record; take down

Distinguishing these various uses of the word とる is not something to be learned by brute memory. If you wish to study it later, there are dictionaries enough to supply you with the necessary information. For now it is best to wait for these distinctions to appear in your reading, as they eventually will.

PREPARING FLASH CARDS

If you made flash cards as indicated in LESSON 5 of VOL. 1, you can use the following details to fill them in with the readings. It will help to know a bit more about how the relevant indexes are laid out and to give some thought to the most efficient way of using the remaining space on your cards. Let us begin with a sample design completely filled in:

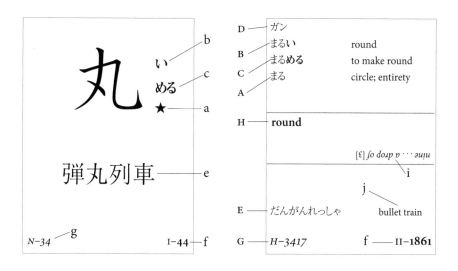

a/A   The asterisk (*) on the FRONT indicates that the kanji has a *kun-yomi* that does not require any inflection. In this case it is the word まる, meaning a circle.

b/B   The い on FRONT indicates a root-word to which the inflection い is

c/C   added. The complete word, given on the BACK, is まるい together with its meaning, round. The same holds for the める.

D   The *katakana* ガン at the top of the BACK indicates the *on-yomi* of the kanji.

e/E   The compound(s) at the bottom illustrate(s) the *on-yomi*.

f/F   The number on the bottom right of the FRONT indicates the frame number in which the kanji appeared in VOL. 1, in which the writing and reading of the character was explained. The number in the same position on the BACK indicates the frame number in VOL. 2.

g/G The numbers on the FRONT and BACK bottom left cross-reference the character to *The New Nelson Japanese-English Character Dictionary* (Tokyo: Charles E. Tuttle, 1997) and Jack Halpern's *New Japanese-English Character Dictionary* (Tokyo: Kenkyūsha, 1990).

H The bold-type word set between the horizontal lines on the BACK of the card indicates the key word assigned to the kanji in VOL. 1.

I The inverted, italicized text gives the primitive elements and number of strokes of the character.

J The meaning of the exemplary compound.

To fill out a card or group of cards, follow these steps:

1. Go to INDEX V and look up the entry corresponding to the number F. Inscribe the *kun-yomi* indicated there at locations A–C on the BACK of your card. If there is some particular reason for learning the meaning(s) of the *kun-yomi* at this time, consult a dictionary before filling them in. Otherwise, leave those areas blank until the word turns up and you need to learn it.

2. In the same entry, you will find a number corresponding to the first appearance of an *on-yomi* for the kanji in question. Look it up and fill in items D, E, and e.

3. If there is an internal cross-reference number in the frame, check it for additional Chinese readings and add them in the same way.

This may be the fastest way to fill in your cards, but you are left with the problem of how to review. Merely by looking at the kanji on the card you cannot know which *kun-yomi* you need to drill and which can be passed over for the time being. You will have to include some small mark on the FRONT alongside each *kun-yomi* you wish to learn or review. Alternatively you can follow these 4 steps to enter new words as you meet them:

1. Look up the Japanese word in INDEX IV. (If it is not there, the word has not been assigned characters in the general-use list.)

2. On the corresponding flash card add the new *kun-yomi* and all the *on-yomi* and exemplary compounds (if you have not already done so).

3. Consult a dictionary to confirm the meaning of the new *kun-yomi* and fill it in accordingly.

4. Set the card aside for drill, together with any other cards whose contents have been completely filled in. To facilitate adding more *kun-yomi* later, you will find it helpful to keep the cards separated in groups from

1–100, 101–200, etc. as we did in VOL. 1. After you have acquired a sizeable number of cards for drill, you will have to set up for yourself a routine for drilling (a) from meaning to writing, (b) from exemplary compound to *on-yomi*, and (c) from inflected kanji to *kun-yomi*. If you worked your way faithfully through VOL. 1, you may feel that there is no longer any need for the first drill. In that case I recommend that you drill the writing directly from the *hiragana kun-yomi* on the BACK.

PRIMITIVE PHONEMES

Unlike the primitive elements of VOL. 1 and the signal primitives of this book, the primitive phonemes presented in the present section are not intended for use *as far as possible,* but only *as far as necessary.* They have been designed as a crutch to help you with words that cause you difficulty. This means that you should not apply them retroactively to words you already know, nor should you use them to learn masses of new vocabulary isolated from the context of your reading or conversation.

Accordingly, the SYLLABARY OF PRIMITIVE PHONEMES displayed below should not be slavishly memorized but only consulted when needed. Once you have studied the examples that follow and experimented with the method on your own, you should be able to determine how best to make use of it or to alter it for your own purposes.

What you *must* take a moment out to memorize before going any further is the 11-syllable "a-b-c" that will enable you to find your way around Japanese dictionaries and word-lists arranged in dictionary order like those of this chapter and the INDEXES. Carry it around with you on a slip of paper and run it through your mind again and again if you must, but do not let another day go by without learning it:[1]

あ・か・さ・た・な・は・ま・や・ら・わ・ん

The table below uses a combination of *on-yomi* and *kun-yomi*, indicated in the pronunciation column by *katakana* and *hiragana* respectively. These are followed by the voiced or "muddied" sounds (see FRAME 1889), lengthened syllables, and finally diphthongs.

---

1. A simple mnemonic device to simplify the learning of this sequence can be found in my *Remembering the Kana* (Honolulu:University of Hawai'i Press, 2006), beginning at the end of LESSON 2 of the *Hiragana.*

PRIMARY PHONEMES

亜	ア	sub-; below
井	い	a well
卯	う	hare; rabbit
江	え	stream; rivulet
尾	お	tail
蚊	か	mosquito
木	き	tree
繰	く (る)	to spin; reel up
毛	け	hair; fur
子	こ	child
刺	さ (す)	to prick; stab
死	し (ぬ)	to die
巣	す	nest
瀬	せ	shoals; torrent
染	そ (める)	to dye; stain
他	た	another (person)
千	ち	1,000
津	つ	harbor
手	て	hand
戸	と	door
菜	な	vegetables
荷	に	luggage; bags
縫	ぬ (う)	to sew
根	ね	roots
野	の	field; plains
歯	は	tooth
火	ひ	fire
吹	ふ (く)	to blow

減	へ (る)	to dwindle; shrink
帆	ほ	a sail
間	ま	a room
実	み	fruit; nut; berry
蒸	む (す)	to steam
目	め	eye
喪	も	mourning
矢	や	arrow
湯	ゆ	hot water
酔	よ (う)	to get drunk
裸	ラ	nude
痢	リ	diarrhea
留	ル	stopover; abroad
礼	レ (イ)	a bow; curtsey
呂	ロ	backbone
輪	わ	a wheel
天	(テ) ン	heavens

VOICED PHONEMES

画	ガ	painting
犠	ギ	animal sacrifice
具	グ	tool
下	ゲ	downwards
碁	ゴ	checkers
座	ザ	a seat
路	じ	a path
図	ズ	a map
是	ゼ	adjusted
象	ゾ (ウ)	elephant

抱	だ (く)	to embrace
出	で (る)	to leave; depart
退	ど (ける)	to remove; set aside
場	ば	a place; spot
鼻	ビ	a nose
打	ぶ (つ)	to beat; slap
辺	べ	vicinity
簿	ボ	notebook

LONG VOWELS

多	おお (い)	many
凍	こお (る)	to freeze
背	せい	height; stature
通	とお (る)	to pass through
設	もう (ける)	to set up; establish
夕	ゆう	night
英国	エイ (コク)	England
空港	クウ (コウ)	airport
警察	ケイ (サツ)	policeman
枢軸	スウ (ジク)	axle
奏する	ソウ (する)	to perform music
交通	(コウ) ツウ	traffic
呈する	テイ (する)	to make a present of
丁寧	(テイ) ネイ	courtesy
脳	ノウ	brain
封じる	フウ (じる)	to seal a letter
紙幣	(シ) ヘイ	paper money
奉ずる	ホウ (ずる)	to dedicate
命じる	メイ (じる)	to give commands to

要する	ヨウ (する)	to need
奴隷	(ド) レイ	a slave
老人	ロウ (ジン)	old man
神宮	(ジン) グウ	Shinto shrine
芸者	ゲイ (シャ)	geisha
号	ゴウ	nickname
税金	ゼイ (キン)	taxes
冷蔵庫	(レイ) ゾウ (コ)	refrigerator
泥土	デイ (ド)	mud
堂	ドウ	public hall
米国	ベイ (コク)	U.S.A.
帽子	ボウ (シ)	hat; cap

DIPHTHONGS

巨人	キョ (ジン)	giant
写真	シャ (シン)	pictograph
洋酒	(ヨウ) シュ	booze
署名	ショ (メイ)	a signature
茶	チャ	tea
著者	チョ (シャ)	author
虜囚	リョ (シュウ)	captive
漁業	ギョ (ギョウ)	fishing
秒	ビョウ	second (of time)
邪	ジャ	malice; evil
儒学者	ジュ (ガクシャ)	Confucian scholar
徐行する	ジョ (コウする)	to slow down
急	キュウ	steep
東京	(トウ) キョウ	Tokyo

修道院	シュウドウ (イン)	monastery
称する	ショウ (する)	to tag; name
駐車場	チュウ (シャジョウ)	parking lot
白鳥	(ハク) チョウ	swan
牛乳	(ギュウ) ニュウ	milk
尿	ニョウ	urine
評する	ヒョウ (する)	criticize
妙	ミョウ	exquisite
竜	リュウ	dragon
寮	リョウ	dormitory
人形	(ニン) ギョウ	puppet
十	ジュウ	ten
嬢	ジョウ	young girl

Before passing on to examples of how the above SYLLABARY OF PRIMITIVE PHONEMES can serve as a mnemonics, there are a couple of points worth noting carefully as you look over the list.

To begin with, there are 3 cases with no character-reading corresponding to a monosyllabic sound. To compensate for this, kanji with diphthongs were chosen and the additional syllable repressed (and set in parentheses).

Secondly, not all possible diphthongs have been included. You may supplement the list or simply break the diphthong up into its composite parts. (For instance, the phoneme りゅ may be reduced to the syllables り and ゅ.)

Finally, where a compound was used to represent a phoneme, the meaning derives from the entire compound rather than from any of its parts. In some cases this means learning a new word, but never a useless one.

THE MNEMONICS AT WORK

The method of memorization based on the SYLLABARY OF PRIMITIVE PHONEMES consists of relating the conglomerate of meanings of the syllabary to the English meaning of the word in the same way that conglomerates of primitive elements were related to English key words in VOL. 1. Without repeating what was said there, a few illustrative examples should make the point.

We begin with a simple example:

弾 ► **bullet** ▷ たま

The relationship indicated by the solid arrow ► was established in VOL. 1. What remains is to move through the second, white arrow ▷, replacing the English key word with a Japanese word.

Begin with the specific connotation of the English word, which we shall take to be "a bullet fired from a gun." Next we consult the SYLLABARY OF PRIMITIVE PHONEMES, where we discover that た means *another* (*person*) and ま means *room*. Finally, we relate the elements imaginatively: Picture yourself sitting in bed, pistol in hand, shooting **bullets** through the wall and into the next room, where *another person* is busily scurrying about collecting the lead and melting it down into new bullets which he then returns to you so you can carry on. If you can see the wall riddled with holes, through which you can see that other person in the next *room,* the picture should be complete. Of course, you may have to learn the meaning of the words た and ま, but that would be necessary in any case.

Let us consider another new word:

墓 ► **grave** ▷ はか

First picture a specific **grave** that you know. The primitive phonemes we have to work with are は (*tooth*) and か (*mosquito*). Now exhume the contents of the grave in memory, turn back the lid on the coffin, and discover a smiling corpse, completely intact except for the fact that it has *mosquitoes* buzzing about in the hollow in its mouth where the *teeth* used to be. (Or, alternatively, you might picture the corpse of a giant *mosquito* smiling through its large, white *teeth*.)

Here is yet another two-syllable word:

絹 ► **silk** ▷ きぬ

The primitive phonemes き and ぬ give us the images *tree* and *sewing* to work with. Picture yourself *sewing* a kimono for the Statue of Liberty by using a tree trunk for a needle, and *silk thread* the thickness of a lumberjack's rope.

The same procedure can be applied to inflected words like this one:

加わる ► **to add** ▷ くわわる

The component phonemes く and わ yield the meanings *spinning* and *wheel.* The word in question may be taken in its transitive or intransitive, or active or passive, form, which is determined in any case by the *hiragana* inflection. Let the special connotation be the **addition** of numbers inside one's head with a complicated set of cogged *wheels,* outfitted with levers and catches galore, *spinning* at high speed to calculate the fact that $1 + 1 = 2$.

滅ぼす ▶ to destroy ▷ ほろぼす

Paint yourself a picture in your mind's eye as vivid as the phantom ship in Coleridge's "Rime of the Ancient Mariner." See the ghosts and demons and goblins flying *kites* stretched with human skin and tailed with *backbones,* fluttering gently in the breeze—a portrait of **destruction.**

Still within the compass of the key words of VOL. 1, notice how the same word can have two meanings—and kanji—and hence require different stories built up of the same primitive phonemes:

塩 ▶ **salt** ▷ しお

潮 ▶ **tide** ▷ しお

The common phonemes are し (*die*) and お (*tail*). If we were obliged to proceed from the word to the meaning we would be in trouble, but since we are learning the readings of the kanji, the duplication does not pose any great problem. In the first case, you may picture **salt** in its function as a ritual purifier in a sumō bout in which one of the wrestlers has been done in. The surviving wrestler takes out a **salt**-shaker and sprinkles the *tail* of a horse, which begins to wave its rear parts over the *dead* wrestler.... And for the second, picture a morning **tide** of *tails* washing ashore, a *death* omen to the surrounding inhabitants.

Lastly, we need to see how an entry in the SYLLABARY OF PRIMITIVE PHONEMES may also be used by itself to represent a word composed of only that sound (minus the inflection). Here is an example:

張る ▶ **to lengthen** ▷ はる

は, we recall from an earlier example, means *tooth.* Imagine that you, like beavers and rats and squirrels, have *teeth* that grow beyond the size of your mouth so that you must constantly be gnawing at something to keep them short. And so you chew away at your desk, your bed, the living room furniture, and most of your house, until one bright morning you discover the cause: you had been using a special toothpaste called **Lengthen** which you mistakenly supposed was intended to give your teeth a "longer life."

We may conclude this introduction to the use of the SYLLABARY OF PRIMARY PHONEMES with a drill of *kun-yomi.* You should have no trouble in any of them if you take your time.

鬼 ▶ **devil** ▷ おに

浮く ▶ **float** ▷ うく

乏しい ▶ **destitute** ▷

株 ▶ **stocks** ▷ かぶ

粘る ▶ **to be sticky** ▷ ねばる

好む ▶ **to be fond of** ▷ このむ

So far all the meanings have been consistent with the key words learned in VOL. 1. If this is not the case—or, as happens more often, if the meaning shifts to a related meaning not covered by the key word—you should not bother adding a second key word to that already learned. It was enough that a single English key word helped you remember how to write the kanji. From here on in, you will have to do what the Japanese themselves do to broaden their knowledge of a given kanji: read as much as you can, look up everything you do not understand, and use what you look up as often as you can.

You may be wondering whether these new primitive meanings and their stories will not confuse what you already learned in VOL. 1. Not to worry. For one thing, most of the meanings assigned to the primitive phonemes did not appear in the first book. For another, the mnemonics described in this chapter is a deliberately short-lived device that is soon let go of once you have begun to use the word in question and to associate it with the object, activity, or quality in your experience that it speaks to. The stories learned in the earlier book, however, will last at least until you have become comfortable with the Chinese and Japanese pronunciations of those kanji and begun to compose with them in Japanese. An example may help.

Let us say you meet the word for "halo," whose Japanese pronunciation and kanji are both new to you and both of which you are determined to learn. The following scheme illustrates the two steps you must go through:

	日 ▶ sun		か ▷ mosquito
暈		かさ	
	軍 ▶ army		さ ▷ stab

All of this you can figure out by consulting a dictionary and applying what you learned in VOL. 1 and in this chapter. The association between the English word **halo** and the Japanese word かさ is supplied at first by the primitive phonemes, and then later—as you begin to use the word—by the context of your thinking and speech. Because you will find yourself writing the kanji rather infrequently, the story you make to relate *sun* and *army* to its writing can be expected to last much, much longer.

There is one more reason why the meanings of the primitive phonemes and the primitive elements are not likely to cause you confusion, and this brings us to the final step in our mnemonics for the Japanese readings. As mentioned in passing, not only the SYLLABARY OF PRIMARY PHONEMES but *any* Japanese word can be used as a sound-and-meaning unit to learn other words. In fact, the more words you learn, the easier it becomes to dispense with the short syllables used in the earlier examples.

Say you have already learned the word へり (縁), meaning the **hem** or **frill** of a garment. And let us suppose also that you learned the word by playing with the phonemes for *shrinking* (へ) and *diarrhea* (リ). We will further assume that you know the word くだる (下だる), meaning *to lower,* which you first memorized by combining the phonemes for *spinning* (く) and *embracing* (だ).

Now when you meet the frightening words へりくだる (謙る), there is no need to break it up into syllables since you already have two parts, *hem* and *lowering* which are most convenient for remembering the meaning of the word: **to humble oneself.**

There is, of course, always the possibility that you will want to learn a word via these larger phonemes even though you were not previously acquainted with them. Take the word ひざまづく (跪く), meaning **kneel down**. Even though you know that ま means *room* and つく means *attached to,* the syllable ひざ is new. You look it up to discover that it means *lap.* The etymological connection is too tempting to pass over, so you learn the new phoneme ひざ together with the original word rather than break it up into its component parts. This procedure is one you will no doubt find yourself using more and more as your vocabulary increases and you develop a greater appetite for new words.

To exercise the principles explained in the last few paragraphs, try your hand at the following five words before reading any further:

盲	▶ **blindness**	▷ めくら
沈む	▶ **to sink**	▷ しずむ
蓄える	▶ **to store up**	▷ たくわえる
鉛	▶ **lead (the metal)**	▷ なまり
唆かす	▶ **to tempt**	▷ そそのかす

Though these are not the only possibilities, you might have used the following new words to learn those just treated:

倉	▶ **storehouse**	▷ くら
桑	▶ **mulberry bush**	▷ くわ
生	▶ **raw**	▷ なま
園	▶ **garden**	▷ その

CONCLUDING REMARKS

With that, the mnemonics for the *kun-yomi* is complete and only remains to be perfected in the practice. But perhaps you are still pestered by the thought: Why not present the whole range of Japanese readings, building up from simple elements to the more complex, in the same way the writing of the kanji was taught in VOL. 1?

Lay the thought to rest once and for all. For one thing, by the time you have reached this page, you will already have at least 2,000 words in tow. To force those words back into a systematic relearning for the sake of another few thousand words seems highly inefficient. A second and more convincing reason is that the habit of isolating vocabulary from the rest of language simply in order to learn new words is a bad one to get into with any language, whether native or acquired. Learning to *write* the kanji presented a special problem that required a special solution: sticking our nose so close to the written form that virtually everything else was lost from view. Learning to *pronounce* the kanji requires another approach, more like keeping a firm finger on systematic study methods while still being able to look up and see the total picture. There is much to be gained by a methodical approach like that outlined in these pages. But when all is said and done, fluent reading and composition is a matter of alert and sustained devotion to the language.

Indexes

INDEX I

Signal Primitives

The following list contains all the signal primitives used in this book, arranged according to number of strokes and primary reading. The numbers refer to the frames in which a given primitive figures in its primary reading. As explained in the text, these primitives do not necessarily coincide with the primitive elements treated in VOL. 1.

2 画

及	R-205-7
二	R-247-9
几	R-551-2
丁	R-1579-86

3 画

化	R-111-14
工	R-115-22
士	R-141-4
凡	R-328-30
毛	R-485-6
亡	R-1283-8
己	R-1323-9
干	R-1372-8
也	R-1395-9

4 画

中	R-57-60
五	R-85-8
元	R-235-7
比	R-381-2
介	R-413-14
气	R-437-8
双	R-481-2
升	R-533-4

亠	R-547-8
牙	R-876-9
毛	R-903-5
屯	R-921-3
夫	R-933-5
文	R-966-8
凶	R-969-71
卆	R-988-90
壬	R-1003-5
氏	R-1012-14
反	R-1330-8
分	R-1343-9
方	R-1424-36
少	R-1526-36
支	R-1520-5
区	R-1591-5
公	R-1602-5
予	R-1627-30

5 画

付	R-69-73
白	R-89-94
包	R-95-100
可	R-105-10
司	R-123-7
申	R-145-8

且	R-149-54
氏	R-155-8
半	R-167-70
	R-1274-7
奴	R-211-13
永	R-214-16
巨	R-238-40
代	R-283-5
丙	R-286-8
玄	R-289-91
末	R-310-12
元	R-339-40
术	R-409-10
冊	R-453-4
民	R-467-8
切	R-527-8
召	R-748-55
令	R-756-61
乍	R-762-6
生	R-775-81
	R-1389-94
旦	R-791-5
圣	R-796-800
奻	R-872-5
加	R-891-3
布	R-924-6
合	R-927-9

6 画

央	R-936-8
広	R-939-41
市	R-957-9
左	R-997-9
史	R-1006-8
未	R-1278-82
正	R-1300-5
古	R-1312-17
矛	R-1339-42
台	R-1367-71
兄	R-1384-8
必	R-1400-2
由	R-1460-5
失	R-1492-5
主	R-1447-52
弔	R-1537-8
皮	R-1539-46

朱	R-196-8
先	R-253-5
州	R-268-70
壮	R-274-6
夹	R-313-15
荔	R-341-2
安	R-351-2

伐	R-353-4
名	R-385-6
旬	R-405-6
刑	R-477-8
此	R-545-6
守	R-539-40
会	R-571-5
次	R-736-41
交	R-742-7
戈	R-812-5
并	R-816-9
旨	R-832-5
列	R-852-5
因	R-880-3
全	R-909-11
争	R-942-4
瓜	R-945-7
吉	R-979-81
充	R-1015-17
同	R-1258-63
兆	R-1264-9
成	R-1270-3
共	R-1295-9
戋	R-1361-6
每	R-1418-24
各	R-1466-74

INDEX II

Kanji

The following list contains all the kanji treated in VOLS. 1 AND 2, *grouped by the number of strokes and ordered according to standard dictionary "radicals." The number following the kanji refers to the first frame in which that character appears in this volume.* INDEX V *provides a cross-reference to* VOL. 1.

爪 R-662
父 R-1204
片 片 R-2083
牙 R-876
牛 R-583
犬 R-1817
王 王 R-1209

5画

丼 R-717
且 R-731
世 R-7
丘 R-2277
丙 R-286
主 R-1450
亻 以 R-11
仕 R-142
他 R-1228
付 R-69
仙 R-1190
代 R-283
令 R-756
兄 R-1384
冊 R-453
冖 写 R-1126
冬 R-1943
処 R-1877
凵 凸 R-2325
出 R-590
凹 R-2326
刊 R-1374
功 R-116
加 R-891
包 R-95
北 R-612
半 R-167
占 R-1841
卯 R-734
去 R-1105
圧 R-575
口 古 R-1312

句 R-1703
只 R-628
叫 R-2131
召 R-748
可 R-105
台 R-1367
号 R-1041
史 R-1006
右 R-1885
司 R-123
叱 R-2151
口 囚 R-1917
四 R-1062
外 R-1057
大 央 R-938
失 R-1494
奴 R-211
尼 R-2399
左 R-997
巧 R-122
巨 R-238
尻 R-681
巾 市 R-957
布 R-924
平 R-1700
幼 R-1767
庁 R-1582
広 R-939
弁 R-1046
弘 R-2409
必 R-1095
打 R-1586
払 R-2268
氾 R-1730
斥 R-1892
旦 R-791
旧 R-1736
木 未 R-1278
末 R-310
本 R-1082
札 R-1842
止 正 R-1300

母 R-1205
民 R-467
氷 R-1930
永 R-214
汁 R-2173
瓜 R-947
犯 R-1745
玄 R-289
玉 R-584
瓦 R-1073
甘 R-2050
生 生 R-775
用 R-1773
田 R-2003
由 R-1460
甲 R-2038
申 R-145
白 R-89
皮 R-1539
皿 R-699
目 R-1225
矛 R-1339
矢 R-2276
石 石 R-1863
示 R-1875
礼 R-51
穴 R-1945
立 R-1682
辶 辺 R-1961
辻 R-646
込 R-666

6画

両 R-1244
争 R-944
亘 R-626
亠 交 R-742
亥 R-705
亻 仮 R-1338
仰 R-1916
仲 R-60

件 R-1779
任 R-1003
企 R-1870
伊 R-33
伏 R-2336
伐 R-353
休 R-1704
会 R-571
伝 R-1232
伎 R-1523
儿 充 R-1015
兆 R-1264
先 R-253
光 R-1196
全 R-911
共 R-1295
再 R-1816
刑 R-477
列 R-852
劣 R-1536
匚 匠 R-1959
印 R-1862
危 R-1250
口 各 R-1466
合 R-1172
吉 R-979
同 R-1258
名 R-385
后 R-1998
吏 R-1008
牟 R-41
吐 R-2034
向 R-1780
吸 R-206
囗 回 R-1185
因 R-880
団 R-1050
土 在 R-1231
圭 R-1503
地 R-1395
壮 R-274
多 R-8

女 好 R-1956
如 R-1985
妃 R-1328
妄 R-2092
子 字 R-1089
存 R-595
宀 宅 R-485
宇 R-30
守 R-539
安 R-52
寸 寺 R-1554
尽 R-2039
州 R-268
彐 当 R-1046
帆 R-329
年 R-1105
戈 式 R-1717
弐 R-248
忙 R-1286
汎 R-330
弋 成 R-1270
扱 R-660
旨 R-832
早 R-587
旬 R-405
旭 R-625
曲 R-1952
肌 R-632
有 R-1164
木 朱 R-196
朴 R-2376
机 R-551
朽 R-2033
次 R-736
歹 死 R-1874
毎 R-1129
気 R-437
汐 R-633
汗 R-1375
汚 R-1807
江 R-118
池 R-1396

INDEX III

Chinese Readings

This index includes all the Chinese readings treated in this book, arranged in standard dictionary order and followed by the number of the frame in which the reading is introduced.

	渋	R-2114	ショウ	青	R-78	抄	R-1528	ショク	職	R-1025

INDEX IV

Japanese Readings

This index includes only the Japanese readings established as standard for the general-use kanji. Characters treated in this book and VOL. 1 that fall outside that list are given only with their most common readings. The numbers refer to frames in the present volume. Only approved readings are given, except for characters that fall outside the list of general-use kanji. Readings used only for personal and place names have been omitted.

あわただしい	慌ただしい	R-444
あわてる	慌てる	R-444
あわれ	哀れ	R-1193
あわれむ	哀れむ	R-1193
あんず	杏	R-642

【い】

い	井	R-44
いう	言う	R-1728
いえ	家	R-307
いえる	癒える	R-195
いおう	硫	R-522
いかす	生かす	R-775
いかる	怒る	R-212
いき	息	R-1941
	粋	R-988
いきおい	勢い	R-1740
いきどおる	憤る	R-218
いきる	生きる	R-775
いく	行く	R-1069
	逝く	R-2349
	幾	R-334
いくさ	戦	R-1155
いけ	池	R-1396
いける	生ける	R-775
いこい	憩い	R-1626
いこう	憩う	R-1626
いさぎよい	潔い	R-1939
いさましい	勇ましい	R-441
いさむ	勇む	R-441
いし	石	R-1863
いしずえ	礎	R-1764
いずみ	泉	R-271
いそがしい	忙しい	R-1286
いそぐ	急ぐ	R-1127
いた	板	R-1332
いたい	痛い	R-1019
いだく	抱く	R-98
いたす	致す	R-2136
いただき	頂	R-1581
いただく	頂く	R-1581
いたむ	悼む	R-2163
	痛む	R-1019
	傷む	R-1491
いためる	痛める	R-1019
	傷める	R-1491

いたる	至る	R-2087
いち	市	R-957
いちじるしい	著しい	R-1480
いつ	五	R-85
いつくしむ	慈しむ	R-226
いつつ	五つ	R-85
いつわる	偽る	R-2081
いと	糸	R-2327
いとなむ	営む	R-1124
いどむ	挑む	R-1266
いな	否	R-1758
	稲	R-2049
いぬ	犬	R-1817
いね	稲	R-2049
いのこ	猪	R-1481
いのしし	猪	R-1481
	亥	R-705
いのち	命	R-1077
いのる	祈る	R-2137
いばら	茨	R-652
いま	今	R-1116
いましめる	戒める	R-415
いまわしい	忌まわしい	R-1327
いむ	忌む	R-1327
いも	芋	R-712
いもうと	妹	R-1281
いや	嫌	R-886
いやしい	卑しい	R-383
いやしむ	卑しむ	R-383
いやしめる	卑しめる	R-383
いやす	癒やす	R-195
いる	入る	R-1690
	居る	R-1317
	要る	R-503
	射る	R-529
	鋳る	R-2225
	煎る	R-1110
いれる	入れる	R-1690
いろ	色	R-1226
いろどる	彩る	R-190
いわ	岩	R-1863
いわう	祝う	R-1387
いわく	曰く	R-657

【う】

う	卯	R-734

【え】

え	江	R-118
	重	R-1755
	柄	R-287
	餌	R-2191
えがく	描く	R-305
えさ	餌	R-2191
えだ	枝	R-1521
えむ	笑む	R-1924
えらい	偉い	R-1319
えらぶ	選ぶ	R-1150
えり	襟	R-476
える	得る	R-1753
	獲る	R-963

【お】

お	小	R-1133
	尾	R-905
	雄	R-2059
	緒	R-1482
おいて	於いて	R-40
おいる	老いる	R-1242
おう	生う	R-775
	負う	R-1737
	追う	R-1772
おうぎ	扇	R-1791
おえる	終える	R-1151
おお	大	R-1055
おおい	多い	R-8
おおいに	大いに	R-1055
おおう	覆う	R-786
おおきい	大きい	R-1055
おおせ	仰せ	R-1916
おおやけ	公	R-1604
おか	丘	R-2277
	岡	R-724
おかす	犯す	R-1745
	侵す	R-259
	冒す	R-357
おがむ	拝む	R-1238
おき	沖	R-59
おぎ	荻	R-645
おぎなう	補う	R-62
おきる	起きる	R-1325
おく	奥	R-2282

	置く	R-1438
おくらす	遅らす	R-2027
おくる	送る	R-1216
	贈る	R-1294
おくれる	後れる	R-1076
	遅れる	R-2027
おける	於ける	R-40
おこす	起こす	R-1325
	興す	R-1727
おごそか	厳か	R-1928
おこたる	怠る	R-1368
おこなう	行う	R-1069
おこる	怒る	R-212
	起こる	R-1325
	興る	R-1727
おさえる	抑える	R-2051
	押さえる	R-1824
おさない	幼い	R-1767
おさまる	収まる	R-1681
	治まる	R-1370
	修まる	R-1901
	納まる	R-1742
おさめる	収める	R-1681
	治める	R-1370
	修める	R-1901
	納める	R-1742
おしい	惜しい	R-1617
おしえる	教える	R-974
おしむ	惜しむ	R-1617
おす	雄	R-2059
	押す	R-1824
	推す	R-1883
おそい	遅い	R-2027
おそう	襲う	R-1894
おそれ	虞	R-726
おそれる	恐れる	R-2044
	畏れる	R-1912
おそろしい	恐ろしい	R-2044
おそわる	教わる	R-974
おだやか	穏やか	R-2109
おちいる	陥る	R-2222
おちる	落ちる	R-1471
おっと	夫	R-933
おと	音	R-1416
おとうと	弟	R-1538
おどかす	脅かす	R-342

おとこ	男	R-1043
おとしいれる	陥れる	R-2222
おとす	落とす	R-1471
おどす	脅す	R-342
おとずれる	訪れる	R-1434
おどり	踊り	R-1020
おとる	劣る	R-1536
おどる	踊る	R-1020
	躍る	R-2228
おとろえる	衰える	R-2303
おどろかす	驚かす	R-987
おどろく	驚く	R-987
おなじ	同じ	R-1258
おに	鬼	R-2062
おのおの	各	R-1466
おのれ	己	R-24
おび	帯	R-483
おびやかす	脅かす	R-342
おびる	帯びる	R-483
おぼえる	覚える	R-1990
おぼれる	溺れる	R-600
おも	主	R-1450
	面	R-369
おもい	重い	R-1755
おもう	思う	R-1697
おもて	表	R-391
	面	R-369
おもむき	趣	R-1588
おもむく	赴く	R-568
おもり	錘	R-1358
おや	親	R-258
およぐ	泳ぐ	R-215
および	及び	R-205
およぶ	及ぶ	R-205
およぼす	及ぼす	R-205
おり	折	R-1763
おりる	下りる	R-1051
	降りる	R-1932
おる	折る	R-1763
	織る	R-1026
おれ	俺	R-677
おれる	折れる	R-1763
おろか	愚か	R-871
おろし	卸	R-697
おろす	下ろす	R-1051
	卸す	R-697

	降ろす	R-1932
おわる	終わる	R-1151
おん	御	R-1035
おんな	女	R-3

【か】

か	日	R-603
	香	R-1845
	蚊	R-716
	鹿	R-727
かい	貝	R-629
かいこ	蚕	R-1799
かう	交う	R-742
	買う	R-1681
	飼う	R-125
かえす	返す	R-1337
	帰す	R-1906
かえりみる	省みる	R-1529
	顧みる	R-544
かえる	返る	R-1337
	帰る	R-1906
	代える	R-283
	変える	R-1171
	換える	R-421
	替える	R-2287
かお	顔	R-1944
かおり	香り	R-1845
かおる	香る	R-1845
	薫る	R-456
かかえる	抱える	R-98
かかげる	掲げる	R-1311
かがみ	鏡	R-462
かがやく	輝く	R-1642
かかり	係	R-976
	掛	R-659
かかる	係る	R-976
	架かる	R-892
	掛かる	R-659
	懸かる	R-436
かかわる	関わる	R-1092
かき	垣	R-635
	柿	R-643
かぎ	鍵	R-326
かぎる	限る	R-1516
かく	欠く	R-1828
	書く	R-1054

がら	柄	R-287
からい	辛い	R-2050
からす	烏	R-2069
からす	枯らす	R-1315
からだ	体	R-1182
からまる	絡まる	R-1470
からむ	絡む	R-1470
からめる	絡める	R-1470
かり	仮	R-1338
	狩り	R-540
	猟り	R-1859
かりる	借りる	R-1619
かる	刈る	R-702
	狩る	R-540
	駆る	R-1594
かるい	軽い	R-797
かれ	彼	R-1541
かれる	枯れる	R-1315
かろやか	軽やか	R-797
かわ	河	R-110
	側	R-282
	皮	R-1539
	革	R-1761
	川	R-1972
がわ	側	R-282
かわかす	乾かす	R-1251
かわく	渇く	R-1309
	乾く	R-1251
かわす	交わす	R-742
かわら	瓦	R-1073
かわる	代わる	R-283
	変わる	R-1171
	換わる	R-421
	替わる	R-2287
かん	神	R-146
かんがえる	考える	R-1675
かんがみる	鑑みる	R-1381
かんばしい	芳しい	R-1433
かんむり	冠	R-1947

【き】

き	木	R-1075
	生	R-775
	黄	R-431
きえる	消える	R-802
きく	利く	R-387
	効く	R-744
	聞く	R-1106
	聴く	R-1720
きこえる	聞こえる	R-1106
きざし	兆し	R-1264
きざす	兆す	R-1264
きざむ	刻む	R-1660
きし	岸	R-1243
きず	傷	R-1491
きずく	築く	R-1747
きせる	着せる	R-1802
きそう	競う	R-1385
きた	北	R-612
きたえる	鍛える	R-2021
きたす	来す	R-1131
きたない	汚い	R-1807
きたる	来る	R-1131
きぬ	絹	R-1942
きば	牙	R-876
きびしい	厳しい	R-1928
きまる	決まる	R-1733
きみ	君	R-956
きめる	決める	R-1733
きも	肝	R-1376
きよい	清い	R-80
きよまる	清まる	R-80
きよめる	清める	R-80
きらう	嫌う	R-886
きり	霧	R-1341
	桐	R-1263
きる	切る	R-527
	着る	R-1802
	伐る	R-353
	斬る	R-411
きれる	切れる	R-527
きわ	際	R-554
きわまる	極まる	R-1937
	窮まる	R-2199
きわみ	極み	R-1937
きわめる	究める	R-1032
	極める	R-1937
	窮める	R-2199

【く】

くいる	悔いる	R-1419
くう	食う	R-1138

さからう	逆らう	R-1832
さかる	盛る	R-1271
さがる	下がる	R-1051
さかん	盛ん	R-1271
	昌ん	R-624
さき	先	R-253
	崎	R-665
さく	咲く	R-730
	割く	R-982
	裂く	R-854
さくら	桜	R-2274
さぐる	探る	R-1896
	捜る	R-569
さけ	酒	R-1792
さげすむ	蔑む	R-2195
さけぶ	叫ぶ	R-2131
さける	裂ける	R-854
	避ける	R-863
さげる	下げる	R-1051
	提げる	R-1606
ささ	笹	R-674
ささえる	支える	R-1520
ささる	刺さる	R-1248
さじ	匕	R-648
さす	刺す	R-1248
	指す	R-833
	挿す	R-2085
	差す	R-1955
さずかる	授かる	R-398
さずける	授ける	R-398
さそう	誘う	R-1884
さだか	定か	R-894
さだまる	定まる	R-894
さだめる	定める	R-894
さち	幸	R-1827
さと	里	R-1256
さとす	諭す	R-194
さとる	悟る	R-87
さばく	裁く	R-812
さび	寂	R-1414
さびしい	寂しい	R-1414
さびれる	寂れる	R-1414
さま	様	R-1572
さます	冷ます	R-757
	覚ます	R-1990
さまたげる	妨げる	R-1428

さむい	寒い	R-1865
さむらい	侍	R-1556
さめる	冷める	R-757
	覚める	R-1990
さら	皿	R-699
	更	R-856
さる	猿	R-297
	申	R-145
	去る	R-1105
さわ	沢	R-1160
さわぐ	騒ぐ	R-2132
さわやか	爽やか	R-2330
さわる	触る	R-2005
	障る	R-264

【し】

じ	路	R-199
しあわせ	幸せ	R-1827
しいたげる	虐げる	R-2156
しいる	強いる	R-1045
しお	潮	R-267
	汐	R-633
	塩	R-1769
しか	鹿	R-727
しかる	叱る	R-2151
しく	敷く	R-1436
しげる	茂る	R-2378
しずしず	静々	R-82
しずか	静か	R-82
しずく	滴	R-162
しずまる	静まる	R-82
	鎮まる	R-1409
しずめる	沈める	R-1858
	静める	R-82
	鎮める	R-1409
しずむ	沈む	R-1858
した	下	R-1051
	舌	R-1623
したう	慕う	R-771
したがう	従う	R-401
したがえる	従える	R-401
したしい	親しい	R-258
したしむ	親しむ	R-258
したたる	滴る	R-162
しな	品	R-1712
しぬ	死ぬ	R-1874

	澄む	R-1568
する	刷る	R-1862
	擦る	R-480
	摩る	R-138
するどい	鋭い	R-1511
すれる	擦れる	R-480
すわる	座る	R-559
	据わる	R-683

【せ】

せ	背	R-2001
	瀬	R-713
せい	背	R-2001
せき	関	R-1092
ぜに	銭	R-1363
せばまる	狭まる	R-314
せばめる	狭める	R-314
せまい	狭い	R-314
せまる	迫る	R-91
せめる	攻める	R-117
	責める	R-848
せる	競る	R-1385

【そ】

そう	沿う	R-927
	添う	R-2128
そうろう	候	R-321
そえる	添える	R-2128
そこ	底	R-157
そこなう	損なう	R-950
そこねる	損ねる	R-950
そそぐ	注ぐ	R-1447
そそのかす	唆す	R-2168
そだつ	育つ	R-577
そだてる	育てる	R-577
そで	袖	R-1465
そと	外	R-1057
そなえる	供える	R-1297
	備える	R-1900
そなわる	備わる	R-1900
その	園	R-296
	苑	R-872
そまる	染まる	R-1807
そむく	背く	R-2001
そむける	背ける	R-2001

そめる	初める	R-1823
	染める	R-1807
そら	空	R-585
そらす	反らす	R-1331
そる	反る	R-1331

【た】

た	手	R-1150
	田	R-2003
たいら	平ら	R-1700
たえる	耐える	R-2046
	堪える	R-951
	絶える	R-1820
たおす	倒す	R-550
たおれる	倒れる	R-550
たか	高	R-439
たかい	高い	R-439
たがい	互い	R-1688
たかまる	高まる	R-439
たかめる	高める	R-439
たがやす	耕す	R-2094
たから	宝	R-2010
たき	滝	R-655
たきぎ	薪	R-257
たく	炊く	R-1984
だく	抱く	R-98
たぐい	類い	R-1695
たくみ	巧み	R-122
たくわえる	蓄える	R-368
たけ	丈	R-1056
	竹	R-2181
	岳	R-2171
たしか	確か	R-1869
たしかめる	確かめる	R-1869
たす	足す	R-301
だす	出す	R-590
たすかる	助かる	R-1687
たすける	助ける	R-1687
たずさえる	携える	R-1775
たずさわる	携わる	R-1775
たずねる	訪ねる	R-1434
	尋ねる	R-2212
たたかう	戦う	R-1155
	闘う	R-1564
ただ	只	R-628
ただし	但し	R-676

ただしい	正しい	R-1300
ただす	正す	R-1300
ただちに	直ちに	R-1441
たたみ	畳	R-1840
たたむ	畳む	R-1840
ただよう	漂う	R-821
たち	達	R-596
たつ	竜	R-2064
	辰	R-806
	立つ	R-1682
	建つ	R-325
	断つ	R-1711
	裁つ	R-812
	絶つ	R-1820
たっとい	尊い	R-1851
	貴い	R-1938
たっとぶ	尊ぶ	R-1851
	貴ぶ	R-1938
たて	盾	R-407
	縦	R-402
たてまつる	奉る	R-888
たてる	立てる	R-1682
	建てる	R-325
たとえる	例える	R-855
たな	棚	R-641
たに	谷	R-1612
たね	種	R-1788
たのしい	楽しい	R-1120
たのしむ	楽しむ	R-1120
たのむ	頼む	R-1601
たのもしい	頼もしい	R-1601
たば	束	R-1596
たび	度	R-495
	旅	R-1070
たべる	食べる	R-1138
たま	玉	R-584
	球	R-246
	弾	R-2002
	霊	R-1853
たまご	卵	R-2056
たましい	魂	R-2055
だまる	黙る	R-1858
たまわる	賜る	R-2214
たみ	民	R-467
ためす	試す	R-1157
ためる	矯める	R-317

たもつ	保つ	R-16
たやす	絶やす	R-1820
たより	便り	R-859
たよる	頼る	R-1601
たらす	垂らす	R-1356
たりる	足りる	R-301
たる	足る	R-301
だれ	誰	R-656
たれる	垂れる	R-1356
たわむれる	戯れる	R-2234
たわら	俵	R-392

【ち】

ち	千	R-4
	血	R-1571
	乳	R-1072
ちいさい	小さい	R-1133
ちかい	近い	R-1112
ちかう	誓う	R-2120
ちがう	違う	R-1318
ちがえる	違える	R-1318
ちかづく	近づく	R-1112
ちから	力	R-1200
ちぎる	契る	R-1782
ちち	父	R-1204
	乳	R-1072
ちぢまる	縮まる	R-518
ちぢむ	縮む	R-518
ちぢめる	縮める	R-518
ちぢらす	縮らす	R-518
ちぢれる	縮れる	R-518
ちらかす	散らかす	R-55
ちらかる	散らかる	R-55
ちらす	散らす	R-55
ちる	散る	R-55

【つ】

つ	津	R-2004
ついえる	費える	R-1773
ついやす	費やす	R-1773
つか	塚	R-680
つかう	使う	R-1007
	遣う	R-1689
つかえる	仕える	R-142
つかす	尽かす	R-2039

【て】

	無い	R-365
なえ	苗	R-304
なえる	萎える	R-1913
なおす	治す	R-1370
	直す	R-1441
なおる	治る	R-1370
	直る	R-1441
なか	中	R-57
	仲	R-60
ながい	永い	R-214
	長い	R-65
ながす	流す	R-521
なかば	半ば	R-167
ながめる	眺める	R-1267
なかれ	勿かれ	R-615
ながれる	流れる	R-521
なぎさ	渚	R-691
なく	泣く	R-2275
	鳴く	R-1951
なぐさむ	慰む	R-394
なぐさめる	慰める	R-394
なぐる	殴る	R-1594
なげかわしい	嘆かわしい	R-1972
なげく	嘆く	R-1972
なげる	投げる	R-1809
なごむ	和む	R-12
なごやか	和やか	R-12
なさけ	情け	R-84
なし	梨	R-670
なす	成す	R-1270
なぞ	謎	R-671
なつ	夏	R-511
なつかしい	懐かしい	R-418
なつかしむ	懐かしむ	R-418
なつく	懐く	R-418
なつける	懐ける	R-418
なな	七	R-1063
ななつ	七つ	R-1063
ななめ	斜め	R-2220
	陀	R-2401
なに	何	R-106
なの	七	R-1063
なべ	鍋	R-694
なま	生	R-775
なまける	怠ける	R-1368
なまめかしい	嬌しい	R-318

なまり	鉛	R-928
なみ	並	R-2078
	波	R-1545
なみだ	涙	R-2043
なめらかだ	滑らかだ	R-450
なやます	悩ます	R-428
なやむ	悩む	R-428
ならう	倣う	R-532
	習う	R-1143
ならす	鳴らす	R-1951
	慣らす	R-420
ならび	並び	R-2078
ならぶ	並ぶ	R-2078
ならべる	並べる	R-2078
なり	也	R-38
なる	成る	R-1270
	鳴る	R-1951
なれる	慣れる	R-420
なわ	苗	R-304
	縄	R-1989
なん	何	R-106

【に】

に	荷	R-108
にい	新	R-256
にえる	煮える	R-1476
におい	臭い	R-2014
におう	臭う	R-2014
	匂う	R-649
にがい	苦い	R-1316
にがす	逃がす	R-1269
にがる	苦る	R-1316
にぎる	握る	R-2014
にくい	憎い	R-1293
にくしみ	憎しみ	R-1293
にくむ	憎む	R-1293
にくらしい	憎らしい	R-1293
にげる	逃げる	R-1269
にごす	濁す	R-2030
にごる	濁る	R-2030
にし	西	R-1146
にしき	錦	R-2291
にじ	虹	R-654
にじゅう	廿	R-687
にせ	偽	R-2081
になう	担う	R-793

	腫れる	R-1789

【ひ】

ひ	日	R-603
	火	R-1071
	氷	R-1930
	灯	R-1584
ひいでる	秀でる	R-2009
ひえる	冷える	R-757
ひかえる	控える	R-2127
ひがし	東	R-1442
ひかり	光	R-1196
ひかる	光る	R-1196
ひき	匹	R-2324
ひきいる	率いる	R-548
ひく	引く	R-1946
	弾く	R-2002
ひくい	低い	R-155
ひくまる	低まる	R-155
ひくめる	低める	R-155
ひこ	彦	R-715
ひける	引ける	R-1946
ひざ	膝	R-672
ひさしい	久しい	R-1768
ひし	菱	R-704
ひじ	肘	R-627
ひそむ	潜む	R-2336
ひたい	額	R-1474
ひたす	浸す	R-260
ひだり	左	R-997
ひたる	浸る	R-260
ひつじ	羊	R-1570
ひと	一	R-1060
	人	R-1057
ひとしい	等しい	R-1560
ひとつ	一つ	R-1060
ひとみ	瞳	R-1047
ひとり	独り	R-1682
ひびき	響き	R-460
ひびく	響く	R-460
ひま	暇	R-1957
ひめ	姫	R-667
ひめる	秘める	R-1400
ひや	冷や	R-757
ひやかす	冷やかす	R-757
ひやす	冷やす	R-757

ひら	平	R-1700
ひらく	開く	R-1724
	披く	R-1543
ひらける	開ける	R-1724
ひる	昼	R-795
	干る	R-1372
ひるがえす	翻す	R-2209
ひるがえる	翻る	R-2209
ひろい	広い	R-939
	弘い	R-2409
ひろう	拾う	R-1953
ひろがる	広がる	R-939
ひろげる	広げる	R-939
ひろまる	広まる	R-939
ひろめる	広める	R-939

【ふ】

ふえ	笛	R-2300
ふえる	殖える	R-1439
	増える	R-1292
ふかい	深い	R-1936
ふかす	更かす	R-856
ふかまる	深まる	R-1936
ふかめる	深める	R-1936
ふく	吹く	R-2280
	噴く	R-217
	拭く	R-2154
ふくむ	含む	R-2227
ふくめる	含める	R-2227
ふくらむ	膨らむ	R-2105
ふくれる	膨れる	R-2105
	脹れる	R-68
ふくろ	袋	R-285
ふける	老ける	R-1242
	更ける	R-856
ふさ	房	R-1431
ふさがる	塞がる	R-2331
ふさぐ	塞ぐ	R-2331
ふし	節	R-1825
ふじ	藤	R-866
ふす	伏す	R-2336
ふせぐ	防ぐ	R-1425
ふせる	伏せる	R-2336
ふた	二	R-1
	双	R-481
	蓋	R-1902

ふだ	札	R-1842
ぶた	豚	R-1678
ふたたび	再び	R-1816
ふたつ	二つ	R-1
ふち	縁	R-2057
ふで	筆	R-1199
ふとい	太い	R-19
ふところ	懐	R-418
ふとる	太る	R-19
ふな	舟	R-2340
	船	R-929
ふね	舟	R-2340
	船	R-929
ふまえる	踏まえる	R-2328
ふみ	文	R-966
ふむ	踏む	R-2328
ふもと	麓	R-2165
ふやす	殖やす	R-1439
	増やす	R-1292
ふゆ	冬	R-1943
ふる	振る	R-809
	降る	R-1932
ふるい	古い	R-1312
ふるう	振るう	R-809
	震う	R-807
	奮う	R-1948
ふるえる	震える	R-807
ふるす	古す	R-1312
ふれる	振れる	R-809
	触れる	R-2005

【へ】

べ	辺	R-1961
ページ	頁	R-631
へだたる	隔たる	R-2123
へだてる	隔てる	R-2123
べに	紅	R-119
へび	蛇	R-1975
へらす	減らす	R-1738
へる	経る	R-796
	減る	R-1738

【ほ】

ほ	火	R-1071
	帆	R-329

	穂	R-2278
ほうる	放る	R-531
ほうむる	葬る	R-1947
ほお	頬	R-692
ほか	他	R-1228
	外	R-1057
ほがらか	朗らか	R-991
ほこ	矛	R-1339
ぼこ	凹	R-2326
ほこる	誇る	R-2116
ほころびる	綻びる	R-896
ほし	星	R-777
ほしい	欲しい	R-1610
ほす	干す	R-1372
ほそい	細い	R-1904
ほそる	細る	R-1904
ほたる	蛍	R-2068
ほっする	欲する	R-1610
ほど	程	R-488
ほとけ	仏	R-1181
ほどこす	施す	R-1397
ほね	骨	R-449
ほのお	炎	R-2175
ほまれ	誉れ	R-2018
ほめる	褒める	R-2338
ほら	洞	R-1261
ほり	堀	R-682
ほる	彫る	R-1653
	掘る	R-323
ほろ	幌	R-647
ほろびる	滅びる	R-614
ほろぼす	滅ぼす	R-614

【ま】

ま	目	R-1225
	真	R-1407
	馬	R-930
	間	R-425
まい	舞	R-366
まいる	参る	R-523
まう	舞う	R-366
まえ	前	R-1109
まかす	任す	R-1003
	負かす	R-1737
まかせる	任せる	R-1003
まかなう	賄う	R-622

まがる	曲がる	R-1952
まき	牧	R-1834
	巻	R-193
まぎらす	紛らす	R-1345
まぎらわしい	紛らわしい	R-1345
まぎらわす	紛らわす	R-1345
まぎれる	紛れる	R-1345
まく	巻く	R-193
まくら	枕	R-720
まける	負ける	R-1737
まげる	曲げる	R-1952
まご	孫	R-977
まこと	誠	R-1272
まさ	正	R-1300
まさる	勝る	R-867
まざる	交ざる	R-742
	混ざる	R-1777
まじえる	交える	R-742
まじる	交じる	R-742
	混じる	R-1777
まじわる	交わる	R-742
ます	升	R-533
	増す	R-1292
まずしい	貧しい	R-1253
まぜる	交ぜる	R-742
	混ぜる	R-1777
また	又	R-661
	股	R-2366
またたく	瞬く	R-1715
まち	町	R-1580
	街	R-1500
まつ	松	R-1602
	待つ	R-1559
まったく	全く	R-1085
まつり	祭り	R-553
まつりごと	政	R-1148
まつる	祭る	R-553
まと	的	R-1225
まど	窓	R-344
まどう	惑う	R-623
まなこ	眼	R-1517
まなぶ	学ぶ	R-1055
まぬかれる	免れる	R-1213
まねく	招く	R-751
まぼろし	幻	R-2215
まめ	豆	R-1562

まもる	守る	R-539
まゆ	繭	R-2327
	眉	R-2202
まよう	迷う	R-1679
まる	丸	R-2002
まるい	丸い	R-2002
	円い	R-1067
まるめる	丸める	R-2002
まわす	回す	R-1185
まわり	周り	R-1654
まわる	回る	R-1185

【み】

み	三	R-2
	身	R-1750
	実	R-1759
	巳	R-735
みえる	見える	R-1111
みがく	磨く	R-139
みき	幹	R-1373
みぎ	右	R-1885
みことのり	詔	R-754
みさお	操	R-242
みさき	岬	R-686
みささぎ	陵	R-2086
みじかい	短い	R-1569
みじめ	惨め	R-524
みず	水	R-1074
みずうみ	湖	R-1313
みずから	自ら	R-1038
みせ	店	R-1107
みせる	見せる	R-1111
みぞ	溝	R-174
みたす	満たす	R-1766
みだす	乱す	R-1144
みだら	淫ら	R-1914
みだり	妄り	R-2092
みだれる	乱れる	R-1144
みち	道	R-375
みちびく	導く	R-376
みちる	満ちる	R-1766
みつ	三	R-2
みつぐ	貢ぐ	R-121
みっつ	三つ	R-2
みとめる	認める	R-348
みどり	緑	R-338

よし	由	R-1460
よせる	寄せる	R-788
よそおう	装う	R-276
よつ	四つ	R-1062
よっつ	四つ	R-1062
よぶ	呼ぶ	R-2007
よむ	詠む	R-216
	読む	R-1201
よめ	嫁	R-308
よる	夜	R-1970
	因る	R-880
	寄る	R-788
よろこぶ	喜ぶ	R-2000
よわい	弱い	R-1923
よわまる	弱まる	R-1923
よわめる	弱める	R-1923
よわる	弱る	R-1923
よん	四	R-1062

【わ】

わが	吾が	R-86
	我が	R-377
	輪	R-1001
わかい	若い	R-604
わかす	沸かす	R-2161
わかつ	分かつ	R-1343
わかる	分かる	R-1343
わかれる	分かれる	R-1343
	別れる	R-1163

わき	脇	R-668
わく	枠	R-639
	沸く	R-2161
	湧く	R-442
わけ	訳	R-1167
わける	分ける	R-1343
	割ける	R-2193
わざ	技	R-1525
	業	R-1124
わざわい	災い	R-1814
わずか	僅か	R-332
わずらう	患う	R-1850
	煩う	R-2293
わずらわしい	煩わしい	R-2293
わずらわす	煩わす	R-2293
わすれる	忘れる	R-1285
わた	綿	R-2012
わたくし	私	R-1793
わたし	私	R-1793
わたす	渡す	R-496
わたる	渡る	R-496
	亘る	R-626
わらう	笑う	R-1924
わらべ	童	R-1701
わり	割	R-982
わる	割る	R-982
わるい	悪い	R-1835
われ	我	R-377
	吾	R-86
われる	割れる	R-982

Cross-Reference List

The purpose of this final index is to facilitate cross-referencing between VOL. 1 *and* VOL. 2. *The index is laid out in the order in which the kanji appear in* VOL. 1. *The column of numbers preceded by an* R- *refer to frames in the present book. The kanji—with Japanese readings and inflection where applicable—are given in the final two columns. As in* INDEX IV, *only approved readings are given, except for characters that fall outside the list of general-use kanji. Readings used only for personal and place names have been omitted.*

1	R-1060	一	ひと
		一つ	ひとつ
2	R-1	二つ	ふたつ
		二	ふた
3	R-2	三つ	みつ
		三	み
		三つ	みっつ
4	R-1062	四	よ
		四つ	よつ
		四	よん
		四つ	よっつ
5	R-85	五	いつ
		五つ	いつつ
6	R-1066	六	む
		六	むつ
		六つ	むっつ
		六	むい
7	R-1063	七	なな
		七つ	ななつ
		七	なの
8	R-607	八	や
		八つ	やつ
		八つ	やっつ
		八	よう
9	R-1064	九	ここの

		九つ	ここのつ
10	R-1066	十	と
		十	とお
11	R-1685	口	くち
12	R-603	日	ひ
		日	か
13	R-586	月	つき
14	R-2003	田	た
15	R-1225	目	ま
		目	め
16	R-1312	古い	ふるい
		古す	ふるす
17	R-86	吾	われ
		吾が	わが
18	R-357	冒す	おかす
19	R-389	朋	
20	R-465	明るい	あかるい
		明るむ	あかるむ
		明く	あく
		明らか	あきらか
		明らむ	あからむ
		明かす	あかす
		明くる	あくる
		明ける	あける
		明かり	あかり

81	R-997	左	ひだり
82	R-1885	右	みぎ
83	R-1164	有る	ある
84	R-622	賄う	まかなう
85	R-121	貢ぐ	みつぐ
86	R-120	項	
87	R-1971	刀	かたな
88	R-2355	刃	は
89	R-527	切る	きる
		切れる	きれる
90	R-748	召す	めす
91	R-749	昭	
92	R-280	則	
93	R-825	副	
94	R-1163	別れる	わかれる
95	R-1579	丁	
96	R-1580	町	まち
97	R-105	可	
98	R-1581	頂	いただき
		頂く	いただく
99	R-1175	子	こ
100	R-1855	孔	
101	R-1732	了	
102	R-3	女	おんな
		女	め
103	R-1956	好む	このむ
		好く	すく
		好き	すき
104	R-1985	如	
105	R-1205	母	はは
106	R-419	貫く	つらぬく
107	R-1384	兄	あに
108	R-1888	呪う	のろう
109	R-1388	克	
110	R-1133	小	こ
		小	お
		小さい	ちいさい
111	R-1526	少ない	すくない
		少し	すこし
112	R-1055	大	おお
		大いに	おおいに
		大きい	おおきい
113	R-8	多い	おおい
114	R-2273	夕	ゆう
115	R-633	汐	しお
		汐	うしお

116	R-1057	外	そと
		外	ほか
		外す	はずす
		外れる	はずれる
117	R-385	名	な
118	R-1863	石	いし
119	R-801	肖	
120	R-803	硝	
121	R-990	砕く	くだく
		砕ける	くだける
122	R-1530	砂	すな
123	R-1698	妬む	ねたむ
124	R-805	削る	けずる
125	R-1196	光	ひかり
		光る	ひかる
126	R-19	太い	ふとい
		太る	ふとる
127	R-2060	器	うつわ
128	R-2014	臭い	くさい
		臭う	におう
		臭い	におい
129	R-2364	嗅ぐ	かぐ
130	R-1533	妙	
131	R-1529	省く	はぶく
		省みる	かえりみる
132	R-1829	厚い	あつい
133	R-787	奇	
134	R-1972	川	かわ
135	R-268	州	す
136	R-1992	順	
137	R-1074	水	みず
138	R-1930	氷	こおり
		氷	ひ
139	R-214	永い	ながい
140	R-271	泉	いずみ
141	R-272	腺	
142	R-915	原	はら
143	R-917	願う	ねがう
144	R-215	泳ぐ	およぐ
145	R-753	沼	ぬま
146	R-59	沖	おき
147	R-330	汎	
148	R-118	江	え
149	R-1053	汰	
150	R-2173	汁	しる
151	R-1531	沙	

223	R-551	机	つくえ
224	R-1082	本	もと
225	R-1842	札	ふだ
226	R-471	暦	こよみ
227	R-352	案	
228	R-241	燥	
229	R-1278	未	
230	R-310	末	すえ
231	R-1282	昧	
232	R-311	沫	あわ
233	R-1279	味	あじ
		味わう	あじわう
234	R-1281	妹	いもうと
235	R-196	朱	
236	R-644	株	かぶ
237	R-604	若い	わかい
		若しくは	もしくは
238	R-1976	草	くさ
239	R-1316	苦しい	くるしい
		苦しむ	くるしむ
		苦しめる	くるしめる
		苦い	にがい
		苦る	にがる
240	R-107	苛	
241	R-2140	寛	
242	R-1497	薄い	うすい
		薄まる	うすまる
		薄める	うすめる
		薄らぐ	うすらぐ
		薄れる	うすれる
243	R-1979	葉	は
244	R-2141	模	
245	R-774	漠	
246	R-767	墓	はか
247	R-768	暮れる	くれる
		暮らす	くらす
248	R-772	膜	
249	R-304	苗	なえ
		苗	なわ
250	R-1264	兆し	きざし
		兆す	きざす
251	R-1268	桃	もも
252	R-1267	眺める	ながめる
253	R-1817	犬	いぬ
254	R-1999	状	
255	R-1858	黙る	だまる
256	R-469	然	
257	R-645	荻	おぎ
258	R-540	狩り	かり
		狩る	かる
259	R-306	猫	ねこ
260	R-583	牛	うし
261	R-1561	特	
262	R-1021	告げる	つげる
263	R-253	先	さき
264	R-254	洗う	あらう
265	R-60	介	
266	R-414	界	
267	R-597	茶	
268	R-2144	脊	
269	R-1172	合う	あう
		合わす	あわす
		合わせる	あわせる
270	R-557	塔	
271	R-1209	王	
272	R-584	玉	たま
273	R-2010	宝	たから
274	R-198	珠	
275	R-1231	現す	あらわす
		現れる	あらわれる
276	R-1810	玩	
277	R-1973	狂う	くるう
		狂おしい	くるおしい
278	R-1918	旺	
279	R-1686	皇	
280	R-487	呈	
281	R-1085	全く	まったく
		全て	すべて
282	R-909	栓	
283	R-1058	理	
284	R-1450	主	おも
		主	ぬし
285	R-1447	注ぐ	そそぐ
286	R-1448	柱	はしら
287	R-1080	金	かね
		金	かな
288	R-255	銑	
289	R-1237	鉢	
290	R-1259	銅	
291	R-2343	釣る	つる
		釣り	つり
292	R-1856	針	はり

293	R-386	銘					高まる	たかまる
294	R-1409	鎮まる	しずまる				高める	たかめる
		鎮める	しずめる	330	R-1968	享		
295	R-375	道	みち	331	R-403	塾		
296	R-376	導く	みちびく	332	R-404	熟れる	うれる
297	R-646	辻	つじ	333	R-491	亭		
298	R-1699	迅		334	R-1030	京		
299	R-1023	造る	つくる	335	R-2330	涼しい	すずしい
300	R-91	迫る	せまる			涼む	すずむ
301	R-1269	逃す	のがす	336	R-960	景		
		逃れる	のがれる	337	R-2058	鯨	くじら
		逃がす	にがす	338	R-1009	舎		
		逃げる	にげる	339	R-1654	周り	まわり
302	R-1961	辺り	あたり	340	R-1655	週		
		辺	べ	341	R-141	士		
303	R-2088	巡る	めぐる	342	R-979	吉		
304	R-1048	車	くるま	343	R-274	壮		
305	R-1803	連なる	つらなる	344	R-275	荘		
		連ねる	つらねる	345	R-1134	売る	うる
		連れる	つれる			売れる	うれる
306	R-1995	軌		346	R-1055	学ぶ	まなぶ
307	R-192	輪		347	R-1990	覚える	おぼえる
308	R-191	喩				覚める	さめる
309	R-1109	前	まえ			覚ます	さます
310	R-1110	煎る	いる	348	R-1830	栄える	さかえる
311	R-1466	各	おのおの			栄え	さかえ
312	R-2312	格				栄え	はえ
313	R-200	略		349	R-1054	書く	かく
314	R-1473	略		350	R-2004	津	つ
315	R-1469	客		351	R-1834	牧	まき
316	R-1474	額	ひたい	352	R-117	攻める	せめる
317	R-511	夏	なつ	353	R-1159	敗れる	やぶれる
318	R-1877	処		354	R-1187	枚		
319	R-1778	条		355	R-1314	故	ゆえ
320	R-1471	落ちる	おちる	356	R-985	敬う	うやまう
		落とす	おとす	357	R-1728	言う	いう
321	R-1090	冗				言	こと
322	R-2297	冥		358	R-986	警		
323	R-1643	軍		359	R-49	計らう	はからう
324	R-1642	輝く	かがやく			計る	はかる
325	R-1165	運ぶ	はこぶ	360	R-910	詮		
326	R-1947	冠	かんむり	361	R-1852	獄		
327	R-2206	夢	ゆめ	362	R-1585	訂		
328	R-235	坑		363	R-567	訃		
329	R-439	高	たか	364	R-1785	討つ	うつ
		高い	たかい	365	R-1905	訓		

366	R-754	詔	みことのり
367	R-980	詰まる	つまる
		詰める	つめる
		詰む	つむ
368	R-1624	話	はなし
		話す	はなす
369	R-216	詠む	よむ
370	R-1560	詩	
371	R-88	語らう	かたらう
		語る	かたる
372	R-1201	読む	よむ
373	R-1652	調べる	しらべる
		調う	ととのう
		調える	ととのえる
374	R-1090	談	
375	R-1891	諾	
376	R-194	諭す	さとす
377	R-1717	式	
378	R-1157	試す	ためす
		試みる	こころみる
379	R-248	弐	
380	R-576	域	
381	R-1996	賊	
382	R-814	栽	
383	R-813	載せる	のせる
		載る	のる
384	R-2378	茂る	しげる
385	R-1078	戚	
386	R-1270	成す	なす
		成る	なる
387	R-1273	城	しろ
388	R-1272	誠	まこと
389	R-2011	威	
390	R-614	滅びる	ほろびる
		滅ぼす	ほろぼす
391	R-1738	減らす	へらす
		減る	へる
392	R-2195	蔑む	さげすむ
393	R-1365	桟	
394	R-1363	銭	ぜに
395	R-1361	浅い	あさい
396	R-1683	止まる	とまる
		止める	とめる
397	R-1534	歩む	あゆむ
		歩く	あるく
398	R-1527	渉	

399	R-2084	頻	
400	R-1897	肯	
401	R-1870	企てる	くわだてる
402	R-472	歴	
403	R-1240	武	
404	R-2159	賦	
405	R-1300	正しい	ただしい
		正す	ただす
		正	まさ
406	R-1304	証	
407	R-1148	政	まつりごと
408	R-894	定か	さだか
		定まる	さだま
		定める	さだめる
409	R-895	錠	
410	R-1889	走る	はしる
411	R-755	超える	こえる
		超す	こす
412	R-568	赴く	おもむく
413	R-2112	越える	こえる
		越す	こす
414	R-1608	是	
415	R-1609	題	
416	R-1607	堤	つつみ
417	R-325	建つ	たつ
		建てる	たてる
418	R-326	鍵	かぎ
419	R-1725	延ばす	のばす
		延びる	のびる
		延べる	のべる
420	R-1161	誕	
421	R-1764	礎	いしずえ
422	R-2289	婿	むこ
423	R-1695	衣	ころも
424	R-812	裁く	さばく
		裁つ	たつ
425	R-276	装う	よそおう
426	R-2076	裏	うら
427	R-417	壊す	こわす
		壊れる	こわれる
428	R-1193	哀れ	あわれ
		哀れむ	あわれむ
429	R-295	遠い	とおい
430	R-297	猿	さる
431	R-1823	初々しい	ういういしい
		初	はつ

		乾く	かわく		536	R-1435	激しい	はげしい
503	R-784	腹	はら		537	R-1512	脱ぐ	ぬぐ
504	R-783	複					脱げる	ぬげる
505	R-1828	欠く	かく		538	R-1509	説く	とく
		欠ける	かける		539	R-1511	鋭い	するどい
506	R-2280	吹く	ふく		540	R-1289	曽	
507	R-1984	炊く	たく		541	R-1292	増す	ます
508	R-109	歌	うた				増やす	ふやす
		歌う	うたう				増える	ふえる
509	R-2218	軟らか	やわらか		542	R-1294	贈る	おくる
		軟らかい	やわらかい		543	R-1029	東	ひがし
510	R-736	次	つぎ		544	R-2099	棟	むな
		次ぐ	つぐ				棟	むね
511	R-652	茨	いばら		545	R-1443	凍る	こおる
512	R-738	資					凍える	こごえる
513	R-737	姿	すがた		546	R-1004	妊	
514	R-740	諮る	はかる		547	R-229	廷	
515	R-166	賠			548	R-1807	染み	しみ
516	R-164	培う	つちかう				染みる	しみる
517	R-2193	剖ける	わける				染まる	そまる
518	R-1416	音	おと				染める	そめる
		音	ね		549	R-470	燃える	もえる
519	R-1417	暗い	くらい				燃す	もす
520	R-949	韻					燃やす	もやす
521	R-1024	識			550	R-2111	賓	
522	R-462	鏡	かがみ		551	R-2162	歳	
523	R-461	境	さかい		552	R-435	県	
524	R-1283	亡い	ない		553	R-653	栃	とち
525	R-1288	盲			554	R-1395	地	
526	R-2092	妄り	みだり		555	R-1396	池	いけ
527	R-443	荒い	あらい		556	R-2167	虫	むし
		荒らす	あらす		557	R-2068	蛍	ほたる
		荒れる	あれる		558	R-1975	蛇	へび
528	R-1284	望む	のぞむ		559	R-654	虹	にじ
529	R-1432	方	かた		560	R-2026	蝶	
530	R-1428	妨げる	さまたげる		561	R-1682	独り	ひとり
531	R-1427	坊			562	R-1799	蚕	かいこ
532	R-1433	芳しい	かんばしい		563	R-1168	風	かざ
533	R-1429	肪					風	かぜ
534	R-1434	訪れる	おとずれる		564	R-24	己	おのれ
		訪ねる	たずねる		565	R-1325	起きる	おきる
		訪う	とう				起こる	おこる
535	R-531	放す	はなす				起こす	おこす
		放つ	はなつ		566	R-1328	妃	
		放れる	はなれる		567	R-1761	改まる	あらたまる
		放る	ほうる				改める	あらためる

641	R-739	恣	
642	R-347	忍ばせる	しのばせる
		忍ぶ	しのぶ
643	R-348	認める	みとめる
644	R-1327	忌まわしい	いまわしい
		忌む	いむ
645	R-143	志	こころざし
		志す	こころざす
646	R-144	誌	
647	R-1987	芯	
648	R-58	忠	
649	R-658	串	くし
650	R-1850	患う	わずらう
651	R-1697	思う	おもう
652	R-883	恩	
653	R-1108	応える	こたえる
654	R-831	意	
655	830	臆	
656	R-278	想	
657	R-1941	息	いき
658	R-1626	憩い	いこい
		憩う	いこう
659	R-31	恵む	めぐむ
660	R-2044	恐れる	おそれる
		恐ろしい	おそろしい
661	R-623	惑う	まどう
662	R-541	感	
663	R-507	憂い	うい
		憂い	うれい
		憂える	うれえる
664	R-512	寡	
665	R-1286	忙しい	いそがしい
666	R-1508	悦	
667	R-1768	恒	
668	R-2163	悼む	いたむ
669	R-87	悟る	さとる
670	R-925	怖い	こわい
671	R-444	慌ただしい	あわただしい
		慌てる	あわてる
672	R-1419	悔いる	くいる
		悔しい	くやしい
		悔やむ	くやむ
673	R-1293	憎い	にくい
		憎しみ	にくしみ
		憎む	にくむ
		憎らしい	にくらしい
674	R-420	慣らす	ならす
		慣れる	なれる
675	R-193	愉	
676	R-999	惰	
677	R-1408	慎む	つつしむ
678	R-542	憾	
679	R-829	憶	
680	R-2158	惧	
681	R-2146	憧れる	あこがれる
682	R-961	憬	
683	R-771	慕う	したう
684	R-2128	添う	そう
		添える	そえる
685	R-1095	必ず	かならず
686	R-1401	泌	
687	R-1150	手	た
		手	て
688	R-1844	看	
689	R-138	摩る	する
690	R-377	我	われ
		我が	わが
691	R-74	義	
692	R-75	議	
693	R-77	犠	
694	R-312	抹	
695	R-2154	拭う	ぬぐう
		拭く	ふく
696	R-2205	拉	
697	R-98	抱える	かかえる
		抱く	だく
		抱く	いだく
698	R-558	搭	
699	R-1528	抄	
700	R-237	抗	
701	R-382	批	
702	R-751	招く	まねく
703	R-1774	拓	
704	R-92	拍	
705	R-1586	打つ	うつ
706	R-2095	拘	
707	R-1010	捨てる	すてる
708	R-1884	拐	
709	R-161	摘む	つむ
710	R-1266	挑む	いどむ
711	R-833	指	ゆび
		指す	さす

712	R-1555	持つ	もつ
713	R-1052	捗	
714	R-1622	括	
715	R-1641	揮	
716	R-1883	推す	おす
717	R-1486	揚げる	あげる
		揚がる	あがる
718	R-1606	提げる	さげる
719	R-950	損なう	そこなう
		損ねる	そこねる
720	R-1953	拾う	ひろう
721	R-793	担う	になう
		担ぐ	かつぐ
722	R-2096	拠	
723	R 305	描く	えがく
		描く	かく
724	R-242	操	みさお
		操る	あやつる
725	R-1709	接ぐ	つぐ
726	R-1311	掲げる	かかげる
727	R-659	掛	かかり
		掛ける	かける
		掛かる	かかる
728	R-1535	捗	
729	R-1031	研ぐ	とぐ
730	R-415	戒める	いましめる
731	R-2374	弄ぶ	もてあそぶ
732	R-416	械	
733	R-1940	鼻	はな
734	R-477	刑	
735	R-478	型	かた
736	R-1639	才	
737	R-1638	財	
738	R-1637	材	
739	R-595	存	
740	R-1231	在る	ある
741	R-36	乃	の
742	R-1775	携える	たずさえる
		携わる	たずさわる
743	R-205	及ぼす	およぼす
		及び	および
		及ぶ	およぶ
744	R-206	吸う	すう
745	R-660	扱う	あつかう
746	R-1056	丈	たけ
747	R-1006	史	

748	R-1008	吏	
749	R-856	更	さら
		更ける	ふける
		更かす	ふかす
750	R-858	硬い	かたい
751	R-857	梗	
752	R-661	又	また
753	R-481	双	ふた
754	R-482	桑	くわ
755	R-1848	隻	
756	R-558	護	
757	R-963	獲る	える
758	R-211	奴	
759	R-212	怒る	おこる
		怒る	いかる
760	R-1909	友	とも
761	R-2208	抜かす	ぬかす
		抜かる	ぬかる
		抜く	ぬく
		抜ける	ぬける
762	R-1809	投げる	なげる
763	R-2269	没	
764	R-2366	股	また
765	R-1746	設ける	もうける
766	R-1770	撃つ	うつ
767	R-2292	殻	から
768	R-1520	支える	ささえる
769	R-1525	技	わざ
770	R-1521	枝	えだ
771	R-1522	肢	
772	R-798	茎	くき
773	R-800	怪しい	あやしい
		怪しむ	あやしむ
774	R-797	軽い	かるい
		軽やか	かろやか
775	R-1411	叔	
776	R-1413	督	
777	R-1414	寂	さび
		寂しい	さびしい
		寂れる	さびれる
778	R-1412	淑	
779	R-1331	反らす	そらす
		反る	そる
780	R-1330	坂	さか
781	R-1332	板	いた
782	R-1337	返す	かえす

846	R-1349	頌	
847	R-1604	公	おおやけ
848	R-1602	松	まつ
849	R-1605	翁	
850	R-1603	訟	
851	R-1612	谷	たに
852	R-1611	浴びせる	あびせる
		浴びる	あびる
853	R-505	容	
854	R-506	溶ける	とける
		溶く	とく
		溶かす	とかす
855	R-1610	欲しい	ほしい
		欲する	ほっする
856	R-1614	裕	
857	R-928	鉛	なまり
858	R-927	沿う	そう
859	R-1454	賞	
860	R-1459	党	
861	R-1138	堂	
862	R-1457	常	つね
		常	とこ
863	R-1453	裳	
864	R-1456	掌	
865	R-1539	皮	かわ
866	R-1545	波	なみ
867	R-1546	婆	
868	R-1543	披く	ひらく
869	R-1544	破る	やぶる
		破れる	やぶれる
870	R-1540	被る	こうむる
871	R-1210	残す	のこす
		残る	のこる
872	R-406	殉	
873	R-197	殊	こと
874	R-1439	殖やす	ふやす
		殖える	ふえる
875	R-852	列	
876	R-854	裂く	さく
		裂ける	さける
877	R-853	烈	
878	R-1874	死ぬ	しぬ
879	R-1947	葬る	ほうむる
880	R-1715	瞬く	またたく
881	R-1974	耳	みみ
882	R-1587	取る	とる

883	R-1588	趣	おもむき
884	R-1589	最も	もっとも
885	R-1590	撮る	とる
886	R-2148	恥	はじ
		恥じらう	はじらう
		恥じる	はじる
		恥ずかしい	はずかしい
887	R-1025	職	
888	R-1141	聖	
889	R-2061	敢	
890	R-1720	聴く	きく
891	R-418	懐かしむ	なつかしむ
		懐かしい	なつかしい
		懐ける	なつける
		懐く	なつく
		懐	ふところ
892	R-463	慢	
893	R-464	漫	
894	R-1681	買う	かう
895	R-1438	置く	おく
896	R-1707	罰	
897	R-605	寧	
898	R-2030	濁す	にごす
		濁る	にごる
899	R-424	環	
900	R-423	還	
901	R-933	夫	おっと
902	R-934	扶	
903	R-433	渓	
904	R-935	規	
905	R-2287	替える	かえる
		替わる	かわる
906	R-1871	賛	
907	R-2336	潜む	ひそむ
		潜る	もぐる
908	R-1494	失う	うしなう
909	R-1492	鉄	
910	R-1493	迭	
911	R-1723	臣	
912	R-667	姫	ひめ
913	R-515	蔵	くら
914	R-516	臓	
915	R-1404	賢い	かしこい
916	R-1406	腎	
917	R-1403	堅い	かたい
918	R-1831	臨む	のぞむ

919	R-1215	覧	
920	R-238	巨	
921	R-239	拒む	こばむ
922	R-1200	力	ちから
923	R-1043	男	おとこ
924	R-1208	労	
925	R-770	募る	つのる
926	R-1536	劣る	おとる
927	R-116	功	
928	R-841	勧める	すすめる
929	R-213	努める	つとめる
930	R-12197	勃	
931	R-2221	励ます	はげます
		励む	はげむ
932	R-891	加える	くわえる
		加わる	くわわる
933	R-893	賀	
934	R-892	架かる	かかる
		架ける	かける
935	R-668	脇	わき
936	R-342	脅かす	おびやかす
		脅す	おどす
		脅かす	おどかす
937	R-341	協	
938	R-1069	行く	いく
		行う	おこなう
		行く	ゆく
939	R-1815	律	
940	R-782	復	
941	R-1753	得る	える
		得る	うる
942	R-401	従う	したがう
		従える	したがえる
943	R-1153	徒	
944	R-1559	待つ	まつ
945	R-1452	往	
946	R-1303	征	
947	R-799	径	
948	R-1541	彼	かれ
		彼	かの
949	R-1705	役	
950	R-1933	徳	
951	R-493	徹	
952	R-371	徴	
953	R-372	懲らしめる	こらしめる
		懲らす	こらす

		懲りる	こりる
954	R-1924	微か	かすか
955	R-1500	街	まち
956	R-669	桁	けた
957	R-2110	衡	
958	R-440	稿	
959	R-309	稼ぐ	かせぐ
960	R-488	程	ほど
961	R-1510	税	
962	R-1767	稚	
963	R-12	和む	なごむ
		和やか	なごやか
		和らぐ	やわらぐ
		和らげる	やわらげる
964	R-1911	移す	うつす
		移る	うつる
965	R-1532	秒	
966	R-509	秋	あき
967	R-510	愁い	うれい
		愁える	うれえる
968	R-1793	私	わたくし
		私	わたし
969	R-1495	秩	
970	R-1400	秘める	ひめる
971	R-2232	称	
972	R-387	利く	きく
973	R-670	梨	なし
974	R-964	穫	
975	R-2278	穂	ほ
976	R-2049	稲	いね
		稲	いな
977	R-1845	香り	かおり
		香る	かおる
		香	か
978	R-1798	季	
979	R-1837	委ねる	ゆだねる
980	R-2009	秀でる	ひいでる
981	R-2138	透かす	すかす
		透く	すく
		透ける	すける
982	R-1884	誘う	さそう
983	R-1899	稽	
984	R-1926	穀	
985	R-2035	菌	
986	R-1913	萎える	なえる
987	R-611	米	こめ

1473	R-1287	網	あみ
1474	R-1405	緊	
1475	R-545	紫	むらさき
1476	R-1498	縛る	しばる
1477	R-1989	縄	なわ
1478	R-1767	幼い	おさない
1479	R-1076	後	のち
		後	あと
		後ろ	うしろ
		後れる	おくれる
1480	R-2229	幽	
1481	R-334	幾	いく
1482	R-336	機	はた
1483	R-335	畿	
1484	R-289	玄	
1485	R-367	畜	
1486	R-368	蓄える	たくわえる
1487	R-290	弦	つる
1488	R-2122	擁	
1489	R-228	滋	
1490	R-226	慈しむ	いつくしむ
1491	R-227	磁	
1492	R-975	系	
1493	R-976	係	かかり
		係る	かかる
1494	R-977	孫	まご
1495	R-436	懸かる	かかる
		懸ける	かける
1496	R-978	遜	
1497	R-457	却	
1498	R-458	脚	あし
1499	R-697	卸	おろし
		卸す	おろす
1500	R-1035	御	おん
1501	R-1174	服	
1502	R-1077	命	いのち
1503	R-756	令	
1504	R-758	零	
1505	R-760	齢	
1506	R-757	冷める	さめる
		冷ます	さます
		冷たい	つめたい
		冷や	ひや
		冷やかす	ひやかす
		冷やす	ひやす
		冷える	ひえる

1507	R-761	領	
1508	R-759	鈴	すず
1509	R-441	勇む	いさむ
		勇ましい	いさましい
1510	R-442	湧く	わく
1511	R-1018	通す	とおす
		通る	とおる
		通う	かよう
1512	R-1020	踊り	おどり
		踊る	おどる
1513	R-918	疑う	うたがう
1514	R-919	擬	
1515	R-920	凝らす	こらす
		凝る	こる
1516	R-1729	範	
1517	R-1745	犯す	おかす
1518	R-1730	氾	
1519	R-1919	厄	
1520	R-1250	危ぶむ	あやぶむ
		危ない	あぶない
		危うい	あやうい
1521	R-874	宛てる	あてる
1522	R-875	腕	うで
1523	R-872	苑	その
1524	R-873	怨	
1525	R-2031	柳	やなぎ
1526	R-2056	卵	たまご
1527	R-1822	留まる	とまる
		留める	とめる
1528	R-2368	瑠	
1529	R-1233	貿	
1530	R-1862	印	しるし
1531	R-2365	臼	うす
1532	R-1980	毀	
1533	R-1727	興す	おこす
		興る	おこる
1534	R-698	酉	とり
1535	R-1792	酒	さけ
		酒	さか
1536	R-2065	酌む	くむ
1537	R-1102	酎	
1538	R-973	酵	
1539	R-1022	酷	
1540	R-270	酬	
1541	R-1472	酪	
1542	R-764	酢	す

		問	とん
1745	R-1507	閲	
1746	R-354	閼	
1747	R-425	間	あいだ
		間	ま
1748	R-711	闇	やみ
1749	R-426	簡	
1750	R-1724	開く	あく
		開ける	あける
		開く	ひらく
		開ける	ひらる
1751	R-1640	閉まる	しまる
		閉める	しめる
		閉ざす	とざす
		閉じる	とじる
1752	R-1468	閣	
1753	R-2296	閑	
1754	R-1106	聞く	きく
		聞こえる	きこえる
1755	R-2143	潤う	うるおう
		潤す	うるおす
		潤む	うるむ
1756	R-2075	欄	
1757	R-1564	闘う	たたかう
1758	R-499	倉	くら
1759	R-500	創る	つくる
1760	R-1550	非	
1761	R-1547	俳	
1762	R-1549	排	
1763	R-1551	悲しい	かなしい
		悲しむ	かなしむ
1764	R-1553	罪	つみ
1765	R-1548	輩	
1766	R-1552	扉	とびら
1767	R-319	侯	
1768	R-320	喉	のど
1769	R-321	候	そうろう
1770	R-1733	決まる	きまる
		決める	きめる
1771	R-1950	快い	こころよい
1772	R-1319	偉い	えらい
1773	R-1318	違う	ちがう
		違える	ちがえる
1774	R-1320	緯	
1775	R-1321	衛	
1776	R-1322	韓	

1777	R-1372	干す	ほす
		干る	ひる
1778	R-1376	肝	きも
1779	R-1374	刊	
1780	R-1375	汗	あせ
1781	R-1377	軒	のき
1782	R-1243	岸	きし
1783	R-1373	幹	みき
1784	R-712	芋	いも
1785	R-30	宇	
1786	R-1636	余す	あます
		余る	あまる
1787	R-1631	除く	のぞく
1788	R-1633	徐	
1789	R-1632	叙	
1790	R-1635	途	
1791	R-2220	斜め	ななめ
1792	R-1634	塗る	ぬる
1793	R-1596	束	たば
1794	R-1601	頼る	たよる
		頼む	たのむ
		頼もしい	たのもしい
1795	R-713	瀬	せ
1796	R-1599	勅	
1797	R-1600	疎い	うとい
		疎む	うとむ
1798	R-617	辣	
1799	R-1597	速める	はやめる
		速やか	すみやか
		速い	はやい
		速まる	はやまる
1800	R-1302	整う	ととのう
		整える	ととのえる
1801	R-136	剣	つるぎ
1802	R-134	険しい	けわしい
1803	R-135	検	
1804	R-132	倹	
1805	R-1755	重い	おもい
		重なる	かさなる
		重ねる	かさねる
		重	え
1806	R-373	動かす	うごかす
		動く	うごく
1807	1789	腫らす	はらす
		腫れる	はれる
1808	R-455	勲	

1809	R-374	働く	はたらく
1810	R-1788	種	たね
1811	R-1763	衝	
1812	R-456	薫る	かおる
1813	R-288	病	やまい
		病む	やむ
1814	R-209	痴	
1815	R-1563	痘	
1816	R-1305	症	
1817	R-1487	瘍	
1818	R-570	痩せる	やせる
1819	R-563	疾	
1820	R-564	嫉	
1821	R-388	痢	
1822	R-1514	痕	あと
1823	R-1542	疲れる	つかれる
1824	R-2217	疫	
1825	R-1019	痛い	いたい
		痛む	いたむ
		痛める	いためる
1826	R-862	癖	くせ
1827	R-2344	匿	
1828	R-1959	匠	
1829	R-1027	医	
1830	R-2324	匹	ひき
1831	R-1591	区	
1832	R-1595	枢	
1833	R-1594	殴る	なぐる
1834	R-1593	欧	
1835	R-2051	抑える	おさえる
1836	R-1916	仰せ	おおせ
		仰ぐ	あおぐ
1837	R-1847	迎える	むかえる
1838	R-1565	登る	のぼる
1839	R-1568	澄ます	すます
		澄む	すむ
1840	R-1671	発	
1841	R-1683	廃る	すたる
		廃れる	すたれる
1842	R-183	僚	
1843	R-185	瞭	
1844	R-184	寮	
1845	R-186	療	
1846	R-1653	彫る	ほる
1847	R-1717	形	かた
		形	かたち

1848	R-962	影	かげ
1849	R-714	杉	すぎ
1850	R-190	彩る	いろどる
1851	R-263	彰	
1852	R-715	彦	ひこ
1853	R-1944	顔	かお
1854	R-35	須	
1855	R-2105	膨らむ	ふくらむ
		膨れる	ふくれる
1856	R-523	参る	まいる
1857	R-524	惨め	みじめ
1858	R-1901	修まる	おさまる
		修める	おさめる
1859	R-2080	珍しい	めずらしい
1860	R-1786	診る	みる
1861	R-966	文	ふみ
1862	R-968	対	
1863	R-967	紋	
1864	R-716	蚊	か
1865	R-490	斑	
1866	R-1663	斉	
1867	R-1664	剤	
1868	R-1661	済む	すむ
		済ます	すます
		済み	すみ
1869	R-1662	斎	
1870	R-2237	粛	
1871	R-2032	塁	
1872	R-1120	楽しい	たのしい
		楽しむ	たのしむ
1873	R-1176	薬	くすり
1874	R-548	率いる	ひきいる
1875	R-2114	渋	しぶ
		渋い	しぶい
		渋る	しぶる
1876	R-2408	摂	
1877	R-938	央	
1878	R-936	英	
1879	R-937	映える	はえる
		映る	うつる
		映す	うつす
1880	R-1965	赤	あか
		赤い	あかい
		赤らむ	あからむ
		赤らめる	あからめる
1881	R-2141	赦	

2017	R-902	盤	
2018	R-901	搬	
2019	R-929	船	ふな
		船	ふね
2020	R-1380	艦	
2021	R-230	艇	
2022	R-947	瓜	うり
2023	R-946	弧	
2024	R-945	孤	
2025	R-2327	繭	まゆ
2026	R-1771	益	
2027	R-1957	暇	ひま
2028	R-1436	敷く	しく
2029	R-1131	来す	きたす
		来る	きたる
		来る	くる
2030	R-437	気	
2031	R-438	汽	
2032	R-1099	飛ばす	とばす
		飛ぶ	とぶ
2033	R-1858	沈める	しずめる
		沈む	しずむ
2034	R-720	枕	まくら
2035	R-2044	妻	つま
2036	R-2147	凄	
2037	R-2303	衰える	おとろえる
2038	R-2380	衷	
2039	R-369	面	つら
		面	おも
		面	おもて
2040	R-370	麺	
2041	R-1761	革	かわ
2042	R-114	靴	くつ
2043	R-1890	覇	
2044	R-1872	声	こえ
		声	こわ
2045	R-2202	眉	まゆ
2046	R-220	呉	
2047	R-221	娯	
2048	R-222	誤る	あやまる
2049	R-2103	蒸す	むす
		蒸らす	むらす
		蒸れる	むれる
2050	R-1878	承る	うけたまわる
2051	R-1963	函	はこ
2052	R-1937	極まる	きわまる

		極める	きわめる
		極み	きわみ
2053	R-876	牙	きば
2054	R-877	芽	め
2055	R-879	邪	
2056	R-878	雅	
2057	R-1702	釈	
2058	R-1041	番	
2059	R-1680	審	
2060	R-2209	翻す	ひるがえす
		翻る	ひるがえる
2061	R-2305	藩	
2062	R-50	毛	け
2063	R-904	耗	
2064	R-905	尾	お
2065	R-485	宅	
2066	R-486	託	
2067	R-26	為	
2068	R-2081	偽る	いつわる
		偽	にせ
2069	R-1912	畏れる	おそれる
2070	R-65	長い	ながい
2071	R-66	張る	はる
2072	R-67	帳	
2073	R-68	脹れる	はれる
		脹れる	ふくれる
2074	R-2152	髪	かみ
2075	R-1751	展	
2076	R-2213	喪	も
2077	R-2056	巣	す
2078	R-1096	単	
2079	R-1155	戦	いくさ
		戦う	たたかう
2080	R-1214	禅	
2081	R-2002	弾く	ひく
		弾む	はずむ
		弾	たま
2082	R-2274	桜	さくら
2083	R-2020	獣	けもの
2084	R-427	脳	
2085	R-428	悩ます	なやます
		悩む	なやむ
2086	R-1928	厳しい	きびしい
		厳か	おごそか
2087	R-2082	鎖	くさり
2088	R-1154	挙げる	あげる

		挙がる	あがる
2089	R-2018	誉れ	ほまれ
2090	R-1859	猟り	かり
2091	R-1978	鳥	とり
2092	R-1951	鳴く	なく
		鳴る	なる
		鳴らす	ならす
2093	R-721	鶴	つる
		鶴	
2094	R-2069	烏	からす
2095	R-722	蔦	つた
2096	R-723	鳩	はと
2097	R-434	鶏	にわとり
2098	R-1714	島	しま
2099	R-1864	暖か	あたたか
		暖かい	あたたかい
		暖まる	あたたまる
		暖める	あたためる
2100	R-1202	媛	
2101	R-1687	援	
2102	R-2216	緩い	ゆるい
		緩む	ゆるむ
		緩める	ゆるめる
		緩やか	ゆるやか
2103	R-1879	属	
2104	R-2198	嘱	
2105	R-868	偶	
2106	R-869	遇	
2107	R-871	愚か	おろか
2108	R-870	隅	すみ
2109	R-1832	逆	さか
		逆らう	さからう
		逆さま	さかさま
2110	R-359	塑	
2111	R-360	遡る	さかのぼる
2112	R-724	岡	おか
2113	R-898	鋼	はがね
2114	R-897	綱	つな
2115	R-899	剛	
2116	R-1920	缶	
2117	R-2060	陶	
2118	R-502	揺さぶる	ゆさぶる
		揺する	ゆする
		揺すぶる	ゆすぶる
		揺らぐ	ゆらぐ
		揺る	ゆる

		揺るぐ	ゆるぐ
		揺れる	ゆれる
2119	R-501	謡	うたい
		謡う	うたう
2120	R-578	鬱	
2121	R-565	就く	つく
		就ける	つける
2122	R-566	蹴る	ける
2123	R-447	懇ろ	ねんごろ
2124	R-448	墾	
2125	R-2196	貌	
2126	R-1213	免れる	まぬかれる
2127	R-2009	逸	
2128	R-1042	晩	
2129	R-1045	勉	
2130	R-513	象	
2131	R-514	像	
2132	R-930	馬	うま
		馬	ま
2133	R-725	駒	こま
2134	R-133	験	
2135	R-789	騎	
2136	R-1449	駐	
2137	R-1592	駆る	かる
		駆ける	かける
2138	R-1170	駅	
2139	R-2132	騒ぐ	さわぐ
2140	R-1921	駄	
2141	R-987	驚かす	おどろかす
		驚く	おどろく
2142	R-932	篤	
2143	R-931	罵る	ののしる
2144	R-865	騰	
2145	R-2063	虎	とら
2146	R-995	虜	
2147	R-996	膚	
2148	R-2081	虚	
2149	R-2234	戯れる	たわむれる
2150	R-726	虞	おそれ
2151	R-994	慮	
2152	R-1147	劇	
2153	R-2156	虐げる	しいたげる
2154	R-727	鹿	しか
		鹿	か
2155	R-2165	麓	ふもと
2156	R-1883	薦める	すすめる

2157	R-1108	慶	
2158	R-1034	麗しい	うるわしい
2159	R-728	熊	くま
2160	R-1670	能	
2161	R-1821	態	
2162	R-729	寅	とら
2163	R-1726	演	
2164	R-806	辰	たつ
2165	R-811	辱める	はずかしめる
2166	R-807	震う	ふるう
		震える	ふるえる
2167	R-809	振る	ふる
		振るう	ふるう
		振れる	ふれる
2168	R-808	娠	
2169	R-810	唇	くちびる
2170	R-473	農	
2171	R-474	濃い	こい
2172	R-1216	送る	おくる
2173	R-1092	関	せき
		関わる	かかわる
2174	R-730	咲く	さく
2175	R-2062	鬼	おに
2176	R-2115	醜い	みにくい
2177	R-2055	魂	たましい
2178	R-140	魔	
2179	R-1280	魅	
2180	R-2126	塊	かたまり
2181	R-1894	襲う	おそう
2182	R-2381	嚇	

2183	R-2286	朕	
2184	R-1346	雰	
2185	R-839	箇	
2186	R-1445	錬	
2187	R-2335	遵	
2188	R-1993	罷	
2189	R-921	屯	
2190	R-731	且つ	かつ
2191	R-243	藻	も
2192	R-1860	隷	
2193	R-195	癒やす	いやす
		癒える	いえる
2194	R-2072	璽	
2195	R-732	潟	かた
2196	R-2382	丹	
2197	R-733	丑	うし
2198	R-2148	羞	
2199	R-734	卯	う
2200	R-735	巳	み

Kanji in VOL. 3

2236	R-1398	也	なり
2386	R-269	洲	す
		洲	しま
2647	R-42	祢	
2909	R-40	於いて	おいて
		於ける	おける
2952	R-2401	陀	ななめ
2965	R-41	牟